LIVING on the MOUNTAIN

LIVING on the MOUNTAIN

Roger C. Palms

Fleming H. Revell Company
Old Tappan, New Jersey

Library of Congress Cataloging in Publication Data

Palms, Roger C.
   Living on the mountain.

   "Portions of this material were previously published
under the title God's promises for you"—T.p. verso.
   1. Devotional calendars.   I. Title.
BV4811.P3   1985   242'.2   85-11911
ISBN 0-8007-1449-0

PREFACE

For more than thirty years I've enjoyed a daily quiet time with God. It has been anything but dull.

Maybe you haven't had an easy time in daily devotions. Maybe it has been a struggle for you—an "ought." I hope that beginning with the first page of this book all that will change.

If you have a high view of God and a commitment to the inspiration and authority of Scripture, you have the makings for interesting times with God. That's why this book was written. I enjoyed writing it. My wife, Andrea, worked right alongside me, editing and doing the finishing work on the manuscript. We pulled together what we've seen and learned on the mountain and have put it on paper for you.

Living on the mountain doesn't mean that you won't have to walk in dusty valleys and wade through depressing swamps. I have. I know what it's like. My shoes get dirty, too. But along the journey I have heard God saying, "Come on. Let's go down this road together."

So come and enjoy a daily time with God. No matter where life takes you, I think you're going to enjoy living on the mountain.

LIVING on the
MOUNTAIN

HOPE

> No man shall be able to stand before you all the days of your life; as I was with Moses, so I will be with you; I will not fail you or forsake you.
>
> Joshua 1:5

This is a time of beginnings, a time of expectation. We are starting a new year, a time of hope.

There are "no-hope" people in the world today, millions of them; but we who are Christians are a people of hope. We are because of the resurrection of Jesus Christ, who gives us "a living hope."

Because God is for us, it doesn't matter who is against us. After all, "Who shall separate us from the love of Christ? Shall tribulation, or distress, or persecution, or famine, or nakedness, or peril, or sword?" (Romans 8:35), or inflation, or high interest rates, or unemployment, or renegade children, or debilitating illness? "No, in all these things we are more than conquerors through him who loved us" (Romans 8:37).

Let this be a year for conquering: Conquering because our Conqueror has already won the supreme battle over sin, death, and its consequences. Conquering, because our Conqueror who lives helps us. We have every assurance of that conquering, because our Conqueror will never fail or forsake us. That is God's promise. He said so.

God is our hope. He always has been, and He always will be. This can be the year we enjoy the most because we enjoy Him the most—no matter what happens to us, no matter what comes.

This year can be a conquering year, a victorious year, a year of hope.

Prayer: Father, I recommit myself to You. Help me to live a victorious, conquering life—this year, beginning now.

❧ JANUARY 2 ☙
WHO?

Who is a God like unto thee . . . ?

Micah 7:18 KJV

That's right—who? There is no product, no drug, no service organization, no government, no military establishment that can begin to do what God can do.

Who is like unto You, Lord? No one, no thing. For everything that we know, even if it were all put together, would still be but a flick of Your finger, from creation to destruction.

Who is a God like unto You? All-knowing, all-powerful, present everywhere, forever eternal? Who?

Prayer: O Lord, there is none like You. And though all man's puny substitutes shout for my attention, I'll always know there is none like You.

❧ JANUARY 3 ☙
TAKING CHARGE

And Elisha prayed, and said, Lord, I pray thee, open his eyes, that he may see. And the Lord opened the eyes of the young man; and he saw: and, behold, the mountain was full of horses and chariots of fire round about Elisha.

2 Kings 6:17 KJV

He shall give his angels charge concerning thee. . . .

Matthew 4:6 KJV

We were doing a TV film to promote our magazine, and I sent a staff member to oversee what was being done. When something involves my work, I take a personal interest and want someone of our own on hand to be involved in what is happening. There is no substitute for someone being there.

God does that, too. Lest we trip, lest we run into something we can't handle, lest we need protection, God sends His angels to keep charge over us. We don't see them any more than the servant standing with Elisha saw them. Elisha had to pray, "Lord, open his eyes that he may see." Then the servant saw: the surrounding mountains were filled with angelic troops.

God looks after His interests. He has a big stake in His own. He knows their value, their importance, what His people are here for, what they are doing, and He doesn't leave any of us unattended.

I took great interest in that promotional film, which would air only a few times. How much more does God take interest in me, who has a life to live. Whenever I feel alone, I remember that I'm not alone, that God has a great interest in me, and the angels are everywhere.

Prayer: Thank You, Lord, for sending Your angels to look after Your interest: me.

❧ JANUARY 4 ❧
SPECIALLY MADE

Know ye that the Lord he is God: it is he that hath made us, and not we ourselves. . . .

Psalm 100:3 KJV

The Lord is God; I am not. He made me; I didn't make myself. When those two related thoughts get hold of my mind, life is focused altogether differently. He is God. Beyond creation, but the Creator. Eternal, but present. Judge, Redeemer, Friend.

He made me. I didn't put together my hands and feet and mind and heart. I didn't assemble all that the world calls "me," when it considers me. I didn't put into me the gifts, talents, skills, mental abilities, appearance, or anything else that is "me." He did it all.

This takes care of bragging. There is no point in it. Knowledge of His creation of me also takes care of the tendency to lament what might have been or could have been or even should have been. He made me. Just as my fingerprints are unique, so is the whole me. He cared enough to make me that way. And His Word makes clear that He cares enough to love me and use me that way.

I am a special creation. We all are.

Prayer: Father, help me to have the great contentment that comes from knowing I am specially created, uniquely gifted, specifically called.

❧ JANUARY 5 ❦

EASY TO FIND

I will meditate in thy precepts, and have respect unto thy ways. I will delight myself in thy statutes: I will not forget thy word.

Psalm 119:15, 16 KJV

One day I was asked to go to the airport to pick up an athlete. I hadn't met him before, but I was told, "You won't have any trouble finding him. He plays basketball." And I didn't have any trouble recognizing him. He was the only one coming off that plane who was seven foot two. He was also the only one carrying a Bible. He had been studying the Scriptures on his trip. As I got to know him I learned that he had a great command of God's truth.

None of us can make it through this life without a solid foundation in the Word of God—even if we play professional basketball. Even if we happen to be seven foot two.

Prayer: What a delight it is, Lord, to meet fellow believers who love You and know Your Word.

❧ JANUARY 6 ❦

AN ALL-FORGIVING MERCY

To the Lord our God belong mercies and forgivenesses. . . .

Daniel 9:9 KJV

It was a mistake, and hundreds of thousands of people saw it. It was an error published in the magazine for which I am responsible.

My sadness wasn't so much that people would see the error and be critical of me; rather, it was that I was responsible for the publication and I had failed at that point of my responsibility. I was far harder on myself than any of the readers would be.

It is the same when I err before God. Though He chastises, He is still a loving Father. What is worse than His chastisement is the sorrow that comes with knowing that I've offended Him. He gives liberty, He gives opportunity, He gives responsibility, He gives a life to live, and how terribly displeasing it is to Him and me when I make a mistake, especially a grievous one.

But God has an all-forgiving mercy. As a Father, He comes to a crying child who confesses his mistake. He comes not so much with a rod as with a caress of love. That makes us want to please Him far more than a rod could ever do.

Prayer: Lord, I don't want to live in fear that I will fail, but I do sincerely want to please You with my life.

⅏ JANUARY 7 ⅏
ROSE-COLORED GLASSES

The Lord is my shepherd; I shall not want. . . . Yea, though I walk through the valley of the shadow of death, I will fear no evil. . . .

Psalm 23:1, 4 KJV

It's nice to read the Bible through rose-colored glasses. That way we can get nice warm fuzzy feelings from it. "The Lord is my shepherd; I'll have everything I want." That's a nice one. We can dream and covet a long time on that.

Or another comfortable verse in Psalm 23: "Yea, though I walk through the valley of the shadow of death, I will face no evil." Think of that! As a follower of God, nothing bad can happen to me.

Except David didn't say that, because God didn't promise it. Reality says I'm not going to get everything I want. It also says I shouldn't. God and I both know I'd never be able to handle it. And David was correct: "Though I walk through the valley of the shadow of death, I will fear no evil." Evil is there—always has been, always will be. I can't be removed from the valleys until I get to heaven, but I don't have to be afraid of what's happening: "for thou art with me." And there's the promise.

David was a realist. Being a realist, he knew life; and being a realist, he knew God.

Prayer: Lord, keep me from the temptation to put on my rose-colored glasses. I need to face reality, because I need to live with You.

ᕗ JANUARY 8 ᕕ

WHAT HAPPENED?

And he continued to seek God. . . .

2 Chronicles 26:5 NAS

He was just a kid, but he was a smart kid. At sixteen, Uzziah became king and reigned for fifty-two years. As long as he sought the Lord, God prospered him. But then he did what too many people do—as he grew older he became proud and acted corruptly. He misunderstood God's blessing for his own ability, God's provision for his own strength. In the end he suffered for it.

There are a lot of Uzziahs in the world, starting out at sixteen faithful to the Lord, then, as God blesses their faithfulness, beginning to assume that it's their own strength and power that got them where they are. Then the blessing of God isn't there anymore.

Uzziah was a smart kid at age sixteen, but he lost his smarts when he was middle-aged. Analysts might call it mid-life crisis or the pressures of leadership. Whatever it was, he failed.

There are a lot of present-day Uzziahs around. People look at them and say what people must have said about Uzziah, "What happened?"

Prayer: Dear Father, help me to learn from the failures of those who have gone before so that I won't repeat their mistakes in my own life.

ᕗ JANUARY 9 ᕕ

BANDIT

Let not sin therefore reign in your mortal bodies, to make •
you obey their passions.

Romans 6:12

He comes in the night, the bandit with the mask over his eyes. Up from the woods near the river, across the deserted streets, over the back fence he comes—our visiting raccoon.

Every night he would succeed in pulling the top off our garbage can. Then, spreading the garbage around the yard, he would feast. We got tired of picking up his trash, so we bought a strong rubber strap, pulled it around the handles of the garbage can and across the top, bracing it firmly. Now he couldn't get it! But he tried, and every morning the garbage can would be somewhere in the yard. During the night he rolled it around, working on the strapped-down lid. We chuckled to ourselves that we had outsmarted him at last! But we hadn't.

One morning once again garbage was strewn over the yard; yet the lid was firmly strapped to the can. How had he done it? Each night he had been working not only on the lid of the can, but on the bottom of it, until he had finally broken through. Then, as neatly as if he had used a can opener, he pulled back the metal.

When garbage beckons, nothing much stops a raccoon. One of our friends suggested, "Why don't you put out a lunch every night?" But would that keep the raccoon from the garbage?

In many ways raccoons are like people. When we want our "garbage," we'll get it. We'll do whatever is necessary to get it, but we will have it. We are built that way.

The raccoon will not take on a new nature, but a person can. To be born from above is to be made a new creation; the old is taken away, the new comes. Until it does, we will always have that drive to get at the "garbage."

Prayer: Lord, so many times I think I am like that raccoon; I want the garbage, and I go after it.

ᥤ JANUARY 10 ᥥ
REVOLVING DOOR

> Go, stand and speak in the temple to the people all the words of this life.
>
> Acts 5:20 KJV

In again, out again; the prison didn't exactly have a revolving door, but almost. When the Apostles were out preaching about Jesus Christ, the Sadducees were so angry they grabbed them and threw them in prison. Then an angel came and opened the door and let them out.

What is interesting is what the angel said to them when he let them out—or rather, what he didn't say, because what he didn't say was, "Now, try to stay out of trouble. I got you out once; I may not be able to do it again." He didn't say that. He said, "Go, stand and speak in the temple to the people all the words of this life."

What life? There was only one life to talk about: that's the life that Jesus offered, the new life, the full life, eternal life, real life, permanent life. That's a lot of sermon material, and they hardly got into it when they were arrested again, beaten, and told not to speak in the name of Jesus.

The minute they were let go, they went back and every day preached Jesus. Prison, beatings, angry words aren't very threatening when the life you have to talk about is "this life."

Prayer: Lord, I don't know if I could keep talking about You if authorities did to me what they did to the Apostles. If that day comes, please make me bold.

≥∢ JANUARY 11 ⊱≤

HE NEVER WILL

"While the earth remains, seedtime and harvest, cold and heat, summer and winter, day and night, shall not cease."
Genesis 8:22

"While the earth remains," there will always be the faithful rhythm of days and seasons.

It's true. Someday—maybe very soon—the earth will pass away because God's timing for the end has come.

But "while the earth remains," so will the promise that He gave.

Seasons and days will come regularly and on schedule. The sun will rise; spring will follow winter.

He is God, and He has made a promise.

That puts a different perspective on running for the bus and missing it,

or planning on a concert and the baby-sitter cancels,

or waiting in a hospital corridor.

God made a promise; He has never broken that promise. He never will.

Prayer: You will always be faithful, and I'm grateful that You will always be near.

❧ JANUARY 12 ❦
BUT I'VE GOT THE FLU

And they said to Moses, "Is it because there are no graves in Egypt that you have taken us away to die in the wilderness? . . ."

Exodus 14:11

Today I've got the flu. I had a miserable night last night and felt sick yesterday, so I'm sitting here thinking about the children of Israel.

We tend to read into the Scriptures. We assume that when the call came to leave Egypt the people were all ready and eager to go. But I doubt that. Mixed into that mass of people there were probably several who had the flu. They were groaning with aches and fever, complaining, "My head hurts," unable to keep food down. Probably they needed to be pulled along in a cart by members of the family, and if one was the man of the house, he probably complained all the way. Everyone knows that if a man has the flu the whole family suffers.

There would have been thousands of people marching through the wilderness and a few on wagons, with the flu, complaining—especially if the wheels hit ruts. And they probably needed to stop from time to time, jump off the wagon, and race to the side of the road while others tried to stay away so they wouldn't get the flu, too.

And in camp at night, did the feverish ones have to trip over two or three hundred sleeping people to reach the public sanitation arrangements?

It isn't mentioned, but God must have provided for them. God doesn't do things halfway. He provided the pillar of fire, the cloud by day. He probably took care of the rest of their needs, too. Maybe He kept them all healthy. Maybe nobody had the flu. It's worth thinking about, because as I lie here groaning, I'm pretty much convinced that had I been there, when the call came to prepare to leave Egypt, I'd have voted to stay.

Prayer: Lord, when I think of what You have to put up with, I realize how long-suffering You are. You even have to put up with me.

❧ JANUARY 13 ❦
WE'RE HUGGED!

See what love the Father has given us, that we should be
called children of God; and so we are. The reason why the
world does not know us is that it did not know him.

1 John 3:1

My daughter and I were riding in the car together when she spot-
ted a bumper sticker that read HAVE YOU HUGGED YOUR KID
TODAY? She asked me, "Have you hugged your kid today?"

I hadn't, so when we stopped, I did.

Two days later, again in the car, we saw the same bumper sticker.
So, paraphrasing it, I asked, "Have you hugged your daddy today?"

It's nice to be hugged. But a hug is only an expression of something much deeper, a love that is inside, a love that makes us give,
even sacrifice, for the one we love.

Love like that has far more content to it than the words "I love
you" tossed out casually in about the same manner as one might
say, "I love chocolate cake."

Real love comes from the experience of being loved. The greater
the love received, the greater will be the expression of love given to
another person. That's the way it works.

The deepest love of all is the love from God that surrounds and
embraces us: "See what love the Father has given us, that we should
be called children of God; and so we are."

That's right, we are! And because we are His children, we are a
loved people. We are given love by the One who created us, emp-
tied Himself for us, came to earth for us, went to the cross for us,
and rose victorious over sin and death for us. Who can describe a
love like that? Who can ever imitate it? But we can try. In fact,
Christians had better try. When the love of God hits us in as many
dimensions of it as we can comprehend and absorb, it keeps on
going, right out to other people. There is no way to stop it. There is
no reason for us to want to stop it.

You have been loved by God today! His love is an all-embracing
hug. Now comes the question: have you hugged someone today?

*Prayer: Thank You, Father, for the love from You to me that I can
give to others. And I want to.*

JANUARY 14

HE KNOWS

Fear not, for I am with you, be not dismayed, for I am your God; I will strengthen you, I will help you, I will uphold you with my victorious right hand.

Isaiah 41:10

Fear!

Like when the word you heard earlier in the day finally sinks in—*malignant.*

Like the way you feel on a dark street in a strange city in a foreign country.

Like when you realize that there won't be a better tomorrow, that what you dreaded might happen is happening.

God knows.

You're not an unknown to God. That's why He responds to you so directly in this verse.

He is clear. "I am," and "I will." He responded to fear in another way, too. He chose to become man: to be alone in the wilderness, to face the hatred of the hostile crowd, to bear the anticipation of what was coming as He saw the heavy mallet and spikes in the hands of a soldier.

He knows!

And the words He gives to Isaiah are not glib; they are carefully thought out.

"Fear not!"

We don't have to be afraid. He has told us so.

And tenderly, but in strength, He has told us why.

"I am your God."

Prayer: When I am gripped by fear, please give me Your strength.

❧ JANUARY 15 ❦
GOOD DEAL!

Ho, every one that thirsteth, come ye to the waters, and he
that hath no money; come ye, buy, and eat; yea, come, buy
wine and milk without money and without price.
                                                    Isaiah 55:1 KJV

One thing is certain. Whenever somebody wants to offer me a
bargain or to save me money, I end up paying more.

I ignore letters from insurance companies, credit offers, even
friends who have "a good deal" for me, because they never do. It
turns out to be a good deal for them. And that makes sense, because
why would anyone choose to save me money? Why not just give me
the money, if it's my welfare they're concerned about?

Maybe I shouldn't be so suspicious, but it's usually the friendly
ones, the ones who come on as if I'm their buddy, who seem to take
my money the quickest. I'm learning that there is no "good deal"
short of hard work and the trade-off of a day's labor for a day's pay.

So why would I or anyone want to respond to Isaiah's plea?

"Wine and milk without money and without price." Sounds suspicious, doesn't it? Except, Isaiah isn't making the offer: God is.
And that it doesn't make human sense, God admits. "For my
thoughts are not your thoughts, neither are your ways my ways,
saith the Lord" (Isaiah 55:8 KJV).

In fact, the whole chapter is a promise, based not on some "bargain" (God doesn't bargain). Nor is it based on a partnership (you
get a little, I get a little). It is a promise made by God, who isn't after
a profit. He just doesn't want to have a great loss: me.

*Prayer: In Your integrity You offer what no person can. Help me to
grasp the difference.*

JANUARY 16
MY FRIEND

Henceforth I call you not servants; for the servant knoweth not what his lord doeth: but I have called you friends; for all things that I have heard of my Father I have made known unto you.

John 15:15 KJV

None of us has too many friends. Most of us have only a few real friends; the rest are just good acquaintances. And though we try hard to keep friendships, even the best of friends can drift apart because of distance or the passing years.

But here is a Friend who is closer than a brother, closer than any friend we have ever had or could hope to have. He has pronounced us His friends. We would be happy to be slaves, servants of our Savior Christ; to be called a friend is more than we can imagine.

But that word says a lot. It says, "Come anytime." It says, "I'm always here." It says, "I understand." It says, "What concerns you concerns Me." And most of all, "I have laid down My life for you, friend."

I would not presume to use that word, had He not used it first. He who is holy, I who am not; He who is very God and very man, I who am created and human and sinful and weak. But He left heaven for me, went to the cross for me, rose from the grave for me, and is coming again for me. He is King, Lord, Savior, Holy God—He is my Friend.

Prayer: Dear Friend, dare I address You as such? Yes, for You have called me Your friend.

JANUARY 17
AT HOME—TOGETHER

I will surely gather all of you, O Jacob, I will gather the remnant of Israel; I will set them together like sheep in a fold, like a flock in its pasture. . . .

Micah 2:12

Feels good, doesn't it!
A fire in the hearth on a blustery winter evening, the secure sense

of well-being when the children are all in and someone suggests popcorn, the comfort of good friends with whom you don't have to pretend anything.

God, being the special Father that He is, understands all that. He has told us: "I will surely gather all of you . . . together like sheep in a fold, like a flock in its pasture . . ." (Micah 2:12).

That's something to think about and look forward to, especially in the sometimes not-so-pleasant "right nows" of living.

It's still ahead for us—His gathering in. But we can think about it now when the penetrating cold, the real kind that comes from fear and worry, creeps inside when the children are not in and we suspect the reason why, or when there is no one with whom we can be real and we are so very lonely.

He will bring us home—together like a flock gathered in and safe. It will feel good.

Prayer: There is security, strength, and a lot of peace in You. I'm glad.

☙ JANUARY 18 ☜
MISERABLE? WHO, ME?

> . . . Thou sayest, I am rich, and increased with goods, and have need of nothing; and knowest not that thou art wretched, and miserable, and poor, and blind, and naked.
> Revelation 3:17 KJV

Miserable? Not me. I've got this new four-wheel-drive pickup truck and a boat with seventy-five horsepower on it. I've got a stereo outfit that shakes the walls, and my apartment has carpeting in all the rooms—even the bathroom. Who's miserable?

All I need now is a little peace of mind. You see, I've got this ulcer. It isn't much, but it does bother me when I eat. And most nights I don't sleep too well either. But there's nothing about me you could call "miserable."

I do worry sometimes about my job. Actually, the company is talking about closing down. And there are those interest payments. I thought if I only used those eighteen credit cards two or three times each, I could keep up.

Miserable? Well, not that miserable. Besides, I'm hoping that Jesus Christ will take care of me. He's here to help me in this life, right? After all, the sermons I hear tell me that Jesus wants me to enjoy myself now.

Don't tell me I'm miserable. It doesn't go with the rest of my theology.

Prayer: Lord, help me to admit what I am and who You are and to find the larger life.

❧ JANUARY 19 ☙

SOMETHING BEAUTIFUL

For I was an hungred, and ye gave me meat: I was thirsty,
and ye gave me drink: I was a stranger, and ye took me in.
Matthew 25:35 KJV

In the back streets of Calcutta is an old temple dedicated to the blood goddess Kali. Next to the temple is a hospital, a different kind of hospital. Outside are the people, part of the millions who live in the streets, poor, simply existing. Inside is a different world. This is the Home for Dying Destitutes, and the person who cares so much about these "discarded" ones is a Roman Catholic nun named Mother Teresa.

What happened to me, what I felt there, was at first like the ripping of my soul. Then a different feeling came, one of calm, even peace, the kind that comes when we are someplace where good is all around.

I watched the nurses tenderly cleansing wounds, touching leprous stumps. It was quiet, there was no crying; the eyes of the bedridden were not fearful, they were the eyes of the secure and the contented. The old people and the little children had a home there, they were wanted, they were loved.

And I remembered, "For I was an hungred, and ye gave me meat: I was thirsty, and ye gave me drink: I was a stranger, and ye took me in" (Matthew 25:35).

Many have tried to honor Mother Teresa for her "sacrifice," but to her there has been no sacrifice. She has a calling and a commitment. Inside the home, on one of the pillars in the hall between the men's ward and the women's ward, is a little sign that reads: LET EVERY ACTION OF MINE BE SOMETHING BEAUTIFUL FOR THEE.

I went into the home a curious editor. I came out knowing that everything about my life and being had to be measured all over again.

Prayer: Lord, I'd like to pray the same: "Let every action of mine be something beautiful for Thee."

JANUARY 20
WE'VE ALL SEEN IT

Because that, when they knew God, they glorified him not as God, neither were thankful; but became vain in their imaginations, and their foolish heart was darkened.

Romans 1:21 KJV

"Apostasy often begins with our unwillingness to be thankful." The person who said that was talking about willing or choosing to be thankful instead of willing or choosing to be critical and bitter. We've all seen it. The drift from God begins with an unwillingness to give thanks to God—to choose to look at what is not, rather than what is; to complain about what should be, rather than what God has given. It's a slow slide, but it is a slide—and before long the ungrateful one becomes the one who has turned his back on God, bitter that he "tried God," but God didn't deliver. He laments his lot, thinking that his cup is half empty, when he could be giving thanks that by God's grace his cup is half full.

Prayer: Lord, may I always be thankful to You for what I have and never become bitter for what I don't have.

JANUARY 21
MUSCLES

... Be strong, and show yourself a man, and keep the charge of the Lord your God, walking in his ways. ...

1 Kings 2:2, 3

Men tend to be insecure about themselves. They don't admit it, but it's true. That's why they like to work on body building, and they do just fine so long as the only other people in the gym are men. Put a woman in there pumping iron and the fellows won't mind, until she lifts more than they do. Then they'll leave. Put men on a squash court and they're just fine, until a woman comes and beats them.

I remember once, when I was running, how pleased I felt with myself, until a gray-haired woman in a sweatsuit went past me as if I were standing still. I quit.

But big biceps don't make men. David knew that, and he made sure Solomon understood it, too. He told Solomon, "Show yourself a man." How was he to do that? David explained, "Keep the charge of the Lord your God, walking in his ways and keeping his statutes, and his commandments, his ordinances, and his testimonies, as it is written in the law of Moses" (1 Kings 2:3).

There is the mark of a man: one who does what David told Solomon to do. It would be fun to put the first part of that Scripture—"Show yourself a man"—on the entrance to a men's gym. It would be even more fun if the rest of that Scripture was on the wall in the weight room.

Prayer: Lord, You made men, and You know what makes a man. Take our eyes off our flexing muscles long enough to see what a real man is.

❧ JANUARY 22 ❦
ANYONE HERE FOUND THE LIGHT SWITCH?

> He will guard the feet of his faithful ones; but the wicked shall be cut off in darkness; for not by might shall a man prevail.
>
> 1 Samuel 2:9

It doesn't matter how strong you are. When the lights go out, strength doesn't mean much. You'll stumble around just like the weaklings.

Everyone is equal in the dark.

God's own, the faithful ones, the people He knows, will be guarded; their feet won't trip.

But the wicked—that's a different story. They will be weak, because they will be thrashing around in the dark.

Some people practice muscle building; they think the most important thing is their own strength.

But it isn't.

The strong one is the faithful one. He's the one who will have the light not because he has been building up his muscles but because he knows God.

God controls the light switch.

Prayer: You are the only true light. I'll stay close to You.

JANUARY 23

WHY SUCH SUFFERING?

In this you rejoice, though now for a little while you may have to suffer various trials.

1 Peter 1:6

Why do the righteous suffer? It was Asaph who asked that question. I've asked it, too. We all have.

There is some terrible suffering endured by people who love God and are faithful to Him. They seem to have so much put on them.

Psalm 34:19 says, "Many are the afflictions of the righteous; but the Lord delivers him out of them all." Like David, Peter doesn't try to explain this; no human being can, and Peter was smart enough not to try. But he did see suffering as more than simple victimizing; he saw it as ministry, even a calling. He urged people who find themselves with that awful ministry to entrust their souls to God, who is faithful.

That's part of the mystery of suffering. God's grace, God's goodness, seem extra rich to those righteous who suffer. There is a grace that goes with the calling, and although I don't know exactly what God gives them, or how they endure, I do know that He is the one giving it.

Why do the righteous suffer? No one knows the answer except God. But God, who knows, is Himself the Answer. The suffering righteous know that and give us a dimension of God that we may never have seen any other way.

Prayer: Thank You, Lord, for what You teach me through the suffering I see. But don't ever let me ignore the suffering ones or take their suffering for granted.

⅗ JANUARY 24 ⅙

A HAPPY MYSTERY

> Submit yourselves therefore to God. Resist the devil and he will flee from you.
>
> James 4:7 KJV

Submission!

"A horrible word," says one person.

"Degrading," says another. "It means control, manipulation, even cruelty."

We like to have a voice in matters that affect us. We want to discuss the options, even cast a vote.

But to come into the Kingdom of God is not to come into a democracy, but a monarchy. We are under God's rule, and the created one doesn't discuss with the Creator how He might best handle His creation. In fact one of the designs of sin and Satan is to bring us to a rebellion against that monarchy or at least to a discussion about the merits of God's absolute rule over us. Satan would like us to be "free enough to decide for ourselves" what is and what is not God's role in our lives.

We don't really have that option. We are told in Scripture: "Submit yourselves therefore to God."

That's it, submit!

We are not liberated when we are free of that submission to God's control or when we decide for ourselves which controls we will obey; we are liberated when we gather up all that we are and submit that to the One who controls. We don't discuss the degree or the quality of submission to His rule—we submit to His rule. To some that is a weak or at least a simplistic view of life, like the reneging of our human strengths and wisdom. But just the opposite is true; submission is the doorway to the most freedom and the greatest strength any of us will ever have.

"Live as free men, . . . live as servants of God" (1 Peter 2:16). That isn't contradictory; that is the basis for real living.

This is a mystery, but it is a happy one. In one sense I have no rights; in another sense under His control I have more rights than the person who does not know Jesus Christ. I am free, yet I am a slave. I can do all things, yet cannot and will not do all things. I can

exercise my feelings, passions, and wants, yet will not be ruled by
them. I am liberated, yet I am owned.

That's the perfect law of liberty.

*Prayer: Lord, I know the more I submit to You, the freer I am. Help
me to be truly free.*

This editorial is taken from "Decision" magazine, May, 1978; © 1978 Billy
Graham Evangelistic Association. Used by permission. All Rights reserved.

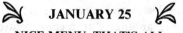

JANUARY 25

NICE MENU, THAT'S ALL

Jesus said unto them, I am the bread of life: he that cometh
to me shall never hunger; and he that believeth on me shall
never thirst.

John 6:35 KJV

It was to be special. A few friends would meet for a quiet dinner
at a nice restaurant. I scouted five restaurants before I chose one. It
seemed to have atmosphere, quiet music, and dress restrictions—
just what I wanted to enhance a good meal. I made the reservation.

When we arrived I gave my name. They couldn't find my reservation, but they would find a table. This created some discussion,
since I had asked for a table along the wall, not out in the middle of
traffic. I was beginning to feel the tension building.

The menu selection was fine, except that when we ordered the
item most of us wanted we were told, "We are sorry; we don't have
that." So we made alternate choices.

Then looking around I noticed that the dress code posted by the
door was just that—a code only posted, not enforced. Sitting next to
us were people who appeared to have come in from a run in the
park or maybe a fishing trip.

The food arrived soaked in grease. But not wanting to say anything more, I ate it, as did the others. We visited, made the best of
the situation, and went home. I sat up until nearly three o'clock in
the morning with an upset stomach. And I thought about plans that
don't work out, food that doesn't satisfy, and unkept rules.

So many things that hold out a promise to us turn out to be a dis-
appointment. Something that we think will be special, isn't. Our an-
ticipations go unmet.

Codes that we expect others to follow are only that—codes, not to be adhered to at all. They are like doctrines or creeds that make nice words to be printed but are not required or even expected to be obeyed.

And food that should at least give nourishment, if not pleasure, ends up leaving a sour stomach.

I wonder about the people who visit our church. The Christian Church is meant to be a banquet hall with fellowship and good spiritual food. But what if visitors are told, "We don't have that," even though they came because they thought what we promoted we offered. What about unkept standards and offers that are promised but not supplied?

Jesus Christ is bread—good bread. He isn't stale, moldy, or unavailable. He who eats of Him won't get an upset stomach. I wonder if anyone has read our "menu," then heard the disappointing words, "Sorry, we don't offer Jesus here."

Prayer: Help me not only to talk about the Bread of Life—but to offer the One who is that Bread of Life.

❧ JANUARY 26 ❧
TRY ME!

Bring the full tithes into the storehouse, that there may be food in my house; and thereby put me to the test, says the Lord of hosts, if I will not open the windows of heaven for you and pour down for you an overflowing blessing.

Malachi 3:10

Inflation, poor stock dividends, higher taxes, and the hot-water heater is starting to leak.

Doesn't God know what it takes just to exist?

Maybe tithing was okay when fifty dollars a week paid the rent, bought the groceries, and left enough for a new Plymouth—but not now. No one can pay a tithe on today's salaries.

One-tenth—that's robbery!

But it isn't.

It's close, but it isn't robbery.

Anything given to the Lord that is less than one-tenth is robbery.

"Will man rob God? Yet you are robbing me. But you say, 'How are we robbing thee?' In your tithes and offerings. You are cursed with a curse, for you are robbing me . . ." (Malachi 3:8, 9).

The tithe is the beginning of giving; it's the end of robbery.

Full tithe? All of it?

He's rather pointed about it, isn't He? That means everything. Nothing held back, not even for contingencies.

But the kids need new shoes!

Funny how that always comes up. Whenever someone mentions tithing, there is always the response, "The kids need new shoes." No matter that we might have just spent an enormous amount on some adult toy or little "extra"—we can explain that: "I work hard for a living, and I need some pleasure. I don't ask for much, and in my situation this isn't a luxury, it's a necessity."

And so it goes. And after we have spent for ourselves, we cry out emotionally, "The kids need new shoes."

It's a shame because most of us have been so busy defending our "needs" and the "kids' shoes" that we've missed the last part of what God says: "Put me to the test . . . if I will not open the windows of heaven for you and pour down for you an overflowing blessing."

Did you notice? It isn't just a general pouring out of His overflowing blessing but an overflowing blessing with your name on it; He keeps stressing "for you." I suppose God repeats it so that if we would ever stop talking about the kids' shoes we might hear what He is saying.

We panic; we scream; we do our own adding and subtracting and are so ready to rebel when we hear *tithe* that we don't hear the rest.

That's too bad! We spend our lives as thieves, robbing God, and miss the overflowing blessing from God's storehouse.

And God's got quite a storehouse!

He is asking only that we stop thieving long enough to "put me to the test" about the blessings.

All He is saying is, "Try me!"

Prayer: Give me the courage to try You, to allow You to do what You said.

JANUARY 27

A GOOD NAME

A good name is better than precious ointment; and the
day of death than the day of one's birth.

Ecclesiastes 7:1 KJV

We cherish the value of a good name more than any other possession. It goes before us every day and lives after us when we die.
The Scripture says that "a good name is better than precious
ointment" and that " a good name is rather to be chosen than great
riches . . ." (Proverbs 22:1 KJV).

But a good name can be destroyed quickly by gossip, innuendo,
or criticism. If I criticize a Christian brother or in any way speak
badly of him, thus tarnishing his reputation, am I not in fact doing
an injustice to the entire Body of Christ—including me?

A brother's name is good because he is God's, and God is good.
Yes, he sins, he falls short of what he ought to be, and we are given
the right sometimes to discipline and sometimes to reach conclusions that we wish we didn't have to reach because of the fruit in his
life, but we don't draw public attention to it. Sadly, we may sometimes have to respond to what is, but we don't have to attack what
isn't.

We all have feet of clay; we aren't always what we want to be. We
pray in our weakness and trust Christ to guide us. But do we really
want Him to work in our own lives? A Christian who is secure in his
own walk with the Lord does not, as Satan does, go around as a
prowling lion looking for someone to devour. He does not act as the
wolf, circling, waiting to go in for the kill. He is a brother, one who
can be trusted to support and protect and hear and cry and pray—
but he will not hurt.

We help a brother. Maybe there is only a little light left in his life,
but that little is still a light.

It is never wrong to assume the best about a Christian brother.
There is a name that is above every other name. If someone is called
by that name, then we cherish him, and we help him. That's why
God put us into fellowship together.

*Prayer: Lord, make me mindful of the good name of another so I
never do anything to tarnish it.*

This editorial is taken from "Decision" magazine, September, 1978; © 1978
Billy Graham Evangelistic Association. Used by permission. All Rights reserved.

❧ JANUARY 28 ❧
FIRST CLASS

As the Father hath loved me, so have I loved you: continue
ye in my love.

John 15:9 KJV

It follows, doesn't it? At least we hear it a lot: "If God loves me
and I remain in His love, certainly He'll find great joy in exercising
that love by fulfilling in my life all that He can do for me. Surely He
wants me happy. Surely He wants me rich. Surely He wants to fulfill all my dreams and satisfy me. Surely that means a big house and
several cars and maybe a boat. What I need to do is remain in His
love, and He's going to love me, give to me 'pressed down and running over' and open up the windows of heaven and pour out such a
blessing I won't be able to contain it, because I'm a child of the
King—and a child of the King, really loved by his Father, would
certainly be invited to go through life first class."

Such ideas and doctrines have been preached a lot lately, but
they're not new. No heresy is new. Satan has always been clever at
patching together selfishness and Scripture and finding people to
teach it. Not only that, he does quite well in finding people who will
listen to it.

*Prayer: Please, Lord, if I ever start to stray like this, pull me back into
the whole of Your Word so that I'm balanced, stable, and mature.*

❧ JANUARY 29 ❧
GOD IS AWAKE

For the eyes of the Lord run to and fro throughout the
whole earth, to show his might in behalf of those whose
heart is blameless toward him. . . .

2 Chronicles 16:9

God doesn't sleep or take a nap or doze in a chair. I can't even
imagine that. By 9:30 at night, I'm shot. But not only does God neither slumber nor sleep (Psalm 121:4), His eyes are moving back and
forth throughout the earth. He's watching, looking, for someone
like me—someone who needs support, someone who can't make it
on his own, someone who finds himself saying, "Where is God?"

If you're like me, you're always looking for God. But this verse tells me that God is looking for me, looking for ways to show His strength, His might, on my behalf.

It's a promise, but there is a small clause that goes with it. He will help those whose "heart is blameless toward Him."

Do I have to run around trying to find God to support me? No, His eyes are looking for ways to support me, if my heart is blameless or right toward Him.

David made sure his heart was right toward God. Even though he did what most of us have never done—followed adultery with murder—he was able to pray, "Create in me a clean heart, O God; and renew a right spirit within me" (Psalm 51:10 KJV).

"The eyes of the Lord run to and fro throughout the whole earth, to show His might in behalf of those whose heart is blameless toward Him." There is a word of comfort in that. Also, there is a plain word of warning. But I'm thankful that for me, as there was for David, there is reconciliation, and I want that. I need His support, and it's nice to know that even when I'm asleep, God is not.

Prayer: Please help me to be sure that my heart is blameless toward You.

 JANUARY 30

FRIENDS

Ye are my friends, if ye do whatsoever I command you.
                                                    John 15:14 KJV

Someone once said, "If you don't have a good friend, you should pray to be sent an enemy." There may be something to that. A good friend, like an enemy, doesn't let us get away with anything. Friends and enemies help us grow. We try to avoid making enemies, of course, but we do need to make friends consciously.

Friendships don't just happen; they have to be cultivated—in short, we have to work at them. They are not built on just taking; they are built on giving. Friends continue to care about us, to be honest, to be loving, and to tell us the truth about ourselves. They won't tell us only what we want to hear.

Jesus chose to say to those who know Him, "I call you friends." And He is a Friend. He is the One who is always there; One who will always help; One whom we do not have to impress; One with whom we can talk whenever the need arises, or with whom we can just be quiet when we don't feel like saying anything at all.

Since He is that kind of Friend, so should His followers be as they relate to each other. All the descriptions of the friendship of God in Christ apply to the Christian Body as well. The Body of believers is more than a spiritual encounter group or assembly meeting—it is friendship with our true Friend as the Head and the other friends functioning together as a whole. We need our Christian friends. Those who do not build friendships often find themselves drying up spiritually. The security of these friendships holds us; the counsel of friends teaches us; and the prayers of our friends support us.

Cultivate your friends, that's why God gave them to you. And be a friend, too, that's why God gave you to them. You will be pleased. So will God.

Prayer: Father, thank You for my friends and for Jesus, who shows me the way to love them.

This editorial is taken from "Decision" magazine, February, 1979; © 1979 Billy Graham Evangelistic Association. Used by permission. All Rights reserved.

❧ JANUARY 31 ❦
RIGHT IN THEIR LAPS

> Give, and it shall be given unto you; good measure, pressed down, and shaken together, and running over, shall men give into your bosom. For with the same measure that ye mete withal it shall be measured to you again.
>
> Luke 6:38 KJV

Who says?

All those sermons go the same way: "Give to God, and He will give more to you"; "You can't outgive God"; "God loves a cheerful giver."

So try it. Everyone knows what will happen.

Instead of steak, you get hot dogs.

Instead of a new car, you drive a rust pile.

Give your time, and there will always be people around to take it and then demand that you give them more.

Right?

Maybe. So what? That's not the measure anyway for either giving or keeping.

The trouble is, instead of looking for that "good measure" that He offers, we look over to the neighbor who keeps everything he gets, gives nothing to anybody, and so has more goods and fun—whatever that is.

No one is ever going to know what Jesus is talking about so long as he keeps measuring that way.

It's interesting. Those who are always looking at their neighbors and backing off from what Jesus is asking are usually the ones who are so certain that what Jesus says won't work.

But those who look to Jesus aren't talking about something that works; they're just talking about Him.

It's always possible, if you push hard enough, to get the steak and the car and keep all your free time for yourself. Then what?

There's something mysteriously wonderful about going the other route—the route with Jesus.

I've never met anyone who can adequately describe what "pressed down, shaken together, and running over" means. But I can't forget the glow on their faces while they try.

It isn't a glow generated by the delicious smell of high-priced steaks or the reflection given by polished, lacquered steel.

It's an inner glow from enjoying God's gift giving—the pressed-down, shaken-together, and running-over gift giving right in their laps.

Prayer: Thank You for being so open with Your great love and Your great gifts.

ꙮ FEBRUARY 1 ꙮ
GOD DOESN'T LAUGH AT ME

But when Jesus heard that, he said unto them, They that be whole need not a physician, but they that are sick.
Matthew 9:12 KJV

I don't go to the doctor very often, but I did today. All night long I had unusual chest pains, and first thing this morning I called the doctor. He took it seriously. So did the nurses. Even when all the tests showed that there was nothing wrong with my heart, he didn't laugh at me; he was glad I came.

When things are not right with my soul, I go to the Great Physician, too. "When in doubt, check it out." And even when it's not as bad as I thought, I'd rather go to Him than stay away and wonder. My Great Physician takes my symptoms seriously. He doesn't laugh at me. When I go to Him, He's glad I came.

Prayer: Thank You, Lord, for being my Great Physician. When I come to You, You never make me feel foolish.

❧ FEBRUARY 2 ❧
ASSURANCE—I NEED THAT

At the beginning of your supplications a word went forth, and I have come to tell it to you, for you are greatly beloved; therefore consider the word and understand the vision.

> Daniel 9:23

That quick!
Not even a little time lag.
Who would have guessed that God would do something like that? But there he stood, God's messenger, with the assurance that for Daniel, as soon as he started praying, the commanding word had already gone out from God.
Humanly, most of us wonder, does God hear?
Will He do anything?
Will He even care?
We know that God isn't mechanical, doing what we tell Him to do just because we tell Him to do it. Still, that's balanced by the repeated messages from Scripture that say: "And call upon me in the day of trouble; I will deliver you . . . (Psalm 50:15); "Ask, and it will be given you . . ." (Matthew 7:7); "If you ask anything in my name, I will do it" (John 14:14).
Well, God is my Father, and He listens.
That means even as I start to pray, He is beginning to work out all of the details to His answers.
Sometimes they may be intricate details, involving several phases. Other times they may be simple.
But it doesn't matter so long as His assurance is there.
When I'm on my knees, that's all I need to know.

Prayer: You are my God, and I know that You are listening to me.

FEBRUARY 3
MERCY

Blessed are the merciful: for they shall obtain mercy. . . .
                                          Matthew 5:7 KJV

Mistakes! At least that's usually what we prefer to call them!
We all make "mistakes," and the punishment is often not so se-
vere as our own self-condemnation. That's why we're glad for
mercy, not only from God, but from those whom we have offended.
Mercy is a rare quality, although it shouldn't be, because mistakes aren't rare. But we do quickly forget how much we have
needed mercy ourselves when someone needs mercy from us.
Buried in the fifth-century records of one of the desert monas-
teries in Egypt is the story of a man who wept when he saw someone
sinning. He said, "He today, I tomorrow." He was a wise man. All
of us, with our clay feet, can fall, and do fall quickly. We need to
remember that.
Jesus told His followers to forgive seventy times seven—in other
words, with a forgiveness that is unlimited. In many of our churches
on Sunday morning we pray the words that are recorded in
Matthew 6:12 (KJV): "And forgive us our debts, as we forgive our
debtors." What we are doing in that prayer is asking God to forgive
us to the same extent that we forgive others.
Forgiving people for their debts, trespasses, "mistakes," is not the
same as condoning what they did. It isn't a compromise with sin.
God neither condones nor compromises. He is firm about sin, what
it means and what it does. But He is also merciful. A strong, un-
compromising view of sin does not also mean a strong, uncompro-
mising, even harsh, view of the sinner.
We help someone all we can before he makes a "mistake," and
then we help him all we can after, if he makes that "mistake" and
falls. Trespasses, our "mistakes," happen often; mercy needs to be
given often, too. That's not a weak view of Christian love, that's
God's view of it.

*Prayer: Lord Jesus, just as You have been merciful to me, help me to
be merciful, too.*

❧ FEBRUARY 4 ❦
MORE AND MORE

Now to him who is able to do immeasurably more than all
we ask or imagine, according to his power that is at work
within us, to him be glory in the church and in Christ Jesus
throughout all generations, for ever and ever! Amen.

Ephesians 3:20, 21 NIV

The Apostle Paul ran out of words when he tried to describe the
"immeasurably more." He was saying in effect that according to the
power of God that is at work within us, God is able to do more and
more and more and more than we can imagine.

Go ahead; try to imagine what God can do. Now imagine more
than that. Now imagine even more than that. Keep going. That's
the power God has at work within us.

On the days when I feel depressed, weak, rundown, I turn to
the "immeasurably more" passage, and I say to myself, "How
much power is at work within me? More and more and more and
more. . . ."

*Prayer: Father, I know I can't measure Your power at work within
me, because I can't measure You.*

❧ FEBRUARY 5 ❦
TEMPTATION—IT'S VERY NICE

No temptation has overtaken you that is not common to
man. God is faithful, and he will not let you be tempted beyond your strength, but with the temptation will also provide the way of escape, that you may be able to endure it.

1 Corinthians 10:13

He savored the temptation and then enjoyed the sin.

It was the consequences that he didn't like; so he prayed to be delivered.

That's the way we are. It's not the temptation or the sin that bothers us; it's the results of giving in.

Sooner or later we learn the cause-and-effect process and begin to
want a life of holiness. We start to resist temptation.

Then we begin to understand what God is talking about.

Temptation will come—all the time. There is no stopping it. It is "common to man." As long as we live, we will face it.

But there is an escape. At the point where we can't withstand it, God answers the cry for help and makes a way out.

Maybe a friend comes along at the right moment, or the phone rings. Whatever, God will do it.

The question is not, "Will God provide a way of escape?" The question is, "Will I take the way of escape that God provides?"

I will if I really want to escape sin.

I won't if I don't.

No one has to succumb.

God has made sure of that.

But we can succumb if we want to. Temptation can be a lot of fun and the sin pleasant for a minute or two.

The consequence of it lasts longer.

Prayer: Keep me steady when the tempting comes. I'm so afraid I'll give in.

⇘ FEBRUARY 6 ⇙
MY DESIRES START SMALL

> . . . We too all formerly lived in the lusts of our flesh, in-
> dulging the desires of the flesh and of the mind, and were
> by nature children of wrath, even as the rest.
>
> Ephesians 2:3 NAS

What we really wanted was a small garbage disposal, but there isn't quite room enough under the sink, where the dishpan goes, and we have to have the dishpan, because we don't have a dishwasher. Of course, a dishwasher would be nice, but the kitchen is too small. There is hardly enough room to turn around now.

But then that's the problem—no room. If we could knock out one of the walls, we could have room for a dishwasher, more cabinets, make an eating area, and have an outside door so we won't have to squeeze past the car when we go out through the garage.

And that's another thing: if we had a two-car garage, we wouldn't have to squeeze at all. And as long as we're extending the garage, we could add onto the back, making a nice sun porch. . . .

I'm glad I can control my wants; some people can't. Their desires get out of hand and lead them on from one want to another. Scripture calls it, "indulging the desires of the flesh and of the mind."

I'm glad I can control my desires. . . . Now, as long as we're adding a sun porch, wouldn't it be nice to build in that fireplace we've always wanted?

Prayer: Lord, I know there's nothing wrong with dreaming, but there is a lot wrong with desiring and craving. Help me to know the difference and to keep my life in perspective.

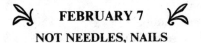

FEBRUARY 7

NOT NEEDLES, NAILS

Set me as a seal upon thine heart, as a seal upon thine arm: for love is strong as death. . . .

Song of Solomon 8:6 KJV

Jeanne Marie Bouvier de la Motte, later known as Madame Jeanne Guyon, wanted so much to please the Lord Jesus that as a young girl she took literally the words of Scripture, "Set me as a seal upon thine heart." She wrote the name *Jesus* on pieces of paper and sewed them to her skin so that they would always be a painful reminder to be repentant and obedient to the Lord. Her action was wrong; her desire was right.

There came a day when she did understand what it meant to be sealed by the Holy Spirit—sealed and preserved, kept not by what she did but by what Christ did.

How far we will go to have forgiveness and peace in our souls, if we could only generate it ourselves. Yet we hesitate to lay claim to the finished work that Christ provided for us on the cross and in the resurrection.

She had the name of Jesus sewed to her skin. Putting needles through our skin adds nothing to redemption, for He has already paid the price for our sin—not with needles, but with nails.

Prayer: O Lord, You went to the cross for me. I can add nothing to it. By faith in what You did for me there, I confess You as my Savior.

FEBRUARY 8

PERSPECTIVE

> ... Lo, I am with you alway, even unto the end of the world.
>
> Matthew 28:20 KJV

"Me? Do without? But I've worked hard, I have a right. ..."
But do we "have a right"? Nowhere does God tell us that we "have a right," even to all that we are enjoying now. Do you have a house, a bed, a furnace, three meals a day? God is good. But He doesn't have to give any of that. What He does have to do is keep His promises—and He always has: "... I will never leave thee, nor forsake thee" (Hebrews 13:5 KJV); "... Neither shall any man pluck them out of my hand" (John 10:28 KJV); "... I am with you alway" (Matthew 28:20 KJV).

It is easy to lose sight of what He does promise when we are so busy looking at all the things that He doesn't have to guarantee. There is little worship in our coupon clipping or figuring what our retirement pension and Social Security benefits will be. Some of us get so involved in accumulating and expecting that we forget God. We don't even bow our heads and offer thanks for lunch. And God doesn't have to provide lunch either.

When a person comes to Christ by faith, he knows: "I have been crucified with Christ; it is no longer I who live, but Christ who lives in me; and the life I now live in the flesh I live by faith in the Son of God, who loved me and gave himself for me" (Galatians 2:20). Does a person who is crucified have any claims? Does a person whose life is no longer his own have a right to make demands?

The greatest thing about being His is exactly that—being His. Everything else is nice, even enjoyable, but it is secondary. It certainly isn't guaranteed.

Prayer: Lord Jesus, sometimes I get so involved in chasing after things, I forget You and Your promises. Please forgive me.

❧ FEBRUARY 9 ❧

BAD SEATS AND A STIFF NECK

And I appoint unto you a kingdom, as my Father hath appointed unto me; That ye may eat and drink at my table in my kingdom. . . .

Luke 22:29, 30 KJV

People talk about having front-row seats in heaven as if heaven is a theater or an auditorium. Heaven isn't an auditorium. Certainly it isn't a theater. And who would want front-row seats there anyway? If heaven were only a theater and we were just going to sit around and watch something happen, that wouldn't be very exciting. Who wants to spend eternity with a stiff neck? Heaven *is* likened to a banquet. It's the marriage supper. We will spend eternity with God, who is the host. We won't be searching or hungry anymore. And at God's banquet table there are no bad seats. The table expands.

I took front-row seats at a concert once. I waited in a long line to get them, and they were the last two seats available. So that's where we sat, looking up to see the shoes of the musicians. I didn't enjoy it so much as I might have. But as I sat there, I kept thinking, *It could be worse. I could be outside.*

When I'm invited to the banquet hall of God, my seat will be a good one, and my name will already be there at my place. I'll spend eternity with God in heaven. I won't be outside, and I won't have a stiff neck.

Prayer: Lord, we can't imagine what eternity is going to be like, but You've given us some hints, and it's exciting.

❧ FEBRUARY 10 ❧

ON TARGET EVERY TIME

The Lord is nigh unto all them that call upon him, to all that call upon him in truth.

Psalm 145:18 KJV

I don't mind doing an occasional interview or talk show; I've done a number of them over the years. But I like radio best.

I have a radio broadcast that is aired on Christian radio stations in several states, and I've learned something doing it. I have learned that God isn't limited by me, the engineer, or the person who plays the tapes on the air. The broadcast comes primarily from material in my books, which means the content is prepared two or three years before it is actually taped. Then we tape it two to three months in advance of its being aired. The engineer packages them, selects the programming time, and then they are aired by whoever is on duty at the station.

Over and over again people have said to me, "What you said last night really spoke to me." Only God could do that. To know their need and how to communicate to them with last night's broadcast, when I had no way of knowing who I was talking to, either when I recorded it or when I prepared it, and had no control over when it would be aired anyway, only proves that before we call, God will answer.

If a person has been praying, "Lord, speak to me," God can use the broadcast to answer that person because He knows the content of it and He knows the person's need. That's the way God has always worked. He gave the Scriptures—sixty-six books, written by more than forty authors, in three languages, over a period of 1,500 years—and when I open the Word and speak from the content of the Word, that Word, inspired by the Holy Spirit, is as fresh as the minute it was given to the writer. It goes straight to my heart or to the heart of the person I'm giving it to. This is a wonder that no one can explain but that all of us have experienced. God is on target every time.

Prayer: Lord, I don't understand the mystery of Your wisdom; I just know that You meet my needs and the needs of others with the right help at the exact moment it's needed, and I believe You'll do that again today.

FEBRUARY 11
TURN AROUND

Wherefore God also gave them up. . . .

Romans 1:24 KJV

What a terrible indictment! Think of the dimensions of it. But God will do that. God will leave us to ourselves if we leave Him first. God will leave us to the outcome of our own choice.

Paul explains in verse 21 that if people will not glorify Him as God or be thankful to Him as God but follow their own ways, becoming foolish enough to think they can serve their own so-called wisdom, exchanging all that God is in His purity for what is ugly and corrupt and defiled—if we insist on that choice, God will let us have the results of our choice

But for every passage of Scripture like that, there is also the wooing, the tender calling back of God. He is there for any who will hear His voice and no longer harden their hearts.

If we want to know what it is to continue to go away from God, Romans 3:12–18 tells us. But if we want to know what it is to come back through faith in Christ, Romans 5:1, 2 tells us that. We can turn our backs on God and walk away, or we can repent and turn around. The choice is ours.

Prayer: Father, I thank You that though Scripture is very clear about the harsh realities of a turned back, it is just as clear about forgiveness and love for those who wake up and see their condition and turn around.

FEBRUARY 12

WHAT'S HIDDEN IN YOUR TENT?

But the people of Israel broke faith in regard to the devoted things; for Achan . . . took some of the devoted things; and the anger of the Lord burned against the people of Israel.
Joshua 7:1

You remember Achan, described in Joshua 7. The plunder or booty of Jericho was devoted to the Lord, according to the passages in Joshua 6, but Achan wasn't satisfied with that. He had to take some of it for himself.

There are some things that belong only to God. Achan couldn't live with that. The Bible says, "he coveted." That's a big word—*coveted*—and it takes in a whole lot more than an expensive suit of clothes and a few shekels of gold and silver. What he did not only changed the course of battle for all his people, it put him down in history as a man who couldn't be trusted. Not only did Achan's sin involve his entire country, he went down forever in history as guilty, listed in the press, if you will, along with his father and his grandfather.

Look at the words used about Achan. He took the devoted things, he stole, he lied, he was the man who "brought trouble on us."

I've thought about Achan. He was caught and punished, but there was an in-between time—I don't know how long it was. I wonder how free he felt. Could he really live happily, knowing what was hidden in his tent? Was he free to let his mind expand on other things, thinking always about that tent? Did he investigate, take new directions, when every thought brought him back to what was in his tent? The stolen goods were buried in his tent, but think about what was buried in his heart. How free can any person be when something forbidden is buried in his tent?

Prayer: Lord, show me whatever is in "my tent" that may be angering You. I want to get rid of it.

❧ FEBRUARY 13 ❧
EMPTY AGAIN

The threshing floors shall be full of grain, and the vats shall overflow with wine and oil.

Joel 2:24 KJV

The gas gauge on my car reads empty again. It always happens one day before I get my paycheck. What I wish I had was one of those new fuel-efficient cars that I read about in the newspaper. If I believe everything that's said about them, the carburetor saves 30 percent, something else saves 50 percent, and so on. It adds up to about 120 percent! The drivers of those cars must have to stop about every 200 miles to let some of the gas out.

Joel talks about God blessing us so much that the vats overflow with the wine and oil. That's the way it is sometimes for a believer. There are times when God gives so much that life seems to be overflowing. But that's all right. When I feel as if I'm going to burst with the goodness of God, I just let some of it out; I give it to those whose tanks have run dry.

Prayer: Father, I know You didn't bless me for me to keep it all to myself anyway. Help me to want to share Your goodness with others.

❧ FEBRUARY 14 ❦
THE BARGAIN

And the peace of God, which passes all understanding, will
keep your hearts and your minds in Christ Jesus.

Philippians 4:7

Worry centers!

At least that is what some people call the heart and mind.

Romantics think of the heart as the seat of emotion; love, hate,
and passion spawn there.

And they think of the mind as holding anxiety, tension, and
worry.

Most people aren't romantics, though. They are practical realists.
But they understand about the heart and the mind. Overload either
one with worry, and sickness will come, even death.

Find a way to produce heart-and-mind peace, and the world will
probably pay anything to get it. But no one can market it. God
alone has the peace and the patent on it.

"Peace"—the kind that can't be destroyed because it is God's
peace, and He can't be destroyed. Anybody want it?

There is no brochure out to describe it; it passes all human understanding. No salesman will call.

The peace that "will keep your hearts and your minds" is in
Christ Jesus.

You can have it when you have Jesus.

Don't ask for peace; ask for Him. When He comes into your heart
and mind, He'll bring His peace with Him.

You get both for the same price—free!

Prayer: You are the bringer of peace. What I want and need is You.

❧ FEBRUARY 15 ❦
BUT WHAT ABOUT CREDENTIALS?

Jesus answered them, and said, My doctrine is not mine,
but his that sent me.

John 7:16 KJV

It's always that way: if you're from one school and somebody else
is from another school, even if you have the same degree, your de-

gree is worth more—your school was tougher; it made more demands. His school was easier; anybody could get a degree from that school. But your school was far more selective to begin with, far more difficult to satisfy on the exams, and if your degree is a graduate degree, your committee was far tougher than his.

When the leaders examined Jesus and questioned His credentials, it wasn't just that they frowned on His academic qualifications. It was worse than that. He didn't have any degrees. They wanted credentials. He answered them simply and truthfully that He was Himself His own credentials. He came from the Father. This is the Son of God talking. "My teaching is not mine, but his that sent me. I say what God has given Me." How could He say that? He was and is God.

Some would water that down by saying, "Well, His truth is truth only if it is true for us," or, "His truth is truth only if we practice it as truth." But Jesus didn't say that about His teachings. The truth He gave was God's truth. If it had been anything else, it would always be relative—relative to the ones hearing it, relative to His academic credentials, relative to any other qualifications people might want to list. We obey Him because He is Truth. We don't make Him Truth simply because we obey Him.

The leaders in His day weren't satisfied with His answer. Many aren't satisfied with it today either.

Prayer: Lord Jesus, You are the Truth of God, and that has absolutely nothing to do with my opinion of it. I acknowledge You as Truth, not because I think so, but because You are one with the Father.

✑ FEBRUARY 16 ✐
SCRUBBED

> But whoever causes one of these little ones who believe in me to sin, it would be better for him to have a great millstone fastened around his neck and to be drowned in the depth of the sea.
>
> Matthew 18:6

"Wipe your feet!"

It's a familiar scene: The kitchen floor has been carefully washed. Mother is just putting away the pail and scrubber when the back door bursts open and children come pouring in from their play in the backyard. From out of the depths of the mop closet comes that panicked scream: "Wipe your feet!" And not only does every child have to go through the ritual, but there is even a rag kept handy to wipe the paws of the dog, lest he, too, track mud onto a clean kitchen floor.

Some of us, who never think that we might warp our children by demanding that they wipe their feet, surrender to the view that we may be too "narrow-minded" if we care at all about the literature that comes into our home. Is our tolerance of muddy books the mark of a broad mind, or is it rather a weak resignation to writers who have amoebic minds? Is clean, uplifting literature that is written to build, educate, strengthen, really less erudite than writings with limited vocabularies and ideas that rarely move to anything more enlightening than bathrooms and motel beds? Have we accepted the notion that the best entertainment is what is given in words that degrade us and negate the work of the Highest, the Holy, the Just, whether first in magazine and book form, or later in a movie or TV script?

We are careful of our clean floors. But an unsoiled floor is not the most important goal to achieve in our homes. What about those unsoiled minds? Think about that the next time your children burst into the house and you yell, "Wipe your feet!"

Floors can always be scrubbed again; how do you scrub a mind?

Prayer: Guide me, Lord, as I seek to guide the children you have placed in my care.

This editorial is taken from "Decision" magazine, May, 1983; © 1983 Billy Graham Evangelistic Association. Used by permission. All Rights reserved.

        FEBRUARY 17

NO SECRETS

... For the accuser of our brethren is cast down, which accused them before our God day and night.
Revelation 12:10 KJV

Satan is the great accuser. Day and night before God he would accuse us, pointing out all that we do, all that we think, all our failures. The thought of that could be terribly depressing, because when I think about it even for a few minutes, there are hundreds of things that Satan could accuse me of; and I can multiply that by every hour of every day.

But wait a minute! What can Satan tell God about me that God doesn't already know? God loves me. God redeemed me. God keeps me. God knows me. Go ahead, Satan; tell God whatever you want. He already knows it; there are no secrets. And that sin that you're enjoying so much has already been confessed and forgiven.

Prayer: Thank You, Lord, that when Satan accuses me, in his whole long list there is not one surprise to You.

FEBRUARY 18

I'M NO PAGAN

Lead me, O Lord, in thy righteousness because of mine enemies; make thy way straight before my face.

Psalm 5:8 KJV

It was one of my favorite Bible verses until somebody showed me that I was quoting it incorrectly. I liked it my way better. I was quoting, "Make my way straight before Your face," and I meant that. I wanted God to bless what I was doing with my life. I had life carefully planned out. I had my affairs arranged. I sincerely wanted God to bless each step I took. I thought that was pretty commendable.

Then somebody showed me what the verse really says: "Make thy way straight before my face." Now I'm not so comfortable anymore, because if I say that, I'm asking God to show me His way, with the implication that if He presents His way clearly before my face, I'll walk His way.

How can I know that I want to do that? Where might God take me? When I plan the way I want God to bless, I wouldn't take me anyplace that might be uncomfortable or difficult. I certainly wouldn't allow hardship or pain to interfere. And by no means would I want any financial difficulties.

I wish my friend had minded his own business. It fit my theology nicely to have God bless my plans. After all, I'm no pagan, wanting to live my life without God's blessing. I want God's blessing—on my terms.

Scripture memorization is fun so long as friends don't bring up accuracy.

Prayer: Father, help me to be sure that I'm building my life on Your Word and not simply on my own interpretation of it.

 FEBRUARY 19

WHO? ME?

For I will give you a mouth and wisdom, which none of your adversaries will be able to withstand or contradict.

Luke 21:15

My adversaries are no dummies.

When they argue, they're logical. I'm the one who gets all twisted up and finds myself wishing that I could go hide somewhere. When my adversaries sneer, they usually have good reason. I come across as a clod.

And it's embarrassing to be a witnessing, Bible-believing, evangelical clod.

So how can I believe a statement like the one in Luke 21:15?

Jesus said it, referring to the roughest part of discipleship—having to answer for what we believe before hostile courts.

He can do what He says, although no matter how I try I can't imagine my mouth and my wisdom confounding anybody.

That's the miracle of belonging to Jesus.

He will do it.

And knowing what's going through my mind, He says as a preface to His promise: "Settle it therefore in your minds, not to meditate beforehand how to answer" (21:14).

It's good He said that, because no amount of thinking beforehand will make me any more clever anyway.

The wisdom isn't in me; it's in Him.

And He's here with me to do the talking.

Let them sneer.

Prayer: I know that I'll be more able to speak if You are the wisdom behind my words.

🍃 FEBRUARY 20 🍃
FOCUSED

But thanks be to God, which giveth us the victory through
our Lord Jesus Christ.

1 Corinthians 15:57 KJV

She was singing with the choir "Thanks Be to God," a beautiful
smile on her face as she expressed the words with deep feeling. Yet
even as I watched her, I knew that two of her three children were
dying of the same rare disease. How could she sing?

She admits that she doesn't understand why such pain and suffering have come to her family. She just knows that God knows and
that someday she may understand. She sings and smiles because she
knows something beyond the everyday suffering, beyond her own
emotions; she knows in her heart what her mind knows; for her
mind is centered on Christ. She is focused on Him.

*Prayer: Father, thank You for those who in the depths of adversity are
still singing "Thanks Be to God."*

🍃 FEBRUARY 21 🍃
GOD DOESN'T HAVE LARYNGITIS

. . . And after the fire a still small voice.

1 Kings 19:12 KJV

It was the writers' guild annual banquet, and I was to be the guest
speaker. Earlier in the day laryngitis had set in, and by the time I
arrived at the banquet I was only able to croak a little bit. So when
it came time to give my speech, I stood close to the microphone and
rasped, "I want to explain my voice. It's changing. I'm a late
bloomer, and this is an event in my life that I've looked forward to
for a long time. So I'm happy that you can share this experience
with me tonight." Then I delivered my speech.

And I noticed something. People were leaning forward in order
to hear what I was saying. I have addressed groups before where the
people have leaned in the opposite direction, with their eyes closed.

God doesn't have laryngitis, and usually we expect Him to speak
to us in a loud voice so that we will hear what He is saying and pay

attention. But He doesn't always do that. He didn't do that with Elijah, and He won't always do that with us.

When I listen to God, sometimes He speaks softly. So I like to get off where it's quiet. Then I can concentrate. I don't want to miss anything.

Many times we have had good fellowship together—me listening and God speaking in that still, small voice. God doesn't require a strong amplification system, but when He speaks, He does ask for, and expect, an attentive ear.

Prayer: Lord, I'm glad You don't have to nearly break my eardrums for me to hear what You are saying.

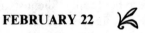

FEBRUARY 22

WEAK!

> But you, take courage! Do not let your hands be weak, for your work shall be rewarded.
>
> 2 Chronicles 15:7

What's the use?

Whenever I try to do something, someone knocks me down.

I'm either not fast enough or good enough; or what I try to do turns out to be unimportant anyway.

That's when I go weak; there isn't much incentive left.

It would help if I could believe God. Maybe I can.

"Take courage!"

Easy words—but not empty.

That would sound like a useless charge if I didn't know that the One who says it is also the One who is promising the reward.

I guess He's saying, "Keep at it."

And I will; it doesn't matter, I guess, how others respond.

I know how God will respond.

He has already told me.

Prayer: Give me the confidence and courage to keep going every day—starting today.

❧ FEBRUARY 23 ❦

GOD HEARS, DOESN'T HE?

But know that the Lord hath set apart him that is godly for
himself: the Lord will hear when I call unto him.

Psalm 4:3 KJV

Does God hear the prayers of everybody? I don't know. And it's
really not my business to try to find out. What is my business is that
He has warned, "But know that the Lord hath set apart him that is
godly for himself: the Lord will hear when I call unto him." We do
know that God will hear the godly. He has set apart the godly and
will listen to them when they call.

I suppose we could make up a rule book for the godly or have
some kind of testing kit, like litmus paper, that determines shades of
godliness. We could put together a council of the godly, with the
more godly and the most godly to examine the rest of us. Then on
the basis of their findings we would determine whose prayers God
hears and to what degree He hears them. But even so, we could
never be sure. We'd never really know.

All we do know is what God has said: that He has set apart the
godly for Himself. So before I can know if my prayers are going to
be answered, I'd better know if I'm godly. And before I can know if
I'm godly, I'm going to have to know about being set apart. God
does the setting apart.

John, in the New Testament, guided by the Spirit of God, told us:
"But to all who received him, who believed in his name, he gave
power to become children of God" (John 1:12). That's my part: re-
ceiving the One who sets us apart and believing in Him. All the rest
follows. And I certainly do like what follows!

*Prayer: Lord, to whatever degree I have received You before, I receive
You now with all my heart and soul.*

54

FEBRUARY 24
PROFANE

Thou shalt not take the name of the Lord thy God in vain;
for the Lord will not hold him guiltless that taketh his
name in vain.

Exodus 20:7 KJV

Profanity bothers me. People who curse, swear, use foul language
in any way trouble me. But I can explain them. Some have a limited
vocabulary. Others are terribly insecure and are pretending to be
tough. They are the frightened ones who are trying to keep people
from discovering just how weak and unsure of themselves they
really are. People who curse are to be pitied.

People who don't swear but whose lives are profane bother me,
too. Those are the ones who deny the ownership of God. Their
bodies are used for profanity; their actions are profane. Their minds
are working on profane practices—cheating, lying, stealing, hurting, using. They are not just polluters of the sound waves, as the
swearers are; they are polluters of society, infecting everybody and
everything around them.

But even worse than that group are those who profess to have
Christ in their lives but do not live Christ. In short, their mouths say
one thing, their actions say another. They are living out a profanity,
hurting people around them, not only temporarily, but sometimes
for eternity, because they drive people away from the Christ they
talk about. Some are cheats, some are liars, some are racist—all the
time talking their talk about Jesus.

God will judge. I don't need to, and I must not. My responsibility
is to keep Exodus 20:7 in mind all the time and govern my tongue
and my life by it.

*Prayer: Lord, may there be no part of me in word or deed that pro-
fanes Your name.*

FEBRUARY 25
MORNING IS COMING

... Weeping may tarry for the night, but joy comes with the morning.

Psalm 30:5

Alone at night with the tears, the deep sobs that make your body shudder—the absolute emptiness of any hope—you say, "God is gone. My name is forgotten in heaven. God has moved away without me. It has to be God's anger. What else can it be?"

Whether or not there is a reason for it isn't the issue. To be so bereft is to feel the utter uselessness of finding any hope at all for tomorrow.

Is God angry? No one fully knows the mind of God. The divinity of God is a curtain; it separates. His revelation gives us some information, but not all.

But God has anticipated our wondering on those sad nights, and there is a word from Him. Through His love that is not reflective of any one moment or event, but comes long before the convulsive sobbing begins, He speaks. The psalmist is His hope bringer: "For his anger is but for a moment, and his favor is for a lifetime. Weeping may tarry for the night, but joy comes with the morning" (Psalm 30:5).

Whether we know why we suffer so or don't know why, the heart of God has a place for our tears. And even before the tears come, His understanding arms are wide open.

The sobbing hours may appear to block the promise of hope, but they won't.

The night may seem to be too dark for any light to ever penetrate, but it isn't.

Morning is coming, and His joy.

They come together.

Prayer: It is comforting to know that Your heart has a place for my fears.

FEBRUARY 26

WINTER IS NOT FOREVER

To every thing there is a season, and a time to every purpose under the heaven: A time to be born, and a time to die; a time to plant, and a time to pluck up that which is planted.

Ecclesiastes 3:1, 2 KJV

Solomon looked around and, in the wisdom that God gave him, stated what at first seems obvious, but is extremely profound: that although there is a season for everything—laughing, crying, sowing, reaping, birth, death—it's all a puff of wind, a vanity. It doesn't last long. Nothing lasts, no matter how long it may seem.

We think about that a lot where I live. We have only two seasons—winter and getting ready for winter. My secretary commented, "If summer falls on a Saturday this year, we're going to have a picnic."

But though our winters go on forever, it seems, there is an end. There is a time to wear boots and a cap, and a time to take them off. There is a time for using a snow shovel and a time for putting it away. Though winter seems permanent, it isn't. Only God is permanent. The cycles and seasons we call nature are what He made, and He did it to help us see that He is the Maker who is beyond what He made. We're going to be lost in the cycles if all we know is the seasons. But they take on new meaning when we look past them to the eternal dimension of being forever with God, where nothing changes.

Solomon was right about there being a time for everything, and he could have added: there will come a point where we will no longer live in time. Forever is not just a long time; forever is forever, and that's what eternity is. We can't decide the time for the coming and going of the seasons. But we can decide where we will spend eternity.

Prayer: Lord, the very way You made the world and its changing seasons points beyond the world to You, the unchanging One. I'm grateful that You pointed me to Yourself.

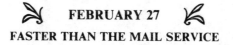

FEBRUARY 27

FASTER THAN THE MAIL SERVICE

And it shall come to pass, that before they call, I will answer; and while they are yet speaking, I will hear.

Isaiah 65:24 KJV

It seems that postage rates are always going up. The last time the postal service added two cents to the postal rate, some people were saying it was for storage. And it might be. But if they are storing mail, they aren't consistent about it.

My bills never get delayed or lost. But the letter I'm looking for from a dear friend usually does. Requests for charitable gifts, investment suggestions, sweepstakes announcements telling me that I might have won $1 million, offers to sell me a waterfront lot in North Dakota or desert property in Moose Jaw always seem to get to my letter box. But not the refund check I'd been hoping would come before the end of the month.

God says, "Before they call, I will answer." How's that for fast service? I don't have to wait for some clerk to finish his coffee break before I get my answer. I can get delivery without waiting for the post-office window to open at 9:00 A.M. And I can even get service after 5:00 P.M. God knows my inner need, and He responds. His loving heart wants to. Even before I can think to express myself, His answer is on the way.

God, of course, isn't a letter carrier, as some people think He is. God is the omnipotent, holy, eternal One who loves me very much. Before I call, He will answer. He promised, and He doesn't even charge an extra two cents.

Prayer: I know You care, I know You listen, I know You love me, and I'm thankful that even now You are answering the inner longings of my soul.

≥ FEBRUARY 28 ≤
RIGHT NOW, THAT'S ALL I WANT

The Lord your God is in your midst, a warrior who gives
victory; he will rejoice over you with gladness, he will
renew you in his love; he will exult over you with loud
singing as on a day of festival. . . .

                                         Zephaniah 3:17, 18

Oh, do I need that!

There are days when I don't need theology, biblical exegesis, or
doctrinal statements. I just need God.

And when He comes with a word like this—clear, personal,
warm—it doesn't matter to me that He said it first to the people of
Jerusalem, because He has said it to me, too, and that promise is big
enough for the whole world.

I can bathe myself in that promise and lean back and enjoy all
that He is and all that He gives.

I have a Warrior who gives victory;
I'm being rejoiced over with gladness;
I'm being exulted over with singing;
I'm being renewed in His love.
And right now, that's all I want to think about.

Prayer: You are all that to me, Father, and so much more.

≥ FEBRUARY 29 ≤
WHICH CHOICE?

And Elijah came unto all the people, and said, How long
halt ye between two opinions? if the Lord be God, follow
him: but if Baal, then follow him. And the people answered
him not a word.

                                         1 Kings 18:21 KJV

Shopping is a chore for me. I think it's because I have so much
trouble making up my mind. I go back and forth from store to store,
comparing price, model, size, color, and I don't know which to
choose. Sometimes I've gone home without choosing anything,
which is in itself a choice. It probably doesn't matter that I'm not

rich; I wouldn't know how to spend lots of money if I had it. I would probably still drive an old car, simply because I hate to face the thought of shopping for a new one.

When Elijah was on Mount Carmel, confronting the people about their choice between God and Baal, he pictured the people as limping between two opinions, going back and forth—uncertain, unable to make a choice, trying to stay on both sides, like a man trying to walk on two sides of a ditch at the same time or trying to go down two forks of a road. Eventually he will be in serious trouble.

"How long will you do that?" Elijah asked. Everyone either chooses God or he doesn't choose God.

Not to make a choice is a choice. When I go shopping I know it. Elijah knew it, too.

Prayer: Lord, You are God. With my whole heart I choose to follow You.

❧ MARCH 1 ❧
WELL ... IT WAS THIS WAY

That I may make it clear, as I ought to speak.
Colossians 4:4

I was reading an article in a magazine in which five famous persons had been brought together in a sort of round-up interview. What struck me was how often all five of them replied to the interviewer's questions with, "Well ...," and then gave their answer. After a while it was like a fingernail on a chalkboard; it was irritating. I realize how fortunate we are that in the Word of God, where God used sixty-six authors, the Holy Spirit didn't allow them to use *well* as a preface to every statement.

Can't you see it: "Well, Jesus was born in Bethlehem." "Well, Paul chose Barnabas," and so forth.

God has a big vocabulary and knows how to use it. His Word is not only good reading because it is His Word—inspired, profitable, a two-edged sword—but also because it is well written.

No wonder good authors, even secular ones who don't believe in the authority of Scripture, read the Bible. Sometimes I wish Christian authors and speakers, who do believe in the authority of God's

Word, would read it as carefully. Well . . . that's all I need to say
about that.

*Prayer: Father, I tend to have lazy habits, too, both verbal and writ-
ten. Help me so that even my communication is a good witness to You.*

MARCH 2

IT'S NOT MY FAULT

And the man said, The woman whom thou gavest to be
with me, she gave me of the tree, and I did eat.

Genesis 3:12 KJV

Just like children. We've all heard it. "It's his fault." "She made
me do it." "It's not my fault."

Adam couldn't blame society, his education, the state of the
economy, the job market, inflation, the government, or anything
else. He and Eve were in a perfect garden, just the two of them. So
Adam blamed Eve for his rebellion against the command of God.
And then to emphasize his own innocence, "The woman *You* gave
me, she gave me of the tree, and I did eat." In other words, "God,
it's Your fault."

People are still doing that, no matter how good their circumstances and surroundings. When they willfully, purposefully, inten-
tionally disobey God, they'll blame somebody else or God Himself.
"Lord, You made me like this. It's Your fault." Irresponsibility
hasn't changed over the centuries. We still talk as Adam talked. He
traded the beauty, the liberty of God's garden for the prison of his
own rebellion and spent the rest of his life doing hard time. Man has
been doing that ever since.

*Prayer: Lord, there is no one to blame. My rebellion is my rebellion. I
confess that and come to You for mercy and forgiveness.*

❧ MARCH 3 ❦
AN AGE-OLD QUESTION

Therefore let those who suffer according to God's will do right and entrust their souls to a faithful Creator.

1 Peter 4:19

Why the good suffer is an age-old question, and no one has the answer to it. Peter, inspired by God, gives the only response that can be given—that those who suffer according to God's will are to do right. They are to entrust their souls to a faithful Creator. Why some suffer and some don't only God knows. The fact that some have a ministry of suffering is obvious. They don't like it, we don't like to see it, but it is so. Yet we've all seen some of the finest saints among the suffering and some of the worst examples of faithfulness to God among those who have been most blessed.

We don't like to think about a ministry of suffering. We even find teachers who will tell us that God wants everybody to be happy and bubbly and high. Tell that to the men and women who are suffering. "Many are the afflictions of the righteous, but the Lord delivers him out of them all" (Psalm 34:19). That's not an explanation of why there is more suffering for some than for others; there is no explanation. That's simply a statement of fact. The good news is that God is there—in suffering. Jesus reemphasized it: "I will never leave you nor forsake you."

Prayer: Lord, help me to minister to those who are suffering. And if the day comes for me to suffer, too, may I entrust my soul to You, my faithful Creator, and may I do what is right.

❧ MARCH 4 ❦
GRAPHIC, ISN'T HE?

He will again have compassion upon us, he will tread our iniquities under foot. Thou wilt cast all our sins into the depths of the sea.

Micah 7:19

Smashed and sunk.

Squashed flat and buried at sea—all as an act of compassion. Hard to understand at first, isn't it?

There must be something alive about iniquity, something about sin that multiplies and grows. Because God takes violent action against it.

"He will again have compassion upon us, he will tread our iniquities under foot. Thou wilt cast all our sins into the depths of the sea" (Micah 7:19).

Graphic, isn't He?

God will treat sin in a way that we can understand.

But He has to; how else will we know how virulent sin is? What better way for us to understand its destruction?

Stepped on and smashed.

Buried and unrecoverable.

And He has promised that to us as an act of merciful love.

Funny how we differ from God. We treat sin kindly; we coddle and caress it.

God smashes it.

He's too compassionate to treat it any other way. It is destroyed so that it can't spread like disease through everything.

And when it's dead, He drops it into the sea like dangerous waste.

Not tender—but compassionate.

He loves us too much to let it live.

Prayer: Thank You for Your tough compassion toward me.

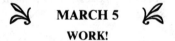

MARCH 5
WORK!

. . . Whatsoever ye do, do all to the glory of God.
1 Corinthians 10:31 KJV

Because God gives us friends, family, and church relationships, we are able to "make it" in what is sometimes an extremely difficult life. But God doesn't stop there, especially for those of us privileged to work with Christians.

To be able to pray together about our work, to be able to minister to one another in our employment needs as well as personal matters, is an extra gift from God. And to be able to help one another is an act of love.

I receive that extra gift in my role as an editor. Assignments take me away from my desk, but not my responsibilities, which go on just as surely as deadlines, preparation, and planning demand.

That's why it is so good to have colleagues who are more than employees. Several times when I've worked late in my office, getting ready for a trip, I've come out to find people in the outer offices, working just as if it were midday. Never mind that they could have gone home; they were giving that up to help me and help the ministry of the magazine. My mind is put at ease, my worries give way to appreciation, as I realize that behind the labor and commitment is prayer.

As I write this, preparing for yet another trip, I wonder how much other Christians give to their jobs. Maybe your supervisor or boss is not a Christian; maybe the job you do does not seem critical to the Kingdom. But your own life and witness are critical. Do you give more than is expected? Do you "go the second mile," even when you feel "used" by another? Do you work only for a paycheck, or do you work as a service unto the Lord? God always sees what we do.

Prayer: Today, Lord, I commit my work to You as a ministry. Be pleased with me and my gift of work.

This editorial is taken from "Decision" magazine, August, 1979; © 1979 Billy Graham Evangelistic Association. Used by permission. All Rights reserved.

❧ MARCH 6 ❧
"AHA" AND "OH, YES"

But these are witten, that ye might believe that Jesus is the Christ, the Son of God; and that believing ye might have life through his name.

John 20:31 KJV

In an advertising magazine there was a story about "Aha" people and "oh, yes" people.

"Aha" people have insight; they see things, their feelings are important, they are creators, idea people. "Oh, yes" people confirm what others say. The world requires both.

But not only are there both types in the world, both types are valuable to God. He created them, He loves them, He wants them in the Kingdom.

In His saving work, Jesus (who knows all minds and hearts) taught, cared for, and went to the cross for both types.

Some people discover Him logically and, with their minds grasping what He did for them on the cross and in the resurrection, say, "Oh, yes."

Others sense, feel, and respond on the basis of intuitive understanding; they say "Aha."

Most of us are a combination, having more of one slant than the other but not totally either. That's okay. We are the ones who can look, see, grasp God's act of redemption in Christ, sense the love of God, and say as we come into deeper and deeper realizations of what He did for us: "Aha . . . oh, yes!"

Prayer: Lord, the more I think about Your saving me, the more awed I am about it. I'm impressed with the logic of redemption's goal.

 MARCH 7

NO MORE "COPE"

Be still, and know that I am God: I will be exalted among the heathen, I will be exalted in the earth.

Psalm 46:10 KJV

Morning came before I was ready for it. In fact, that's the way time has been for me all week.

Rush, hurry, and get farther behind.

So maybe it was God's purpose that I saw that simple sentence: "Be still, and know that I am God. . . ."

Is that an order—"Be still. Know that I am God"?

Or a request—"Be still, please, and know"?

Or a question—"When will you be still and know?" I could go any direction with it. But I won't. As the Holy Spirit takes those words and expresses them, I see a promise: "Be still, and [you will] know that I am God."

One thing is certain. I can't cope, and I can't catch up. I need Him, His peace, His "cope," and He knows it. That's why, I think, in His loving concern He comes to me with that text.

Lord, I am so busy that I'm going to stop and sit here and be still until I know, really know, that You are God.

I don't need to catch up; I need You.

Prayer: When I can't cope with all that's happening, I'm that much more glad that You are my God.

⤳ MARCH 8 ↰

BUT IS IT GOING TO RAIN?

Where wast thou when I laid the foundations of the earth?
declare, if thou hast understanding.

Job 38:4 KJV

I came bursting through the door, soaking wet, and as I stood dripping on the floor announced with great authority, "The way that rain is settling in, it's going to pour all night." Five minutes later the rain stopped.

Some people know a lot more about weather than I do. My grandfather did. He could tell from the sky whether or not it was going to rain or how the weather would be twenty-four hours from then. He was right more often than the weatherman I watch on the evening news. But then my grandfather wasn't encumbered by all the fancy, expensive equipment that the weather caster boasts about. As a farmer, he had a lot of experience. Most farmers do.

Still, neither fancy equipment, rheumatic knees, sinus headaches, nor the experienced eye of an outdoorsman equip us to be experts. They only make us better than average guessers. We aren't that smart about the weather—or a lot of things.

When everything was going wrong for Job and he wasn't happy about it, God asked him a question: "Where were you when I laid the foundations of the earth?" Job couldn't answer. We can't answer either. There comes a time when we cannot make pronouncements. All we can know is that God is God. He made our world, He made us. He alone knows what's happening to our world and to us. But then it's not so absolutely important that we know what's going to happen tomorrow—to us or to the weather. What is important is that we keep our eye on God and have enough sense to come in out of the rain.

Prayer: There is so much I don't know. Help me act wisely in what I do know and be smart enough to trust You.

⚛ MARCH 9 ⚛

WHY ARE PEOPLE STILL LONELY?

What agreement has the temple of God with idols? For we are the temple of the living God; as God said, "I will live in them and move among them, and I will be their God, and they shall be my people."

2 Corinthians 6:16

He's talking to us—the people who have experienced and know that they are God's temple and God's Spirit dwells in them (1 Corinthians 3:16). His words are personal.

". . . I will live in them and move among them, and I will be their God, and they shall be my people" (2 Corinthians 6:16).

If this was all the Bible we had—if nothing more was ever said to us—generations of people could ponder the implications of this for centuries and never comprehend it all.

"I will live in them."

"I will . . . move among them."

"I will be their God."

"They shall be my people."

There isn't any way to think through a love like that; there isn't anything with which to compare it. God, who is totally other, the Creator, the omnipotent One, has come to tell us that He won't be separate and apart. He will live and move in the midst of His people.

Then why are people still lonely? No one has to be.

He says, "I will."

He doesn't have to say any more.

Prayer: You want to live in me; You said so. Help me to believe that so I won't be lonely anymore.

❧ MARCH 10 ❧
DON'T JUST LISTEN

And he was teaching daily in the temple. The chief priests and the scribes and the principal men of the people sought to destroy him; but they did not find anything they could do, for all the people hung upon his words.

Luke 19:47, 48

There are always people who hang upon the words of a speaker; any celebrity or person of note gets a hearing from them. And that might have been something of what was happening in this report that Luke gives. But not entirely. Because in the original text the Scripture says more than that. It reports that "the people hung upon him, hearing."

It's possible to hear the words of Jesus and not hear Jesus. There are people who quote His sayings but don't obey Him. But Luke reports, the people hung upon Him, hearing—not just listening to words, but hearing Him. Jesus said, ". . . My brethren are these which hear the word of God, and do it" (Luke 8:21 KJV).

To hang upon the words of Jesus is good, but there is always the chance that that's all we're doing—hanging upon His words, impressed with what He says, willing to quote Him, referring to Him, even being awed by the wisdom of Him. But always the question has to come, "Am I hanging onto Him?"

We can have the best hearing in the whole crowd and still be deaf.

Prayer: Lord, help me to hear and obey Your words. I don't want to be a listener only.

❧ MARCH 11 ❧
CRAWLING IN THE DARK

Then spake Jesus again unto them, saying, I am the light of the world: he that followeth me shall not walk in darkness, but shall have the light of life.

John 8:12 KJV

Jesus didn't have the benefit of standing under a streetlight that would come on as darkness fell. When it got dark, it got dark! He knew exactly what He was talking about when He said, "Whoever follows me will never walk in darkness but will have the light of life."

He lights up the world. He's the Son. We can run in sunlight without tripping. But try it in the dark. You'll trip, you'll fall, you'll hurt yourself.

There are a lot of people around who are either hurting themselves as they trip and fall or they are crawling through life irritated because they can't get anywhere very fast. Jesus doesn't want that. He didn't put us on this earth for that. He came to be the light of the world. It must sadden Him to see so many people with scraped hands and knees trying to find their way in the dark.

Prayer: Help me to walk in the light and to demonstrate to others what it is to live in Your light. My friends need to see.

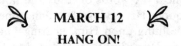

MARCH 12

HANG ON!

I am coming soon; hold fast what you have, so that no one
    may seize your crown.

Revelation 3:11

You've earned it!

So why give up that crown so cheaply?

The temptations have come, and you have spent time on your knees and even sought the counsel and prayers of other believers because you couldn't resist. And you've made it.

Don't give that up!

There's a little twist to Satan's way. After years of faithfulness to the commands of Christ, we can be tripped. And it's usually over something that we once had conquered.

The Holy One, the True One, the One who says, "I came that they may have life," says, "Hang on! There's only a little way to go; don't give in now."

Don't surrender that crown that is so special.

Sounds like a plea, doesn't it? Well, it is! He's concerned, very concerned about those latter-year temptations. Maybe He's burdened about you right now—at this moment. Too many who have been faithful all their lives have tripped and fallen into Satan's snares—right when they thought they had those temptations licked.

Jesus cries out, because He doesn't want it to happen to you: "I am coming soon; hold fast what you have, so that no one may seize your crown" (Revelation 3:11).

Hang on!

"I am coming soon."

Prayer: This crown You have for me is precious. Don't let me give it away right at the end.

⤙ MARCH 13 ⤚

CRAZY DRIVERS

> For we ourselves also were sometimes foolish, disobedient, deceived, serving divers lusts and pleasures, living in malice and envy, hateful, and hating one another.
>
> Titus 3:3 KJV

Driving on the freeway during rush hour is wild. People swerve in and out, zooming ahead on the break-down lane then cutting in ahead of me, with someone else right on my rear bumper. I'm afraid to put my brakes on; the tension is building; the anger at those who keep cutting in and out mounts; my nerves are jangled. By the time I get home, I hate everybody.

I looked up *hate* in my concordance. There are a lot of references to it, because there is a lot of hatred recorded in the Scriptures, especially among some of the people in the Old Testament. But then comes Titus, in the New Testament, who puts hatred into perspective. He says, in describing hatred, that's what we once were like—hateful and hating one another—but not now. We are to speak evil of no one, we're not to be brawlers, we are to be gentle, meek. Why? Because of the kindness and the love of God our Savior that has appeared. Which means, if I'm in Christ I'm not an Old Testament person anymore. If I'm in Christ I'm a New Testament person, changed by the "love of God our Savior."

Now I've got to learn how to be a New Testament person, even on the freeway.

Prayer: Father, I know You want me to serve You in the context of life, not in some ivory tower. Help me then to love people, no matter where I am or what they do.

❧ MARCH 14 ❧
EVERYTHING WORKED

In the beginning God created the heaven and the earth.

Genesis 1:1 KJV

Very few things go the way I plan them. When I schedule a workday, I find that every job seems to take twice as long as I thought it would. The stepladder isn't tall enough, and I have to borrow the neighbor's. I don't have the right tool and try to make do. An item that I thought I had is the wrong size, and I have to stop what I am doing to make a trip to the hardware store. And when I'm in an awkward position, trying to hold two things at the same time while reaching for the hammer, the phone rings. So I put down the hammer, let everything else fall to the floor, and run to the phone, only to hear someone on the other end ask if I would like to take advantage of their special sale on carpet cleaning.

Then I think about Genesis 1:1: "In the beginning God created the heaven and the earth." That's it. No fuss, no wrong tools, no stopping for a trip to the hardware store. He spoke, and it was so. From nothing He created all things. The thought became the fact. Everything fit together, and everything worked.

Whenever I start to take God for granted or stand in a little less awe of Him, I schedule another workday. Then I realize afresh who He is and who I am and the difference.

Prayer: Father, I thank You that You are who You are and not some projection of myself, with all of my human weaknesses.

❧ MARCH 15 ❧
SLEEP DIDN'T COME—BUT GOD DID

I, I am the Lord, and besides me there is no savior.

Isaiah 43:11

Alone and quiet.

Outside even the night sounds diminish as earth's scenery changes from dark to dawn.

It's quiet here, too, where I'm sitting, hours yet before the family rises. Even the dog doesn't realize that it is more morning than night.

I don't miss the bed; sleep wasn't there anyway. I needed to get up, needed to pray.

There isn't much that I want from God, not so much as I need to know that He is here. And I thought, as I sat here in the silence, meditating, that if He spoke to me or if my mind recalled His Scripture, it would be a sign, a call, a word of direction.

But it wasn't.

Instead He began quietly to remind me, "I, I am the Lord, and besides me there is no savior" (Isaiah 43:11).

Not so much, really. No stirring command. No "this is the way." Just a quiet fact: "I am the Lord." Yet to my mind so full of those wakeful things, it's more than a statement of fact. It's a promise. In the truth of those words every part of my life holds together. He is Lord. His word is a promise that even my worries can't change. In relief I pray, and peace comes.

"I am," is all He had to say.

I can go back to bed.

Prayer: You are Lord; I can rest in that and be thankful.

MARCH 16
MESS

For God sent not his Son into the world to condemn the world; but that the world through him might be saved.
John 3:17 KJV

"What a mess!"

The person who said that to me the other day wasn't talking about a spill on the kitchen floor or the chaos of his teenager's clothes closet; he was talking about the world.

And how does one respond to that? Of course the world is a mess. That's not news. That's the way the world has always been, even though we try to recall selectively "the good ol' days" rather than look at those days in the same way that we are forced to do every hour of every day in the present.

The world is a mess, and sometimes I begin my reading of John 3:17 with my own paraphrase, "For God did not send His Son into the world to condemn this mess. . . ." I don't mean that He likes the mess we have made of things; if I read my Bible correctly, He weeps over what we have done. Nor do I mean that He approves messed-up human lives. He is the One who redeems, reorganizes, and re-directs messed-up lives. Rather, I read John 3:17 this way because God loves the world—mankind, His creation, each individual in it—even though He, better than any of us, knows how ugly, how utterly evil, how wrong things are in this world. He knows because He is pure, holy, just, true, and orderly—and He entered into this world with us.

The incarnate Christ is our secure balance, our wholeness, our order not only for eternity but for right now in the day-to-day struggle of being here. The Prince of Peace is the only Sense in this non-sense world. He is Light in the confusion of our darkness; He is Truth in the midst of what lies all around us; He is Clarity in what is otherwise not clear at all as we travel through what is at best a cor-rosive and corruptive sin fog. We can't step out of all this, but in Him we have the only way of navigating within it and through it.

Prayer: Thank You, Lord Jesus, for coming to us; thank You for giv-ing me direction in this mess.

This editorial is taken from "Decision" magazine, December, 1982; © 1982 Billy Graham Evangelistic Association. Used by permission. All Rights reserved.

⍝   MARCH 17   ⍤

ME, MAKE MISTAKES?

The soul that sinneth, it shall die. . . .

Ezekiel 18:20 KJV

I can spot the mistakes of other people quite well. In fact, I spot them in a hurry. But not my own. Yet when someone shows me one of my own mistakes, it is usually a big one. Then all I can say is, "Yes, I did it," and go on, having learned from it and trying hard not to repeat that mistake again. Even high-priced batters strike out occasionally. Business people say, "You can't be right all the time. You had just better be right more times than you are wrong."

When I make a mistake I can lament the circumstances, deny my errors, blame other people, or admit that I did it. I find that the last way is the fastest way to getting on with life. The Scripture says, "The soul that sins shall die." God said that, and it's true. But knowing that can lead to wholeness, because the same God who gave the warning about sin and death gave the deliverance from it through the atoning work of Jesus Christ.

Because we know God's statement, we can seek the forgiveness offered in the remedy God provides. The biggest mistake comes when we think we make no mistakes. When we don't recognize our sin, we find no reason to confess, and there comes no wholeness; worse, we don't see death coming.

I don't like to admit my wrongs, but I like the consequences of not admitting them even less.

Prayer: Help me, Lord, to be honest with myself so that I can be honest with You.

⊰ MARCH 18 ⊱

OFF THE ROLLER COASTER

So you have sorrow now, but I will see you again and your
hearts will rejoice, and no one will take your joy from you.
John 16:22

You've probably noticed.

You get filled up by a joyous experience and then something bad happens.

It's not healthy to go around anticipating trouble or acting like gloomy Eeyore in *Winnie-the-Pooh,* who can't even enjoy the sunshine today because it will probably rain tomorrow.

But we do get philosophical as we get older and take joy in stride, quite aware that tomorrow is another day—an uncertain one.

That's why this promise of Jesus means so much.

He knows what our *nows* are like.

But He also knows what joy is ahead for us when He returns. That joy will last forever; no one can take it away.

Think of it, joy because God is with us—permanently. The excitement will build to pleasure, and the pleasure will become great joy.

And no collapse the next day!

The Source of joy will never leave.

No more uncontrolled roller-coaster feelings.

No more continuous emotional tides.

"I will see you again."

Jesus is coming back—permanently!

Prayer: Thank You that the emotions that throw me off balance now will someday be fully under Your control.

❧ MARCH 19 ❧
EAR TROUBLE

An evildoer listens to wicked lips; and a liar gives heed to a
mischievous tongue.

Proverbs 17:4

One morning I was petting a beautiful, honey-colored cocker
spaniel, and when I ran my fingers down his long ears, they stung
me. At least it seemed that way, because along the bottom edge of
his ears were thick burrs. Obviously he had been running through a
field and had picked up burrs along the way. Now they were embedded in his ears. They could cause him a lot of trouble unless his
owner takes a pair of scissors and cuts away the hair to get rid of the
burrs.

It's not always that easy to get rid of some of the things that our
ears pick up. Sometimes I've gone certain places and wished I had
left my ears at home. I've found that I can't run through a weed
patch without something sticking.

God gave that cocker spaniel beautiful, silky, long ears, but
sometimes, in the wrong places, those ears get him into trouble.
God gave me ears, too, and sometimes, in the wrong places, my ears
bring me trouble, too.

*Prayer: Lord, I'm glad You gave me ears. Sometimes I'm not very
happy about where I take them or what they pick up.*

❧ MARCH 20 ❧
SHEEP KNOW BETTER

I am the good shepherd: the good shepherd giveth his life
for the sheep.

John 10:11 KJV

We were walking through the fields when we saw him. A large
ram lay right where he had fallen the night before. He had rolled
over onto his back and couldn't get up by himself. We lifted him to
his feet, but he fell again. Finally we held him while the circulation
returned to his legs. Then he trotted off.

Try to tell sheep that they can live without a shepherd; they know
better. But there are people who still don't.

Jesus calls Himself "the good shepherd." That's a term that communicates, especially to people who have been around a little and have observed sheep.

He's not just any shepherd, but the *good* one, who guards the sheep, because they're precious to Him. He finds the best grass and checks the water. He salves the wounds and takes the irritating foreign bodies out of their fleece.

There is no other shepherd like that. God only sent the One.

Some of us prefer to listen to undershepherds, which is all right if they are listening to the Shepherd. But there is only one Good Shepherd, and He wants to take care of us.

That boggles the mind.

Why would God bother with us sheep? Why is He gathering His flock?

I'm glad that He is, because when the wolves are out prowling or the food is short, it's good to look up and see Him there. He is my Shepherd—the Good One.

And He's always there, even when I fall on my back.

Prayer: Thank You for always being willing to go ahead of me.

⅔ MARCH 21 ⅓
THEY'RE LOOSE AGAIN

There is a way which seemeth right unto a man, but the end thereof are the ways of death.

Proverbs 14:12 KJV

My eyeglasses keep sliding down my nose. It's time for an adjustment again. It seems as if I just had them fixed; now they're loose again. "You're taking them off the wrong way," my friends tell me. "You spread them when you do that."

"When I do what? It seems the right way to me."

When someone showed me what he called the correct way to remove my glasses and put them on again, I tried it, but my glasses still got loose and slipped down my nose. All I want is to be able to put on my glasses and take them off again without their getting loose and slipping. I want to do what I want to do the way I want to do it, but I don't want the consequences.

That's like sin. What I want to do is follow my way, my methods, without any of the results. I want to flout the system, disobey the correct way, but still have everything comfortable.

Life isn't that way—not for eyeglasses, not for anything. "There is a way that seemeth right unto a man, but the end thereof are the ways of death." In other words, my way of doing things may seem all right to me, but the results aren't going to be all right at all.

There is a wrong way and a right way, a broad road and a narrow road; there is God's way and my way. I need to be reminded of that every day. Fortunately, I get that reminder. I wear eyeglasses.

Prayer: Lord, help me not only to learn Your way but to live Your way.

✌ MARCH 22 ✌
LET'S HAVE A SHOW OF HANDS

> I will instruct you (says the Lord) and guide you along the best pathway for your life; I will advise you and watch your progress.
>
> Psalm 32:8 TLB

Think of it! Not just *any* pathway, but the *best* pathway. The omnipotent, all-knowing God wants to guide you, advise you, and lead you, and watch your progress on "the best pathway."

If we were to ask a roomful of people, "How many here want God to do that?" we'd probably get a strong show of hands. Yet in practice, we tend to ignore Him.

God is saying, "I want to guide you," and we believe He can. But by our actions, we are saying, "Leave me alone."

We want His guidance, but we don't necessarily want to follow Him—at least not very much. We say, "I'll do anything You tell me to do," but forget to go to Him for instructions. We stress, "I want God to run my life," but won't take His orders.

There could be a lot of better days for all of us if we acted as we say we want to act. Certainly there would be better days if we stopped saying with our words or by our actions, "Leave me alone," "Mind Your own business"—because we are God's business.

It takes a lot of nerve to say some of the things we say to God.

Prayer: Lord, I do want You to lead my life; please don't let me cut You out.

⤳ MARCH 23 ⤶

TRY THE DOOR

I am the door; if any one enters by me, he will be saved,
and will go in and out and find pasture.

John 10:9

It happens.

We can know where something is but not be able to get to it; or
we can see an object, but it is just out of reach; or an opportunity is
missed because of sickness or a broken promise; or we see a door
and find it locked.

That's frustration—seeing yet not having, wanting but not being
able to get. Seems as if that is characteristic of most of life's desires—unfulfilled.

So what Jesus says is more than just an answer; it's psychologically soothing. It is also the way to spiritual contentment.

"I am the door; if any one enters by me, he will be saved, and will
go in and out and find pasture."

Jesus is the Doorway to the pasture—a Doorway without locks.
"Anyone," He says, can enter and be saved.

People tend to dislike other people telling them who can be
saved. But this is the Savior telling who will be saved. It's simple;
those who enter by Him are the ones who will be saved. Once
through the Door, the pasture is waiting. "In and out," Jesus said—
as many times a day as we want to. Nobody has to take everything
at once, as one does when he thinks he might not come that way
again. God won't be annoyed by our trafficking in and out, as a
mother is with four children on a day when the ground is thawing
and she's trying to scrub the kitchen floor.

The pasture is there—lush, green, and inviting. And we can go in
and out.

That pasture is waiting; so is the Savior. He's the Door: Frustrating if we are just looking and wishing for what is on the other side,
but so satisfying if we go through the Door.

Why stand wondering what to do next?

The pasture isn't out of reach; try the Door.

Prayer: Why are we so foolish? Can't we just believe You?

❧ MARCH 24 ❧

HOT

But they were urgent, demanding with loud cries that he
should be crucified. And their voices prevailed.

Luke 23:23

In our office an article that needs editing in the next few hours is
labeled HOT. One due in the next few minutes is VERY HOT. Sometimes the HOTS and the VERY HOTS start piling up on each other.
But not every day has such rush orders. We try to be organized
enough so that we can avoid the VERY HOT, even the HOT. That way
we can work along at a steady pace and only push extra hard when
we see one of those labels.

Someone has to determine what is HOT or VERY HOT. That someone handles our production schedules. No one argues with the
label; if it says HOT, it must be hot, and we act on it.

I wonder why we have so much difficulty believing God when He
brings up something HOT—such as the need for turning around, the
need to take seriously the condition of a lost soul. God labels the
need HOT, VERY HOT, URGENT; read the Gospels—it's there plain
enough.

It's interesting that in Scripture one place where people were urgent is recorded in Luke 23:23. "But they were urgent . . ."; they de-
manded that Christ be crucified. "And their voices prevailed."

Crucifixion was a VERY HOT item. Salvation is, too, but Satan
keeps saying, "Tomorrow is soon enough." He succeeds a lot of
times, too. The label VERY HOT is scribbled over by some people,
and as a result the most important decision of their lives never gets
made.

*Prayer: Lord Jesus, just as there was urgency to have You crucified, I
will receive You, Risen Christ, as my Savior—and I'll do it now.*

MARCH 25

WHERE?

> Simon Peter said to him, "Lord, where are you going?"
> Jesus answered, "Where I am going you cannot follow me
> now; but you shall follow afterward."
>
> John 13:36

Sounds familiar, doesn't it? "What are you doing, Lord? Where
are You taking me? What's going on? What's happening?"

In other words, "Tell me, Lord; I need an explanation."

God cannot give me an explanation, for the simple reason that I
can't grasp it. He is the God of history. He is outside time and space.
The whole movement of the whole world is in His hand. I can't
grasp that, so there's no way for Him to explain to me my part in
His plan. He cannot give an explanation for the very reason that He
is God. What He knows can't be explained to me. Perhaps a part of
it, but not all of it.

My responsibility is to place my hand in His hand and trust. The
question is really a statement. It is not, "Where are You going,
Lord?" but "Lord, wherever it is, I want to be with You."

*Prayer: Father, my finite mind can't grasp all that's happening. I can
trust You, and I will.*

MARCH 26

A RUSTY SPIKE

> . . . There they crucified him, and the malefactors, one on
> the right hand, and the other on the left.
>
> Luke 23:33 KJV

Sometimes when I am working in my basement study, I hold in
my hand a rough-cast railroad spike. It's a spike that was used in
building the railroad line on the bridge over the River Kwai, in
Thailand. A missionary gathered them, numbered them, and
brought them to the States. Mine is #649.

When I look at that spike and see where the rust has eaten it
away, its shape, its size, I find myself reflecting on who the prisoner

was who drove this spike into that railroad line. Perhaps he was sick, starving, forced to work at bayonet point.

And then I begin to think about the spikes that were driven into Jesus' hands and feet. Who pounded the nails in, perhaps without even thinking much about it, because he'd done it to others before and would do it again? Did he go back afterward and remove the spikes? Nails were expensive; they were saved and used over and over again. How many people were crucified with those same spikes? And for how many centuries was one of those spikes used before it rusted or broke or lay buried someplace where Roman armies ruled? It's good we don't know where Jesus' crucifixion spike is, or some people would worship it; others would sell it at a high price. That spike had a part in God's eternal plan of redemption, arranged before the foundation of the world.

I hold a spike in my hand and realize that something so physically simple can have such consequences. What simple, man-made things God uses. What simple thing is God using even now in His great plan for the ages?

Prayer: Lord, help me to see as I use the everyday things around me that You use those things, too. Even a spike can have eternal consequences.

☙ MARCH 27 ☙
HE DIDN'T DELEGATE

Who his own self bare our sins in his own body on the tree,
that we, being dead to sins, should live unto righteousness:
by whose stripes ye were healed.

1 Peter 2:24 KJV

In some ways it is easier to be a manager in a business than an employee in it. A manager can delegate almost everything; in fact, he should. A manager shouldn't be doing anything that somebody else in his employ can do, because there are some things that can't be delegated, that only the manager can do because he has both the authority and the responsibility. Then it's all on his shoulders.

Jesus knew that. The Incarnate Son of God, with all the universe made by His hands at His disposal, could not and did not delegate our redemption. There could be no other one who could take His place. He Himself bore our sins in His body on the tree. He did it

Himself. He carried our sins onto the cross in His own body. He couldn't and didn't pass that responsibility on to anybody else. He alone had the authority. He alone took the responsibility. He alone redeems. "... For there is none other name under heaven given among men, whereby we must be saved" (Acts 4:12 KJV).

Prayer: Thank You, Lord Jesus, that when it came to my eternal redemption, You did Yourself what only You could do.

MARCH 28

NOISE

> And the apostles, when they were returned, told him all that they had done. And he took them, and went aside privately into a desert place belonging to the city called Bethsaida.
>
> Luke 9:10 KJV

We live near the airport. Sometimes the noise of the planes is (*vroom*) so loud that we have to stop our (*vroom*) conversation because one person (*vroom*) can't hear what another person is saying. The worst part is Saturday morning, when we want to sleep in. Then the mechanics test the engines, revving them up to a high pitch that shakes the bedroom walls. And they seem to have a need to do this between 5:00 and 6:00 A.M.

Jesus knew the need that His followers had of going aside, resting, being alone and quiet to pray. We all need that. He had a desert place in the quiet area near Bethsaida where He took His followers; I envy the disciples.

But He also knew the noise of the crowd: Jerusalem, Golgotha; the shouting, the screaming, the raucousness of people yelling, "Crucify Him, crucify Him"; the cross, with the people shouting obscenities. He went into the noise and the clamor and the pain for me, a far cry from the silent hills of Galilee.

When I start to complain, "Jesus didn't have to listen to jet planes," I'm reminded, "And you don't have to face a mob saying, 'Crucify him.' He went through that for you."

Prayer: Lord, when I start to feel sorry for myself, help me to remember.

MARCH 29

THANK YOU, LORD

And so Pilate, willing to content the people, released
Barabbas unto them, and delivered Jesus, when he had
scourged him, to be crucified.

Mark 15:15 KJV

When they came to get Barabbas, he had no idea that that day
wouldn't be his death day, but his release day. He thought he was
going to a cross. He was given liberty, set free to do whatever he
wanted.

What did he do? One thing is certain. He didn't go find Jesus and
say thank You. There is no evidence in Scripture that he stayed
around at all. If he was grateful for being spared his life, there is no
record of his ever having said so.

Jesus spared my life. He went to the cross for me. It was my sin
that put Him there. That I'm pleased with the substitution, He
surely knows. But like Barabbas, have I slipped away without saying thank You? Barabbas was given a few more years. When I
placed my sins on Jesus, He gave me eternal life. If I spent every
hour of every day saying thank You, it wouldn't be too much.

*Prayer: Lord, I don't know when I said it last, but I want to say it
now. Thank You for dying in my place. Thank You for being my Savior.*

 MARCH 30

UNSHAKABLE

But now is Christ risen from the dead, and become the
firstfruits of them that slept.

1 Corinthians 15:20 KJV

I missed the news this morning; now I feel as if I don't know anything. Last night's news is like ancient history. Nothing seems to
hold steady, and I feel as if I am standing on ground rocked by an
earthquake. I think, *Surely this cannot change,* but then it does.
What once was stable for generations, and then at least for decades,

now heaves and shifts, rebounds and echoes, as events surge and churn in every direction—and we are all in the middle of it.

But Easter is here, bringing me and my world back into focus. Some will think that the focus is only mythical, or at best a bit of nostalgia. To them my clinging is an attempt at eye closing, a holding on to something that perhaps was capable of giving comfort once, but not anymore.

Not so, because the resurrection is connected to the living God, who is beyond the ages, beyond current time, and outside man's destructive works. God has brought Jesus Christ from the dead. The Risen Lord is the eternal Christ.

Don't look to people, governments, or things for something firm to hang on to while everything around you shifts and tumbles—you won't find it. There is only one unshakable reality. That reality is succinctly stated in a greeting on the tongues of people from hundreds of tribes and nations around the world:

"The Lord is risen."

"He is risen, indeed."

Prayer: O Risen Christ, I give thanks to You for bringing victory over sin, the grave, and life's uncertainties.

This editorial is taken from "Decision" magazine, April, 1984; © 1984 Billy Graham Evangelistic Association. Used by permission. All Rights reserved.

MARCH 31
CAN'T IT WAIT UNTIL MORNING?

And their eyes were opened and they knew him. . . .

Luke 24:31 KJV

Suddenly it all came together for them. They had been on their journey from Jerusalem to Emmaus. One of the men was named Cleopas; we don't know the name of the other. But they were despondent, distressed. Everything they had hoped for in Jesus seemed ended at the crucifixion. But when Jesus met them on the road and then stayed with them for the evening meal, suddenly all He said about Himself from the Scriptures and what they saw fit together. They knew it was the Lord. Now suddenly they were not two unhappy men whose lives were purposeless and without direction. Now they had good news, and even though it was night and they had already shut the door and were having their evening meal, they went back to Jerusalem.

Robbers could have been on the streets. They were the only people who tended to be out at night. These two men went out anyway. There were no streetlights; they had to find their way over dark roads. They went anyway. Even wild beasts tended to lie low during the day but would be out at night. They went anyway. They had good news, and good news can't wait until morning.

There are still faithful men and women like that, who don't care that it's dangerous outside, who don't talk themselves into staying with the comforts of home and hearth. They've met the Risen Christ; they have good news, and it can't wait.

Prayer: Lord, don't let me ever get so comfortable or so afraid to go out that I start to think that the news I have about You can wait until morning—or next year or. . . .

≥᎒ APRIL 1 ᎒≤
IT'S STILL THERE

As far as the east is from the west, so far hath he removed our transgressions from us.

Psalm 103:12 KJV

I thought it was gone. I was practicing with my new computer and erased the text, I thought; but then my teacher came over and said, "No, it's still there," and brought it back. I tried again. This time I was sure. The screen was blank; I couldn't find the text; but once again he did. There it was, just as I had typed it, back on the screen.

Then he showed me what was required to erase something. There is a series of questions where essentially the computer is asking me, "Are you sure you really want to do this?" I had to tell the machine that indeed I did want that text removed. Then it was gone, erased from memory. It required a conscious decision and a conscious act.

When I sought forgiveness, cleansing from the guilt and penalty of sin, it was a conscious decision, not one lightly taken. I couldn't erase my past simply. In spite of what I tried myself, the sin wasn't gone yet, even though "the screen was clean" and I couldn't see it anymore; it was still there in the memory.

A cleansed person is a forgiven person. God does the erasing, and the sin is removed as far as the east is from the west, forever gone—from my memory and His. It is not just out of sight; it is totally and forever removed.

That takes a conscious decision. Do I really want this to happen? It isn't a decision lightly made, but it is a forever decision.

Prayer: Lord, what I can't do, You can do—and You have removed my sin, not only from my memory but from Yours, and I'm grateful.

❧ APRIL 2 ❦
WHAT AN OFFER!

> Seeing the crowds, he went up on the mountain, and when he sat down his disciples came to him. And he opened his mouth and taught them. . . .
>
> Matthew 5:1, 2

I'm a little slow, because I just now figured it out.

It's about the Sermon on the Mount.

Jesus isn't just making statements of fact, although they are powerful statements.

He's making promises—a lot of them.

And in His conclusion He says that whoever ". . . does them and teaches them shall be called great in the kingdom of heaven" (Matthew 5:19).

Not only do we get the promise that we will be "blessed" when or if certain things happen; we will also be called "great"!

You can't beat an offer like that.

So really, what difference does it make if in a genuine, honest attempt to be faithful to the Lord Jesus some ". . . revile you and persecute you and utter all kinds of evil against you falsely on my account" (Matthew 5:11)?

The better part is the "blesseds."

Prayer: Thank You for all the "blesseds" that have my name on them.

❧ APRIL 3 ❦
SLURS

> Can a fig tree bear olives, or a grapevine bear figs? . . .
>
> James 3:12 NIV

Increasingly of late I am hearing ethnic slurs, racial jokes, and anti-Semitic remarks, and I shudder. I hurt not only because of the words spoken but because I hear professing Christians saying those words. It would be easy to say, "People who speak that way are not really Christians," and maybe they aren't. But they tell me that they are. Some are even in Christian ministry!

How can that be? I have asked that question, and I hear comments such as, "I don't see any bigotry or racial prejudice in that." Or worse, "You don't know 'them' as well as I do." And I'm reminded of the people who said similar things in Europe just before millions of Jewish people were shipped off to Auschwitz, Mauthausen, Bergen-Belsen and Dachau.

The Apostle James said of the tongue: "With the tongue we praise our Lord and Father, and with it we curse men, who have been made in God's likeness. Out of the same mouth come praise and cursing. My brothers, this should not be. Can both fresh water and salt water flow from the same spring? My brothers, can a fig tree bear olives, or a grapevine bear figs? Neither can a salt spring produce fresh water" (James 3:9–12 NIV).

Three times, in James 4:11, the writer refers to "brethren" and "brothers" to make his emphasis clear that he is speaking to Christians. In short, evil speech is not only a pagan problem.

James is right when he states that the same spring cannot bring out fresh water and brackish water. No matter how we paint the pump, no matter how attractive the pumphouse, the water that comes out is the water that is in the well. You can tell what a person believes by the jokes and slurs that come from his mouth. No matter what he says about obedience to Jesus Christ, you can tell whom he really follows.

Slurs give clear evidence that something is impure inside . . . and Satan is delighted.

Prayer: Control not only my tongue, Lord, but my mind, which dictates what I say.

APRIL 4

A BAG FULL OF MARBLES

... Who knoweth whether thou art come to the kingdom
for such a time as this?

Esther 4:14 KJV

"How did the message go?" someone asked me, knowing I had
spoken earlier in the day at a college chapel.

"Well," I replied, "no one dropped the marbles." I had been told
that as a prank some students had planned to drop a bag of marbles
during my morning message, when the auditorium was at its quiet-
est. But it didn't happen. Apparently whoever held the marbles was
listening and forgot about what he had planned to do. I wonder if
he was surprised, at the close of the chapel service, to find that he
still had the marbles.

There are a lot of surprises in life, a lot of things that change for
us. That happened to Esther. She came to a place of influence at the
right time to change the course of Jewish events. God knew the
time; He also knew the woman. She didn't think of herself as ex-
ceptional. She probably hadn't planned for her life to go the way it
went. In fact, if she had kept a diary as a schoolgirl or a teenager, it
probably wouldn't have contained any dreams or wishes of what
eventually took place.

Life is full of surprises. We meet a person, enter a building, make
a right turn instead of a left, and life changes. We grow, we stretch,
we learn, we influence—we may even change the course of history. I
wonder what ever happened to the student with the bag in his hand.
All he planned to do that morning was drop the marbles.

*Prayer: Lord, I realize I have no way of knowing what You're going
to do next or even what You're going to do with my life today.*

APRIL 5

TOO BUSY

Refrain from anger, and forsake wrath! Fret not yourself; it
tends only to evil.

Psalm 37:8

"Sorry, God. No time for instruction now. No time for counsel;
I'm busy."

So I ran for my interview appointment, waited through the supper hour, and my appointment didn't come. I was hungry and angry. But I didn't learn.

I tried again, made another appointment, and once more he didn't show up.

Back in my hotel, desperate—"Lord, what I need is Your help. You know how I can find this man. I'm wasting all my time."

Then, looking at my tape recorder, I discovered that it wasn't working properly. I wouldn't have gotten that interview anyway. Only I probably wouldn't have known that until after I'd spent the time taping.

In quick succession I borrowed a recorder, the phone rang, and my appointment was saying, "Sorry about not making it. May I come to your hotel, and we will do that interview?"

All my running around. All my anger and spent energy—unnecessary.

Too busy?

Too frantic?

God isn't too busy: "I will instruct you and teach you the way you should go; I will counsel you with my eye upon you" (Psalm 32:8).

While He has been saying, "I could help you. I could counsel, teach, and keep My eye on you," I've been running right past Him saying, "Sorry, God. I'm too busy."

Prayer: I am foolish, I admit it. Help me to live by Your guidance. That's the only way that makes sense.

APRIL 6
GOD ISN'T A SKYCAP

For he spake, and it was done; he commanded, and it stood fast.

Psalm 33:9 KJV

A woman was anticipating the arrival of her husband's flight from the West Coast. "What airline is he on?" I asked. When she told me, I said, "Oh! Well, he'll be on time, but his luggage will be about an hour and a half late."

"How do you know that?" she asked.

"Because I think this airline has only one baggage handler, and he's on his lunch break."

"Are you sure he's on his lunch break?"

"He's always on his lunch break. That same airline has often had to deliver baggage to my home, because it came in so late."

What God promises to do, He does. He doesn't disappear on His lunch break. Yet some people expect God to be on the spot, doing His job, because they think of Him as a divine baggage handler, ready to follow after them, loaded down with the things they want to carry on their journey through this life. They even think He will be happy for any occasion when they give Him a nice tip.

But God is not a hired porter; He never has been and never will be. He's God, and because He's God, when He says He'll do something, He does it. And He doesn't even have to offer disclaimers about scratches or dents.

Prayer: Thank You that You are faithful, that You always keep Your word.

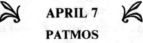

APRIL 7

PATMOS

... "The kingdom of the world has become the kingdom of our Lord and of his Christ, and he shall reign for ever and ever."

Revelation 11:15

This is a promise and a proclamation!

John was on a desolate, rocky piece of land stuck out in the Aegean sea. He couldn't get off.

Pounding surf, sea gulls, and dead fish on the beach were his company. He lived there in his old age. And that's where he died.

But that lonely island was the place where God met him and gave him a lot more than escape. When he wrote down what he learned there, it challenged believers in the seven churches on the mainland and has undergirded the Church all over the world ever since.

Some of us have had a "Patmos," too.

Someone may even be on "Patmos" right now—an exile just as lonely as John's, where God seems far away.

But the Lord comes to our island, too, in a beautiful, life-changing way.

John must have been ready for His coming, being "... in the Spirit on the Lord's day ..." (Revelation 1:10). That's the value of a "Patmos"—to be alone and prayerfully listening.

No island is too far away for Him. And when He comes, as He will, our "Patmos" will no longer be a desolate, lonely island. It will be a special, holy place.

Prayer: You know where I am, Lord, even when I feel so alone.

❧ APRIL 8 ❧

HE WASN'T ON TELEVISION

> He is despised and rejected of men; a man of sorrows, and acquainted with grief: and we hid as it were our faces from him; he was despised, and we esteemed him not.
>
> Isaiah 53:3 KJV

Whenever I'm to appear on television, I first have to have makeup applied to my face, not because of vanity, but because the deep creases and lines, particularly in my forehead, cast shadows under the bright lights. Somebody once told me that I have a good face for radio.

But no matter how any of us may look on television or off, very few of us have ever had people turn away because they couldn't look. But it happened to Jesus. When His accusers had beaten Him, when they had pushed down those long thorns into His forehead, when they had spit upon Him, when His face was contorted from the excruciating pain of the nails through the skin and cartilage and bone of His hands and feet, some, as Isaiah predicted, turned away; they couldn't look at His face.

With that pain, suffering in the flesh as any person would but added to by the ugliness of the sin of the world placed upon Him, this One, pure and spotless, who was without sin, must have been in awful agony—an agony so extreme that people were indeed full of awe, and they turned away from this "awe-full" sight.

Jesus wasn't acting; He wasn't on television. He was on a rugged hill that looked like a skull, and He hung there before the crowd. They couldn't stand to look; the sight was so ugly. And the best makeup artist in the world could not have made Him appear any different. He hurt, and He hurt for us.

Prayer: Father, though some may turn from the cross because of its ugliness, I turn to the cross for the beauty of what Jesus did there for me.

❧ APRIL 9 ❧
RIGHT THROUGH THE FIRE

> When you pass through the waters I will be with you; and
> through the rivers, they shall not overwhelm you; when you
> walk through fire you shall not be burned, and the flame
> shall not consume you.
>
> Isaiah 43:2

Did you hear that?

Somebody might hear that and start playing with fire. But if he
does, he has missed the point, and he'll get burned.

God is saying something far more profound than, "Feel free to
mess around, because I'm going to protect you."

When the floods come upon me and I'm trying to get out, when
the enemy is pressing behind me and I need a Red Sea miracle,
when the flame is suddenly all around like a prairie fire on a hot,
windy day and I have no safe place to go. . . .

That has happened and will probably happen again, not just for
me; you've had it happen, too.

That's when His promise means something, not an academic
topic for interesting Sunday-night discussions or a license to defy
the self-preserving rules of common sense, but because it's God's
Word and has come for us to hold on to.

In the water and in the fire maybe that's all we'll have. But in that
flood or in that burning that's all we need.

*Prayer: Thank You for the promise of Your protection even when the
unexpected happens.*

❧ APRIL 10 ❧
NOT HOPELESS AT ALL

> Come and see the works of God. . . .
>
> Psalm 66:5 KJV

Somewhere I read a reference to the wonder of spring, not only as
the miraculous but as a multiplication of the miraculous. And it is.
Over there is a tree. It seemed to die last autumn. And here is a
flower, bent over, having given up its strength. Plants in my vegeta-

ble garden all lost in their battle with the frost. Yet there's life in the roots of that tree. The bulb underground will sprout again, and each seed from my garden contains a harvest in itself.

A seed is a miracle. Millions of seeds are millions of miracles. And the result of sap rising in a tree fills me with awe.

What seemed to be hopeless was not hopeless at all. Look what God can do. No wonder the psalmist's words, "Come and see the works of God," are really part of a song. In the spring, when I look around, I feel like singing, too.

Prayer: Lord, the miraculous is all around me. May I never stop being amazed.

❧ APRIL 11 ❧
FOR ALWAYS

The grass withers, the flower fades; but the word of our God will stand for ever.

Isaiah 40:8

God isn't seasonal.

The grass comes and goes; God's promises don't.

Flowers spring up and die; they're seasonal. God isn't.

His Word is forever; it stands—not just sometimes, not just when conditions are favorable; it stands. All the time!

And since it does:

It's always a guide.

It's always a light.

It's always a standard, because God is always God, and His Word is always His Word.

It doesn't matter how seasonal other things are, like grass and flowers or even each one of us, for that matter. His Word isn't dependent on anything, even seasons.

His Word is independent of everything, even me—just as God is.

Prayer: Thank You that no matter what else dies, You never will.

APRIL 12
GIVERS

Each one should use whatever gift he has received to serve others, faithfully administering God's grace in its various forms.

1 Peter 4:10 NIV

The person who takes will never know about giving. He is self-centered. His world is himself. But the giver, because he knows the value of a gift, is also able to receive. He knows the value of what he gives, therefore recognizes value in what another gives to him. A taker only exploits; he knows nothing of value given.

What would become of our society if people were all takers? What would society be like if the primary goal in life were to get what we could from any person, group, or situation? People can take, consume, and manipulate only so long as there are others who will not. But if the day comes when we are all takers, who will do the giving? Who will know the value of a gift, especially the Gift that is above every other gift—the Gift of God?

Prayer: Thank You, Lord, for the greatest Gift to me—Jesus. Help me to be a giver, too.

This article is taken from "Decision" magazine, May, 1982; © 1982 Billy Graham Evangelistic Association. Used by permission. All Rights reserved.

APRIL 13
VENGEANCE!

For I lift up my hand to heaven, and swear, As I live for ever, if I whet my glittering sword, and my hand takes hold on judgment, I will take vengeance on my adversaries, and will requite those who hate me.

Deuteronomy 32:40, 41

Every now and then He reemphasizes it. God is a God of love; nothing is uncertain about that.

But He is also a God of vengeance—when He has to be.

If that wasn't so, we'd play games with the Almighty One.

Or, if it was so but He never told us—never gave warning—not one of us would survive.

God is love, and God is just. But if sooner or later He has to whet His sword, if He has to "take hold on judgment," He will do it.

That isn't pleasant to think about. But God is God—beyond every dimension of our knowing, and that includes His consistency. The wise person understands that.

Prayer: You will do what has to be done; I know that. Keep me from thinking that You won't.

≥ঽ APRIL 14 Ɀ
YOU MADE A MISTAKE!

There is none righteous, no, not one.

Romans 3:10 KJV

Just when I think I've done a job perfectly, someone shows me a glaring error. In the publishing business, any error is multiplied thousands, even millions of times. We write and rewrite, then edit and check and reedit and recheck, then publish material. Then, when the printing is done, there for all the world to see is a big mistake. And the complaints begin to come.

People like to point out errors. It makes us feel good when we can find an error in someone else's work, especially if their errors are bigger than our own. That's the way we are. Somehow what we do is not quite so bad if we can find someone who did it worse.

But no matter how tiny our flaws, or how large theirs, we are all the same before God. We are all less than what God wants. "There is none righteous, no, not one." He said that. None of us could say it of another, but He in His purity and righteousness can and does say it of all of us. And there is no arguing it; there is no pointing at someone else and saying, "But I'm not as bad as . . . ," because that's not the point. There are none righteous, and He is the measure of righteousness. That's why all we can do is first shut our mouths before the obvious evidence of our sin, then pray, "Wash me, and I shall be whiter than snow." We have to mean it. It has to be real. And when it is real, God promises to do that washing.

We'll still make errors in our work, of course, but righteousness is another matter. We can be washed, then reclothed in His righteousness.

Even though I can't cover over my work errors, even though I have to live with them and admit my mistakes, I don't have to live with unrighteousness. The righteous Christ who chooses to live in the confessing believer offers another way—the washed, cleansed way.

Prayer: Father, I know I will always make errors that others will point to, but I also know on the basis of Your redemptive work that the errors in my eternal soul have been covered over.

✎ APRIL 15 ✎
REAL SATISFACTION

Heal the sick, cleanse the lepers, raise the dead, cast out devils: freely ye have received, freely give.
Matthew 10:8 KJV

Once I joked, "If God wants to make me rich, He's going to have to work hard at it, because I like to give money away."

Jesus was talking about spiritual matters when He said, "Freely ye have received, freely give." But it's not a great transition from spiritual matters to material things, because we're not to lay up treasures for ourselves. We can't read the New Testament without realizing that our responsibility is not to gain for personal purposes but to be content and give to the poor, give for the proclamation of the Gospel, give to any who have need who ask of us.

There is real satisfaction in giving money away. I suppose for those who don't know Christ there is a great satisfaction in gaining huge profits. For the believer, money can be invested in more than profit-making ventures. Money can be invested in profitable lives. It can also be invested in those who may never ever do anything noteworthy for Christ but who need to stay alive, eat decent food, and have a roof over their heads.

God didn't give me the ability to earn income to spend it only on myself, and if I ever think that, He's just as likely to take it away and give it to somebody whom He can trust to share it.

Years ago I made up my mind that tithing was an absolute necessity, and after that there comes the joy of giving. There is a special satisfaction in it that those who have never done it can't understand.

Prayer: Father, You have given freely to me. Help me to give freely to others. Help me to be a channel to those in need, with none of it sticking to my fingers as I pass it along.

❧ APRIL 16 ❧
EVERY DAY

Then said the Lord unto Moses, Behold, I will rain bread
from heaven for you; and the people shall go out and
gather a certain rate every day, that I may prove them,
whether they will walk in my law, or no.

                                                    Exodus 16:4 KJV

That's frustrating for the "can-do" types of people. The manna
came every day, twice as much on Friday for the Sabbath—no
more, no less.

Entrepreneurs couldn't gather it and invest it, hoping to live off
the dividends. Middle-aged people couldn't save some for their retirement years. God provided every day, and everyone had to look
to Him. No one could go up to heaven and bring more down, no
matter how capable he thought he was. The businessman with the
calculating mind couldn't multiply it. The creative genius couldn't
invent more of it. Politicians couldn't talk God into any extra. What
frustration.

There were a lot of people on that wilderness journey. And there
are a lot on their journey of faith today, too. God says, "Look to
Me," and then reminds us, "I'll rain down the manna."

*Prayer: I stand before You with empty hands every day, and every day
I need You to provide for me.*

❧ APRIL 17 ❧
CAFETERIA STYLE

How sweet are thy words unto my taste! yea, sweeter than
honey to my mouth!

                                                    Psalm 119:103 KJV

I meet cafeteria-style Bible students all the time. They're the ones
who say, "This passage of Scripture really speaks to me," or "I like
this passage," or "I didn't get much out of this part of the Bible."

Cafeteria-style Bible study is the kind where you can select any
Scriptures you like, as if you were going through a cafeteria line.
And, as in most cafeteria lines, we usually find the desserts first.

Why not? Why not take the parts that are pleasant, enjoyable, before all the others? Didn't the psalmist say, "How sweet are thy words unto my taste! yea, sweeter than honey to my mouth!"?

Except he said a whole lot more. Take a look. He talks of meditating on the law all day (v. 97), of being wise through the commandments (v. 98), of meditating on the testimonies (v. 99), keeping the precepts (v. 100), keeping God's Word as a whole (v. 101), never departing from God's ordinances (v. 102). And then after all that solid food, he comes to the exclamation, "How sweet are thy words unto my taste!"

Dessert is a nice part of any meal, but it's not the whole meal. The psalmist loved God's Word. He was nourished by it and enjoyed every part, because God's Word isn't a quick "pick and choose" cafeteria snack; it's a full-course banquet.

Prayer: Lord, help me to love and obey Your Word—every part of it.

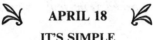

APRIL 18

IT'S SIMPLE

> Do not be deceived; God is not mocked, for whatever a man sows, that he will also reap. For he who sows to his own flesh will from the flesh reap corruption; but he who sows to the Spirit will from the Spirit reap eternal life.
>
> Galatians 6:7, 8

It's a matter of choice.

A person can elect which way he will go. God won't beat anyone over the head and force him to go in some direction against his own wishes.

Anyone can move into the world of decay if he wants to and go right on into hell that way.

Or a person can be always newly freshened by the Spirit of God and go into heaven that way.

It's not a confusing choice; it's not difficult at all. The difference between the two is quite distinct.

Paul, under the inspiration of God, said: "Do not be deceived; God is not mocked, for whatever a man sows, that he will also reap. For he who sows to his own flesh will from the flesh reap corruption; but he who sows to the Spirit will from the Spirit reap eternal life" (Galatians 6:7, 8).

No one mocks God.

If we plant a crop of corruption, we harvest a crop of corruption. We get what we plant. It's the same for everyone.

God isn't fooled; He knows what we planted. It's people who are deceived; they deceive themselves. By a strange turnabout "logic," some people say, "Plant corn, harvest grapes; plant beans, get potatoes; plant corruption, reap eternal life."

And on what basis are these wonderful deductions made? "I'm sincere." "I meant well."

But it doesn't work that way!

You plant corn; you harvest corn. No matter how you feel about it. If you want to harvest something else, you plant something else. It's a simple principle.

No one ever has to go through life wondering what he will harvest.

Just look at the label on the seed package.

Prayer: You won't be mocked by my foolishness. I can't fool You; help me not to try.

❧ APRIL 19 ❦

A SECOND REVOLUTION

Behold ye among the heathen, and regard, and wonder marvellously: for I will work a work in your days, which ye will not believe, though it be told you.

Habakkuk 1:5 KJV

When Major John Pitcairn marched his troops into Lexington Village on the morning of April 19, 1775, he walked into a battle with minutemen that set in motion events leading to the American Revolution and the birth of these United States.

But there are always "preliminaries" to a revolution. Peyton Randolph, John Jay, George Washington, and the fifty-two other delegates to the First Continental Congress wrestled with issues and argued liberty in their own colonial assemblies long before they met in Philadelphia. These meetings of the patriots were as much a part of the ensuing struggle for independence as the more dramatic events that followed.

It's unlikely that most of the people at the time understood the whole picture. How many would have announced, "A new nation is being born"? They only saw pieces—the mosaic was still coming together.

I don't see my life so completely either. And I sure don't see the work of God very well—only little pieces of it. I can't be too dogmatic about "what God is doing" or "what God will do," because my worldview is just that, "my view of my world." It is not the whole view of the whole world. Only God sees that.

"Behold . . . I will work a work in your days, which ye will not believe, though it be told you." He said that to Habakkuk, and it was too much for him to grasp. He says it to me, and I can't grasp it either. I can believe it—and to whatever degree I can understand, I can behold it.

I can stay close to Him today and obey. And I will. Because, besides the fact that I like being close to God, I don't want to miss the big picture.

Prayer: You are much bigger than I am; keep me from thinking that You are not.

⊱ APRIL 20 ⊰
THE BEST UMBRELLA

For it is written, He shall give his angels charge over thee,
to keep thee.

Luke 4:10 KJV

Fortunately, angry dogs don't know about umbrellas, at least one angry dog doesn't. I was walking in the rain with my umbrella when a dog came racing out from around the corner of the house where he lived, growling and snarling as he lunged toward me. I quickly dropped my umbrella down between me and him. When he saw that black umbrella, he came tumbling to a halt, tripping over his own feet, then backed off. He didn't know what the umbrella was. No one had ever explained to him that he could tear it apart in an instant. I hope he never finds out.

God has a special umbrella that is not flimsy or weak; it is awesome. It's the guarding of His angels over us. The psalmist explained, "For he shall give his angels charge over thee, to keep thee in all thy ways" (Psalm 91:11 KJV). Satan tried using that passage of Scripture with Jesus, but Satan being Satan, he quoted it wrong. We have an umbrella of angels guarding us always, in all our ways. That's good to know when suddenly terror comes charging at us. We've got the umbrella of God—His angels—and even Satan can't change what they do. Read Psalm 91, then read Luke 4, then remember whose you are and the strong umbrella of protection He has put around you—not cloth, but angels.

Prayer: Father, I know Satan would like to fool me about the angels. Thank You that they're there at Your command.

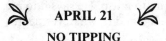

APRIL 21

NO TIPPING

. . . You shall be redeemed without money.

Isaiah 52:3

The streets of Calcutta were dark when I got back to my room. Then I remembered that I had left my tape recorder under a chair at the meeting where I had been earlier in the evening. So I went outside, found the car and driver who had been hired by our host, and he took me back through the crowded streets to the building where we had been. I found my tape recorder still under the chair.

Returning to the hotel, I reached into my pocket to give the driver some money for his kindness. There was no streetlight, and in the darkness I pulled out what I thought would be enough bills and gave them to him. He was not happy and let me know how unhappy he was. But I knew it was a good tip and thanked him again and went to my room. Later, as I was drifting off to sleep, I realized why he was unhappy. What was in my pocket was not Indian currency but Thai currency.

The next day I told my host what I had done. He said, "Oh, the drivers always complain; they want more money."

I tried to explain, "That's not the point. It's not that I didn't give him enough money, it's that I gave him the wrong currency."

He replied, "But you were not supposed to pay him at all. He was hired for this period of time."

I wasn't completely satisfied, but it was a new day, and we had a new driver, and I never did see the previous driver again.

Everything is paid for in our redemption, too. God paid the price through His Son, the Lord Jesus Christ. I can't reach into my pocket and add to it. It doesn't matter how big the tip I offer God or what currency I have; tippng isn't necessary. Isaiah knew that: "You shall be redeemed without money." I can't tip, but I can say, "Thank You."

Prayer: Father, I know there's not enough money in the whole world to pay for my redemption. You paid the price with Your Son on the cross, and You did it for me. I am empty-handed and grateful.

APRIL 22
PROMOTION

... He hath no form nor comeliness; and when we shall see him, there is no beauty that we should desire him.

Isaiah 53:2 KJV

At a dinner recently, the owner of a Christian bookstore, who was sitting next to me, said with authority based on years of experience, "Cover and title. That's what sells a book. It doesn't matter what is inside."

Jesus didn't come with a great title. In Philippians 2 we read about a self-emptying. He left the glory of the Father. That He is King of kings and Lord of lords has always been true as a fact, but that the title was not given to Him for publicity reasons is also a fact. Jesus didn't need Madison Avenue techniques, advertising budgets, or retouched photos. We don't have to package Him, either, to make Him "sell."

Transfer your trust from yourself to Jesus Christ, then tell another person what He means to you. Don't wait for some kind of media promotion. We are His witnesses. We can tell about Him with plain talk.

Promotion? He didn't come with great promotion. He was attractive because of who He is, who He was, and what He did.

Prayer: Lord Jesus, You are not a commodity; You are my Savior. When I speak of You, keep me from adding to who You are, because anything I add would really be a detraction.

APRIL 23

GOD DOESN'T MEAN THAT—DOES HE?

God doesn't listen to the prayers of men who flout the law.

Proverbs 28:9 TLB

There it is!

Right in the middle of *The Living Bible.*

No apologies, no "I'm sorry to have to tell you this, but . . . ," no easing into it.

Flat out, Solomon gives us God's Word: "God doesn't listen to the prayers of men who flout the law."

Of course He will hear my prayer if I flout the law just this once and then hurry to ask forgiveness—won't He?

And if I flout the law and make a couple of dollars, I could tithe on them; that would make my praying acceptable, wouldn't it?

He couldn't mean every law, all the time—could He?

I guess the decision to make is: Do I want to skin the law a little and maybe profit somehow by it, or do I want to know that God is listening when I pray?

The results of the first choice, at best, are temporary; the results of the second are for always.

Frankly, it isn't even a choice. I need God more than I need those couple of dollars.

Prayer: When You make a statement, it is straight out. Now I want to heed what You say.

APRIL 24

WHAT HAPPENED TO THE LIGHTS?

Ye are the light of the world. A city that is set on an hill cannot be hid. Neither do men light a candle, and put it under a bushel, but on a candlestick; and it giveth light to all that are in the house. Let your light so shine before men, that they may see your good works, and glorify your Father which is in heaven.

Matthew 5:14-16 KJV

We were having a get-together with friends when suddenly all the lights went out.

"Why don't you pay your light bill?" one of our visitors joked. We guessed that someone had hit a utility pole, since there was no storm and the entire neighborhood was dark.

Candles were lit, and we went on with our talking. But something was different—we were aware of the poor light and the darkness outside. Yet we had not been conscious of the light before.

I see a lot of light around me, and most of the time I don't pay any attention to it. There are a lot of Christians in my circle of friends and associates. I don't get away from light very much. Still, I don't really notice the light, because I'm used to it. I'm not so conscious of the dark.

But others are. Their surrounding night is so dark that even a pinprick of light is noticed. They turn to the light because there is so little of it.

I didn't mind the candle glow for visiting. I knew the lights would come back on soon, and they did. But were I living in the dark all the time, I'd sure hope for some light. And if someone had it covered or, worse, blew it out when I was trying to find it, I'd feel frustrated.

I suspect many of us who are used to a lot of light know very little about the frustrations of those who have little. Next time all your lights go out, light a candle; you'll learn something.

Prayer: You have given me a good light. Please keep me from switching it off or covering it up, not only because I need it, but because there are others looking for it.

APRIL 25

SAFE WALKING, EVEN WITHOUT GLASSES

They saw not one another, neither rose any from his place for three days: but all the children of Israel had light in their dwellings.

Exodus 10:23 KJV

When you wear bifocals (as I do) and walk at night (as I sometimes do), if it's raining (as it tends to do when I'm walking), the streetlights that normally offer so much help become a hazard. The light, diffused by the rain and the water drops on my glasses, makes it hard for me to see. So unless I invent windshield wipers for my spectacles, I'll have to keep on doing what I do now: I take them off and put them in my pocket and walk without them. Unfortunately, walking in the rain at night without my bifocals, I'm a hazard, too.

There was no hazard for the children of Israel in Egypt when God placed darkness over the land for three days. The Scripture says, "But all the children of Israel had light in their dwellings." No one else could see, but they could. There was darkness everywhere; God caused it. But there was light in their houses. God gave that light. They didn't have poor lighting or diffused lighting; they had God's lighting, which is good lighting, for God is good.

We live in dark surroundings; sometimes it is so dark that if it weren't for the good light of God, we'd stumble as the Egyptians did. When God gives light, then "we walk in the light as He is in the light." We won't stumble then, no matter how dark, even if it's raining. With God's light we never have to take off our eyeglasses and take our chances.

Prayer: Thank You, Lord, that in Your light I can see.

❧ APRIL 26 ❦
YOU CAN DO WHAT?

> And the Lord said, "If you had faith as a grain of mustard seed, you could say to this sycamine tree, 'Be rooted up, and be planted in the sea,' and it would obey you."
>
> Luke 17:6

Pardon me for laughing, but that's the most unbelievable. . . .

Go ahead, read it: "If you had faith as a grain of mustard seed, you could say to this sycamine tree, 'Be rooted up, and be planted in the sea,' and it would obey you" (Luke 17:6).

See what I mean?

Mustard seed! That's one of the smallest seeds there is. And did you ever try to overpower the root system of a full-grown tree?

It must have been a joke that Jesus was telling. He had to be teasing.

Except, He had recently healed quite a few people and fed a crowd. Because of that, His disciples were making an honest and serious request: "Increase our faith!" (Luke 17:5). That's not something to joke about.

Was He joking?

That example about the tree, it's so peculiar. He could have chosen hundreds of examples that are more realistic—more plausible—but He didn't.

My faith couldn't do the thing He said. Nobody's faith could; only God could do that.

Maybe He purposely chose that example. Maybe He was talking not so much about my faith (which I tend to measure all the time) or faith in doing some great feat but faith in God who can do anything.

I'd better read that Scripture again.

Prayer: I know You meant it, or You wouldn't have said it.

৯ে   APRIL 27   ৬

AN ACCOUNT I CAN'T OVERDRAW

It is of the Lord's mercies that we are not consumed, because his compassions fail not. They are new every morning: great is thy faithfulness.

Lamentations 3:22, 23 KJV

Praying at night is difficult for me. After a long day of opportunities for Satan, when he can point out to me all the times I stumbled, the mistakes I made, my failure to do what I should have done, the times that I did exactly the opposite to what I wished I would have done, the times temptation had its victories, I find my bedtime praying to be mostly apology. So I really feel a kinship with Jeremiah. He must have been praying at night when God gave him the awareness, "It is of the Lord's mercies that we are not consumed, because his compassions fail not." I can go to sleep on that. And, I make it through the day by the mercies of God. His compassions don't fail.

More than that, His compassions are new every morning. When I put my head on the pillow and shut my eyes and recollect how God mercifully helped when I so desperately needed Him and thank Him for His compassion, there is the awareness that when I wake up there will be a whole new checking account full of compassion to draw upon. If I overdraw my personal checking account, nobody puts more money in for me the next morning. But I cannot overdraw God's compassion, because every morning His compassions are renewed. No wonder Jeremiah could say with great exclamation, "Great is thy faithfulness." That's what I want to say, too.

Prayer: Truly, Lord, Your faithfulness is great. Thank You for Your compassion, which is new for me every morning.

⤳ APRIL 28 ⤵

RESTORED, EVEN AFTER MY BROOM BREAKS

> And I will restore to you the years that the locust hath eaten, the cankerworm, and the caterpiller, and the palmerworm, my great army which I sent among you.
>
> Joel 2:25 KJV

I've never seen what locusts can do—but there are people who have. They've looked at the land afterwards and have seen nothing but dust and the dead locusts they killed with their brooms. Around them everything was gone.

But I've met people who have "lost it all" to other "locusts"—a devastating and costly illness, a career ended by a robot replacement, a family destroyed by hate and anger.

What can anyone do? Very little. What can God do? Everything that we can't do. When all is gone, He isn't.

Over the horizon they come, those locusts. No warning, no way to stop them, our energies for fighting soon gone. We can't do any more. There are too many; we are overcome. I'm not sure that's happened to me yet. With my broom and a lot of effort I've batted down the few annoying locusts that have invaded my life. My efforts have overcome them. I've prayed as I've swatted my locusts and thanked God for the strength to keep going.

But the day may come when my efforts won't be enough and my broom will break. When that day comes, I won't put down my broom, and I won't go hide under the bed. I won't quit, and I certainly won't stop praying. But I'll look again at those words of God, and I'll be glad He made that promise.

Prayer: Thank You, Lord, that even when I've fought and lost, You will restore.

৯৬ APRIL 29 ৬৯
CHIPPED PILLARS

He who conquers, I will make him a pillar in the temple of
my God; never shall he go out of it, and I will write on him
the name of my God, and the name of the city of my God,
the new Jerusalem which comes down from my God out of
heaven, and my own new name.

Revelation 3:12

Think about that! Quite a picture, isn't it?

But then, how else would God describe us?

"He who conquers, I will make him a pillar in the temple of my
God; never shall he go out of it. . . ."

Not a floor or a ceiling but the part that holds it all together—a
pillar—that's what I am. And every believer can say that.

And apparently these aren't hollowed out, gilded ornaments—
not picturesque for-decoration-only pillars. John was given these
words to share with the body of believers who were under persecution; they were in a war.

It is a battle for believers now, too; things haven't changed. There
are some scarred, chipped, and tarnished pillars in His temple—all
His.

Some people look at Christians and laugh and say, "They're
weak," because they are God's pillars. Pillars don't have to argue
the point or prove what they are—not when they've already fought
the fight and have come out conquerors.

Pillars only have to be pillars.

Let the scoffers kick or slam their fists against one. They'll know!

Prayer: Help me to be a conqueror and a pillar.

৯৬ APRIL 30 ৬৯
YOUR WAY OR MY WAY?

You search the scriptures, because you think that in them
you have eternal life; and it is they that bear witness to me.

John 5:39

We all tend to see things from a different perspective. While flying across America's heartland, I looked down and saw all the pat-

terns of the fields and marveled at the variety of forms. My wife looked down and saw ideas for a patchwork quilt. That's because she sews, and I don't.

We all do that; we see something and get one idea, while someone else sees the same thing and gets another idea. Because that happens, we realize that no one has the final word or interpretation of what we see.

Some try to carry that over to matters of faith. "You see God your way; I see God my way." Except there's a problem with that. If I see God my way, I'm in trouble. I have created God in my image. I have determined God. But God reveals Himself to us not in our way but in His way, with the same person—the Holy Spirit—being the interpreter of who He is.

We can debate with each other about who God is and what He says, but we'd be a whole lot better off if we would look at the revelation of Himself as given in Scripture and ask the Holy Spirit to explain it to us. If we don't, we may have a lot of different religious ideas about God, but we won't have God.

Prayer: Father, help me to seek You, on Your terms, in Your way, being aware that I tend to get into my own ideas too much.

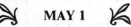

MAY 1

BUT I DIDN'T HEAR YOU KNOCK

> Behold, I stand at the door and knock; if any one hears my voice and opens the door, I will come in to him and eat with him, and he with me.
>
> Revelation 3:20

We've all done it.

We pass the front door and notice somebody patiently standing out there. We open the door and, embarrassed, exclaim: "How long have you been out here?"

Then come the apologies:

"The TV must have been too loud."

"I was busy in the kitchen."

"The kids were yelling."

We admit it: Our failure to open the door wasn't because the visitor didn't knock; it was that he knocked, and we didn't hear.

Jesus said, "Behold, I stand at the door and knock; if any one hears my voice and opens the door, I will come in to him and eat with him, and he with me."

And we stand there telling Jesus:

"But I didn't hear Your knock."

"Too many other things were going on."

"Why didn't You just come in?"

Yes, why doesn't Jesus just come in? What if He did? Would you have welcomed Him? Would you have even noticed that He was there?

Jesus said, "Eat with him, and he with me," meaning to be together. He wants to be close. Would you be ready for that kind of relationship if you hadn't even invited Him in, if He'd surprised you?

For many people, Jesus never does come in. Some don't hear Him knocking; some aren't ready for Him; some don't want Him—and He'll never break the lock.

There is a way to have Jesus come in.

It's very simple.

Listen for His knock.

Invite Him in.

Prayer: Please let my ears be attuned to Your knock. I don't want to miss You.

MAY 2

ACCOUNTABLE

> Blessed is he who considers the poor! The Lord delivers
> him in the day of trouble.
>
> Psalm 41:1

It is true that Christians, like everybody else, tend to be faddish, getting on and off bandwagons as they come along. You can sometimes predict what pastors will preach by knowing what years they were in seminary. You can guess fairly accurately how some people will vote by knowing when they were in college and where. There are political, social, and theological influences. Every book publisher knows that there are definite trends in people's interests and thinking, and they hope that their authors will hit each trend as it is rising, not after it has peaked.

But the rise and fall of interest in an issue is not the measure of the importance of that issue. The attention paid to a problem is not the determiner of how important or unimportant that problem is. Certainly not when it comes to looking at the way we live.

We are accountable to God for the way we live. To ignore this is to be guilty of the same heresy that infected the early church when, in a division of soul and body, it was implied that it didn't matter what the body did so long as the soul was saved.

No one can dictate what we are to do about our goods, our way of life, and our values—that is God's place. But we can and must encourage people to hear what God is saying.

Each of us can deny that there is any problem and go on taking, using, and consuming. In our shrinking world, that is exploitive—but we can do it. Or we can reevaluate our lives and our commitment to Christ and begin to change.

Prayer: Father, I don't want to be one of the takers and exploiters; I want to be a giver of my goods and my life.

৵ MAY 3 ৶

SOMEBODY NEEDS TO EMPTY THAT

> . . . If any one does sin, we have an advocate with the Father, Jesus Christ the righteous.
>
> 1 John 2:1

My wastebasket needs emptying again. It's a lot like me.

Trash has a way of piling up: stuff of no value, clutter. It all multiplies in my life.

I'm a contradiction. Forgiveness, cleansing, removal of sin and its consequences were done by Jesus. I trust Him as Redeemer. I believe in His righteousness to clothe me. Yet, like Paul, there are a lot of things I don't want to do that I do. Soon, though I try to keep short accounts, my life—like my wastebasket—is full.

Scripture shows the way for regular emptying to happen. John's letter tells us, "If we confess our sins, he is faithful and just, and will forgive our sins and cleanse us from all unrighteousness" (1 John 1:9). Then he goes on with the hope that "you may not sin." Yet understanding his readers, and especially with an understanding of

me, there follow the words, "If any one does sin, we have an advocate with the Father, Jesus Christ the righteous."

He is there—my Lawyer, my Advocate, the One who makes
atonement for me. He shows me where I fail and when. Best of all,
He does what He alone can do—He gets rid of the trash.

*Prayer: Thank You, Lord, for Christ my Advocate, who continues to
stand by my side and help me.*

﹋ MAY 4 ﹌
GOD'S ONE-LINER

> For God so loved the world that he gave his only Son, that
> whoever believes in him should not perish but have eternal
> life.
>
> John 3:16

Now, there's fame for you!

How would you like to have your name remembered by millions
of people?

How would you like to have children told by their teachers that
they must memorize what you wrote?

That's John!

Only John is not really the author, even though he signed the
writing; God is. And that's the reason that people remember the
words.

Being inspired by God, John wrote what is sometimes called the
Gospel in one sentence.

"For God so loved the world that he gave his only Son, that whoever believes in him should not perish but have eternal life."

That's God's promise, and we can act on it because:

God does love the world;

He has sent His Son—His Only One.

That means that the "whoever" part can include me. If I believe
in Him (the Only Son), I will not perish; I will have eternal life.

Improve on that, and your words will be remembered by millions
of people, too.

Only you can't improve on it, because there will never be another
Jesus to make possible that once-for-all forgiveness.

There is only one Eternal One. His atonement is a one-time
event.

John has the written Word about the living *Word*—the Logos, who is Jesus Christ.

John points to Jesus.

You can memorize what John wrote, talk about John, and quote John, but you can be saved only by Jesus.

Prayer: You gave Your Word to your servants so they could give it to me. Now help me to live by it and pass it on.

ᴪ MAY 5 ᴪ

NO MORE

He will wipe away every tear from their eyes, and death shall be no more, neither shall there be mourning nor crying nor pain any more. . . .

Revelation 21:4

"No more" is a nice Bible term. I suppose the "no mores" give me as much comfort as any other part of Scripture. In looking at the new Jerusalem, the new dwelling place with God, the city coming down out of heaven when God Himself will be with us, John said, "God will wipe away every tear from their eyes." Every tear. That's personal. It's not a statement—"Buck up and stop crying." But with the tenderness of a parent, He's carefully soothing and wiping away all the tears.

Then come the "no mores": no more death, no more mourning, no more crying, no more pain—because that's part of the old order, and we aren't going to be in that old order anymore; all will be passed away.

When life gets hard, my mind goes back to those two simple words. Someday there will be "no more."

Prayer: Lord, Your Word is so encouraging to me. Thank You.

◈ MAY 6 ◈
RUST

Lay not up for yourselves treasures upon earth, where moth and rust doth corrupt, and where thieves break through and steal: But lay up for yourselves treasures in heaven, where neither moth nor rust doth corrupt, and where thieves do not break through nor steal.

Matthew 6:19, 20 KJV

Was the Lord thinking about my car when He said that? The motor in my nine-year-old car is fine, but the body is falling apart. In the northern climates where I live, they like to put lots of salt on the roads. And even though I try to wash the car frequently, the salt still starts to eat at the metal. The body of my car has that filigreed, lacy look of Spanish grillwork. Everyone I know has the same problem, but people keep investing in new cars. Like me, they have to. Someday, my nine-year-old vehicle with the lacy fenders will probably lie down and die. But when I get another car, I won't need the newest, the best. I know what's going to happen to it anyway, when winter comes.

But a few people I know still keep wanting a bigger or newer car all the time. Some trade every year or two. For them it's a status symbol. It "proves" (at least to them) that they've made it; they have a good income, they can afford nice things.

Jesus gave an alternative. He talked about laying up treasures in heaven, where the rust can't get them. There are a lot of ways to do that. I like to invest in people's lives—needy people who are faithful to Christ. Moth and rust can't do a thing about that kind of investment.

And the more I give like that, the more my ancient, lacy, filigreed car begins to look as if it could make it through yet another winter.

Prayer: Lord, help me to keep my priorities straight and put my treasure where it's going to do the most good.

❧ MAY 7 ❧

ROBOTS ARE QUICK THINKERS

And the Lord God formed man of the dust of the ground, and breathed into his nostrils the breath of life; and man became a living soul.

Genesis 2:7 KJV

In a creative advertising display, I watched a robot talking to people. He would comment on what they were wearing, flirt, walk along, and argue. I went back and watched several times. The computerized ability to respond to different people in different ways was fascinating. People tried to trap him with statements or comments. But he was up to it and always replied with a snappy response.

I wondered, though, what would have happened if I'd talked to him about his soul. Probably I'd have drawn a blank. He doesn't have a soul; his programmer didn't give him one. In fact his programmer couldn't.

God gave man a mind, the ability to think and give snappy replies—and He also gave him a soul. There is a reason for that. He wants man to have His "in breathed" part, the very essence of God. He wants man's soul to distinguish him from the rest of creation— to love and be loved in return.

God wasn't creating a computerized robot when He made us. He wanted something special and designed us that way. He wasn't just looking for snappy answers to His questions and comments; He wanted people to share the very content of His heart.

Some people, though, still don't know why God made them. They think their quick thinking makes them smart enough not to need God. They don't know that without God they aren't much different from a robot. So they keep on polishing their snappy answers and impressing themselves.

Prayer: Lord, I don't want to be only a mind with quick answers. I want to have You fill my soul and be my Answer.

❧ MAY 8 ❧
A LITTLE SCRAP OF PAPER

And the Lord said unto him, What is that in thine hand?
And he said, A rod.

Exodus 4:2 KJV

A lot of books get written on scraps of paper, at least the early drafts do. Some of the notes for this book were jotted on a piece of hotel stationery that I stuck in my pocket. I kept adding to the notes throughout the day. Basically that's the way most of us live—a little here, a little there, using what we have at the moment, adding as we go along. But even though we tend to live patchy lives, that doesn't surprise God or alter His leading. He knows what we have with us at the moment, and He knows how to use it. What is a scrap of paper to us is a part of His plan to Him.

He asked Moses, "What is that in your hand?" Moses had a stick, a common, ordinary stick picked up from the ground. It was enough to scare Pharaoh, because God used that stick.

What's in your pocket? Are you using what you have now, or are you lamenting that you're not where you produce your best work; you're not at your office with a good typewriter and research books. You're not in the best of health. You're not at home. You don't have your family around. You're lonely.

Maybe you're like me: all you've got is a wrinkled piece of hotel stationery. Well, use it. It's common things that God often puts to work. And because that's true, we can never doubt that God did the using.

What's in your pocket now? Or in your hand? Use it. What do you think it's there for?

Prayer: Father, I always look for the best, the ideal circumstances, while all the time You want to use what's in my hand right now.

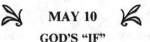

MAY 9
WAITING

> . . . Why stand ye gazing up into heaven? this same Jesus,
> which is taken up from you into heaven, shall so come in
> like manner as ye have seen him go into heaven.
>
> Acts 1:11 KJV

They might have stood there a long time. It was a normal reaction to an unusual once-ever event. Jesus was risen, and they saw Him disappear into heaven. They didn't budge; their eyes were riveted, their necks locked in place. But He didn't reappear.

Instead two men—angels, certainly—told them that Jesus would come again just as He left. They had work to do, and until He came back, they were to do that work.

We are two thousand years closer to His return. If anything, the waiting has made us more alert than ever that the time of His coming could be today, maybe in the next few minutes.

But unlike the disciples then, we aren't outside, looking up at the sky; we have work to do. There are still too many who have either not heard that Jesus is coming, or they've heard and don't care.

When He comes, Jesus wants to find us proclaiming the good news, being faithful in well doing. He expects us to be redeeming the time. We're to look around us and get busy, not be standing around looking skyward, waiting. Faithful followers may be tired when He comes, but they won't have stiff necks.

Prayer: Perhaps today, Lord, You'll come back. If You do, I want to be busy at work for You.

MAY 10
GOD'S "IF"

> If we are faithless, he remains faithful—for he cannot deny
> himself.
>
> 2 Timothy 2:13

He was sitting over against the wall, complaining, "My faith is too small."

The reply from his friend was immediate: "So what!"

That'll shake a person, and it did. But then came his friend's explanation. "Think how capricious and unsteady God would be if what He did depended only on your belief in His power to do it!"

Then he opened his Bible to the "if" passage:

"The saying is sure:
If we have died with him, we shall also live with him;
if we endure, we shall also reign with him;
if we deny him, he also will deny us;
if we are faithless, he remains faithful—for he cannot
deny himself" (2 Timothy 2:11–13).

God is His own promise, His own surety, His own guarantor. He wants my faith; He promises to respond to my trust, but to be God, He doesn't require my faith. He is God who will keep His word whether I or anybody else has enough faith that He will keep it.

That "if" passage is not too well-known.

A lot of lives would be different if it were.

Prayer: I'm so grateful that Your faithfulness is not governed by mine.

MAY 11

BLACK TIE AND BLUE SOCKS

> Study to shew thyself approved unto God, a workman that needeth not to be ashamed, rightly dividing the word of truth.
>
> 2 Timothy 2:15 KJV

The orchestra was playing Mozart and Tchaikovsky. It was beautiful. The acoustics were excellent, the conductor outstanding, and each member of the symphony orchestra was dressed in formal black attire—almost. Right in front of me, at eye level, sat one of the violinists, wearing blue socks. As the orchestra began to play, my eyes kept going back to those blue socks.

But even though my mind was wandering, pulling me back to those blue socks, the music was still being played flawlessly. Each musician was concentrating on either the music or the maestro. Each had obviously studied well and determined to be workmen who needed not to be ashamed. The eyes of each musician were moving back and forth—from the conductor to the music and back to the conductor. And I thought of the words of Jesus, ". . . My brethren are these which hear the word of God, and do it" (Luke 8:21 KJV).

Here was a collection of men and women, each with a different instrument to play, each producing a different sound, each playing according to the text in front of him and the direction of the maestro. The result was a symphony of sound. After a while I didn't notice the different instruments. I didn't notice the different shapes and sizes of the performers, for some were bald and some were fat and some were skinny. And after a while, as I concentrated on the music, I didn't even notice the blue socks.

Prayer: Father, keep my mind on what is important—Your Word and Your direction.

 MAY 12

CAN'T I?

All scripture is given by inspiration of God, and is profitable for doctrine, for reproof, for correction, for instruction in righteousness.
2 Timothy 3:16 KJV

That's what I like to do—correct the Scriptures—and I'm so glad there's a verse that gives me the authority to do that. It does, doesn't it? Scripture is given for doctrine, for reproof, for correction. I can use Scripture to show other people where their doctrine is wrong. I can use Scripture to reprove them, when I don't like their behavior. And I can correct the Scripture to make it say what I like it to say—can't I? And as a result I am "perfect, throughly furnished unto all good works" (v. 17 KJV)—aren't I?

Someone told me that the Bible was inspired by God to reprove me, to correct me, to instruct me, and to give me doctrinal teaching from God so that I can be complete. But that can't be so—can it? Because the Bible is living and active, a two-edged sword. What is a sword but something to slash with? The Bible is a great weapon; I handle it like a machete. That's okay, isn't it?

I do have one concern. If all Scripture is given by inspiration of God, how can verse 13 be inspired? After all, how can there be imposters and deceivers if everybody did as I do and corrected the Scriptures; no one would be deceived—would they? Scripture we correct ourselves is easy to live up to. How can anyone be deceived or get worse and worse? That's confusing . . . unless I've misunderstood something. Maybe that's a verse I need to correct, too.

Prayer: Lord, whenever we do that to Your Word, make us so uneasy that we have to come back to You and plead, "Teach me Your truth."

✝ MAY 13 ✝

A WASTE OF TIME?

So shall my word be that goeth forth out of my mouth: it shall not return unto me void, but it shall accomplish that which I please, and it shall prosper in the thing whereto I sent it.

Isaiah 55:11 KJV

What a waste of time, or so it seemed. Jeremiah dictated the words, Baruch wrote them down, Jehudi read them to Jehoiakim the king, and Jehoiakim the king burned them up in his fireplace (*see* Jeremiah 36). Was Jeremiah frustrated?

Then Jeremiah did it all over again. That's the way it has to be. You have to do what you're told to do when God does the telling.

I was invited once to speak at a morning worship service conducted by a national organization. The only problem was, when I stood up to speak following breakfast, I discovered that most of the men hadn't been to bed yet. Many were still drunk from the Saturday night before. As I preached, people were joking and yelling, table-hopping and slapping one another on the back, gathering in groups and having their own conversations. Only a few were looking in my direction—some glassy eyed and a few others who, I assume, were trying to listen. I wanted to quit, but I had to go on and finish my sermon. What a waste of time.

I could only think about Jeremiah. His word, as God gave it, is still bearing fruit. I tried to preach God's Word and believe on the basis of what He said that somehow just telling forth His Word would bear some fruit. God told Isaiah that it would.

Prayer: Father, even when I see no results in my service to You, keep me faithful

MAY 14
HOW TO GET ATTENTION

He must increase, but I must decrease.

John 3:30 KJV

For two weeks the college swim team surreptitiously slipped knives out of the college cafeteria, then one night put a knife in each hymnbook in the college chapel. The next morning, when the chapel hymn was announced, 3,000 knives fell to the floor.

When I heard about that prank, I asked, "Why the chapel?" The answer showed an interesting principle. "Because that's the one place where everybody gathers." The principle is, if you want to grab attention, go where everyone is. Politicians know that. People seeking public attention know that. And college students know that.

John the Baptist always drew a crowd, but not purposely. People gathered around him because they wanted to hear what he was saying and watch what he was doing. When something is happening, people gather. That's still true. When God is at work, people notice. God and His work are attractive.

Some people try all kinds of gimmicks to attract attention; John the Baptist never did. His purpose was to do the will of the Father, and in doing that he drew a crowd. John didn't have to put knives in hymnbooks. All he had to do was point to Jesus.

Prayer: Lord, some of the things I see Christians do are as comical as college pranks. Help me not to seek attention, but to point to You.

MAY 15
ANNUAL REVIEW TIME

But God commendeth his love toward us, in that, while we were yet sinners, Christ died for us.

Romans 5:8 KJV

Salary review time, for those who are not on a collective bargaining contract, can be difficult. There is a loneliness about it—just the individual and the one who reviews him. There is a time when the employee is wondering, *What is my worth?* and his self-esteem is usually measured by the increase in pay that comes. It's hard for the reviewer, too, who feels a tremendous responsibility to be faithful to the guidelines given to him and yet to do the best he can for the employee.

What is a person worth? That's difficult to measure, especially when the primary measure given in our society is salary. "But God commendeth his love toward us, in that, while we were yet sinners, Christ died for us."

What does that have to do with my self-worth? God has shown us our worth. Determine in your mind what Jesus, the Son of God, is worth to God the Father, and you'll know what you're worth to God the Father, because Jesus is the price He paid for you. And when you get into the mystery of the Trinity, you'll recognize that God Himself paid God Himself for you.

Contemplate that, and you'll begin to have some sense of what you're worth to God. You are priceless. Try to measure that with an annual salary review.

Prayer: Thank You, Father, that though there was nothing in me to merit Your love, You do love me, and You paid the price of Jesus for my redemption.

⅀ MAY 16 ⅂

MAXIMUM SECURITY

> Turn you to the strong hold, ye prisoners of hope: even to day do I declare that I will render double unto thee.
>
> Zechariah 9:12 KJV

Getting inside a maximum-security prison is difficult. The visitor goes through several electronic doors, a series of inspection points, his hand is marked with dye to show up under special lighting—all to get in. Getting out is even harder. Prisoners don't think of security the way we do. They don't want to be "secure." They want to be free.

Those who belong to the Lord Jesus Christ by faith in His redemptive work have maximum security; they are also free. Zechariah calls those of us who have turned to the stronghold "prisoners of hope." Hope surrounds us on all sides. We are *inside* hope. We can't get out of hope. Our hope is in God—our eternal hope, a hope based on a covenant, God's promise. Sometimes we think all hope is gone, but it isn't. Hope isn't conditional to our holding onto it. Hope holds onto us.

Prisoners of hope are prisoners of God. That's maximum security.

Prayer: Thank You, Lord, for the hope with all its eternal dimensions that is mine in Christ Jesus.

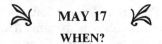

MAY 17
WHEN?

> Because you have made the Lord your refuge, the Most High your habitation, no evil shall befall you, no scourge come near your tent. For he will give his angels charge of you to guard you in all your ways.
>
> Psalm 91:9–11

"Because you have. . . ."

That can be the beginning of a gift presentation or a sentencing to life imprisonment.

You have done something; and because you have, something follows. In this case, you are getting a gift. God has a special gift for you. It's in three parts. Here it is:

"No evil shall befall you,
No scourge come near.
He will give his angels charge of you to guard you in all your ways."

That's the promise. It's in Psalm 91:10, 11, and it's all yours.

But wait a minute!

Don't be presumptuous, saying, "When, when?" or nasty with, "If it's true, then why am I unhappy?"

Don't, because there is more to this promise. There is an introduction, too: "Because you have made the Lord your refuge, the Most High your habitation." That's in verse 9. "Because you have," then the gift.

Still asking, "When do I get the gift?"

There's a prior question: When will the Lord be my refuge? When will the Most High become my habitation?

Still want to react with a, "If it's true, why . . . '"?

Because it is true; it's spoken by the True One, the Holy God.

If you suspect that you aren't on God's gift list, you may want to check that "because" clause again.

Prayer: Be my refuge, Lord; be my habitation, my secure place of living.

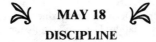

MAY 18

DISCIPLINE

But I pommel my body and subdue it, lest after preaching to others I myself should be disqualified.

1 Corinthians 9:27

We conquer outer space and body-devastating diseases and apply ourselves to finding alternative fuel sources, but there is a frontier, a mountain called discipline, that many have never conquered. Some have never even tried to conquer it.

If drug abuse, alcoholism, and other "escapes" are some people's response to pain or anything else that is disagreeable, then so is the self-indulgence and the leaking out at the edges that characterize so many others in our Western world. There is a weakness, a basic unwillingness to cope with unpleasantness or difficulty, an inability to endure, and we see it everywhere. Some call it the freedom to be, but it isn't freedom. Lack of discipline is slavery.

When I cannot or will not say no, I offer myself to be shackled by any impulse, yearning, or fleeting pleasure that comes along.

When I allow myself to be directed by whatever is easy or promises immediate gratification, I am as incapable of standing as a rootless tree.

When I trade duty for pleasure, honor for expediency, God's call for my wants, I deal in the business of human failure.

Temptations come; of course they do. Situations present themselves, escape from emotional or physical unpleasantness is attractive, the broad path offers fewer obstacles. But strength comes in the moral and spiritual muscle building that demands effort, even strain—it is a pushing against or a pulling back.

The Apostle Paul said, "I pommel my body and subdue it. . . ." Sometimes it comes to that. It isn't easy, it isn't pleasant, and it may not be immediately rewarding. But because God is King, the discipline of honesty, morality, faithfulness, truthfulness, and honor offers a greater satisfaction: the awareness of no longer being victims—not even of ourselves—but of being conquerors. And, as conquerors, we build other strengths for an even tougher discipline tomorrow.

Prayer: Lord, help me to be a disciplined person. I don't want to be a "me" person; I want to be Your person.

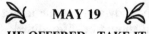

MAY 19

HE OFFERED—TAKE IT

And you will know the truth, and the truth will make you free.

John 8:32

Those are two things that people are always struggling to get—truth and freedom.

Jesus offers both, ours for the asking. But so many still miss out.

We study to find truth, when it comes from Him.

We fight for freedom while all the time real freedom is being offered to us if we will take it.

Funny how people go through life missing what they want the most. If He didn't want us to have truth and freedom, He wouldn't have offered them.

Prayer: Thank You that You want me to have truth and freedom. I want them, too.

 MAY 20

THOSE TINY BICYCLE SEATS

... Whither thou goest, I will go; and where thou lodgest, I will lodge: thy people shall be my people, and thy God my God.

Ruth 1:16 KJV

I'm a biker.

I don't have a black leather jacket (it's blue, and it isn't leather), and I don't have a motorcycle. What I have is a bicycle, maroon.

Riding it is good exercise. At least it is for a while. Then something happens. I notice it before my wife does. When she rides with me, she can keep going even after I'm ready to stop.

The words of Ruth to Naomi come to mind on rides like that. "Whither thou goest, I will go." Ruth was willing, and she did it. I'm willing, but I can't do it. But then Ruth wasn't riding a bike, and she wasn't middle-aged. And no one yet has made a bicycle seat for the middle-aged, at least not one for long rides.

So as my wife rides on, I stop and walk a little and think about God being with Ruth and Naomi. She proved faithful, and her faithfulness resulted eventually in her marriage to Boaz. From that line came the genealogy of Jesus.

God had a faithful woman in Ruth, and He blessed her for it. But then, keeping up with Naomi must have been easier for her. Ruth wasn't a bike rider; she didn't have to contend with an undersized bicycle seat. Ruth walked.

Prayer: I marvel, Lord, that even when I'm walking my bike, You are there and have Your truth to teach me.

MAY 21

SEEMS SIMPLE

Draw near to God and he will draw near to you. Cleanse your hands, you sinners, and purify your hearts, you men of double mind.

James 4:8

Like two magnets, the closer they get, the closer they want to be.

It's the same with God. As I start to move toward Him, He is already moving toward me, just as He said He would.

"Draw near to God and he will draw near to you."

Even a little movement assures that promise.

It may be only a slight glance, a decision not to argue with Him anymore, an honest question about His forgiveness, a cry, a prayer, a beginning attempt at reading the Bible, a visit to the church on the corner.

Sometimes, if that drawing near is ever going to happen, a person has to stop running in the opposite direction, stand still, and listen.

Then, hearing God and knowing that He is serious about what He says, turn around and start back.

"Draw near to God and he will draw near to you." He will!
Seem simple? Almost too easy?

God doesn't want us to be separated from Him. He built a bridge
to us with a cross that had Jesus on it. When you think about that,
you realize that it's easy for us to come, because our coming was so
costly for Him.

Drawing near to God is a free trip.

God has already picked up the tab.

*Prayer: I struggled as I drew near, but You kept coming toward me.
Thank You.*

MAY 22
EXAM TIME

... Be ready always to give an answer to every man that
asketh you a reason of the hope that is in you. ...

1 Peter 3:15 KJV

It was just like college exam time, only I have been out of college
more than twenty-five years. I was to give a progress report on
my work, complete with budgets, predictions for the future, personnel needs, and so on, and be prepared to answer any questions
that the board of directors might ask. I studied; morning, noon,
and night I studied, and I was ready. For five hours I waited to be
called. When the phone rang and I gathered up my notes, I learned
that the board had approved my plans and that I wouldn't have to
appear.

Two months later, when some board members casually asked me
questions that I had been prepared to answer at that earlier meeting, I stumbled around, grasping for the answers that I once knew
so well, and it was embarrassing.

We're told as Christians to be prepared always to give a reason
for the hope that is in us. People don't ask us about Christ right at
the moment when we think we're the most prepared to witness.
They ask us about the Savior when other things are on our minds,
when we haven't crammed for the questions. Then we start stumbling.

We're obliged, because we believe what we believe, to be ready
always. We do this not as one preparing for a test but to be able to

respond quietly when somebody asks, "What is this hope that is in you?"

Prayer: Father, help me to see witnessing not as a test to be passed but as a faith to be passed along.

⤷ MAY 23 ⤶
PUBLICLY

> Because, if you confess with your lips that Jesus is Lord and believe in your heart that God raised him from the dead, you will be saved. For man believes with his heart and so is justified, and he confesses with his lips and so is saved.
>
> Romans 10:9, 10

"Ifs" often precede something special in the Bible. This one certainly does.

"If you confess with your lips that Jesus is Lord and believe in your heart that God raised him from the dead, you will be saved. For man believes with his heart and so is justified, and he confesses with his lips and so is saved."

Confession by itself? That won't do; it's not enough.

Belief without confession? That's not enough either.

The two go together. That's the way God wants it.

Belief—in the inner part of our very being, where life is, where the real self is, and confession—the thing that is so hard to do if we only "sort of" believe.

So sooner or later someone will ask you the question: "Do you believe in Jesus?"

And you will answer indignantly, "Of course I do. I'm no pagan!"

But that won't stop the question: "Have you confessed Him as your Savior—publicly?"

Now that's going a bit too far. God doesn't expect all this public-display stuff.

But He does!

Jesus called Matthew publicly.

When He called the sons of Zebedee, it wasn't privately.

Check out the other disciples. And keep going, right past the resurrection and ascension. In fact, look where Paul was when he met Jesus—in the middle of the freeway.

Our salvation wasn't meant to be a secret. The cross wasn't put
up in a back alley.

No one will confess Jesus publicly as Savior if he doesn't believe
in Him as Savior.

But when belief is real and the confession is, too, then the "if"
gives way to the promise—
"and so is justified . . .
and so is saved."
It's in Scripture.

*Prayer: Don't let me go through life being a secret disciple. People
need to know.*

COLORISM

Therefore if any man be in Christ, he is a new creature: old
things are passed away; behold, all things are become new.
2 Corinthians 5:17 KJV

It was a discussion on racism, and I found myself listening carefully. Some participants referred to economics as the basis for racism. An argument can be made for that. Some spoke of cultural
reasons and had points to substantiate their position. Others referred to racism as a sickness; certainly there is evidence for that.
But one man caught my attention particularly when he said,
"Though the other points are true, I believe that racism is 'colorism.' It's a religion, a secular belief."

He went on to explain that no changes economically or legally,
no social pressures, no upward mobility, no programs will in the
long run make a lot of difference, because people will believe what
they believe. And even if they try to keep their beliefs hidden, "colorism" will come through at critical moments, at emotional times.
People's beliefs always do.

I pondered what that man said, because so much of it fits religion.
The actions of individuals who are caught up in "colorism" do in-
dicate a religious system. It is what they believe, and they find evidence to support their beliefs.

Why then, I wondered, doesn't all that change when people are
converted to Jesus Christ? For some, change does come. For others,
it does not. Conversion to Christ does not instantly erase all of a be-

liever's former manner of behaving or believing. There is still, for many who claim to be "new creatures" in Christ, a clinging to old beliefs. Some people can sing praises to God, witness to His saving power, and still practice their old religion—even "colorism."

Prayer: Father, help me to be the new creation Christ saved me to be in every part of my life.

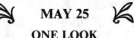

MAY 25
ONE LOOK

The stone which the builders refused is become the head stone of the corner.

Psalm 118:22 KJV

There it was, the whole Gospel at one look. Near Sedona, Arizona, stands a huge cross, the crosspiece embedded in two rock buttes. That says it all. There's the cross—God in Christ paid the penalty for our sins on a cross, taking upon Himself the punishment we deserved. And there's the rock, symbol of the Risen Christ—victorious, eternal, who is the foundation of His Body, the Church. I only saw that cross between the two rocks for a minute as we drove by, but I'll never forget it.

Prayer: Thank You, Lord, for the crucified and Risen Christ who is my life and my rock.

MAY 26
CLEVER MERCHANTS

But you shall receive power when the Holy Spirit has come upon you; and you shall be my witnesses in Jerusalem and in all Judea and Samaria and to the end of the earth.

Acts 1:8

I got one!

It's one of those automobile batteries that's guaranteed to go on and on for the life of the car.

They told me that even in my decrepit, old wreck, the battery will stay strong.

Even when the climate is too much for me, the power in the battery will always be there.

That gives peace of mind. I never have to wonder if I will have enough power in an emergency. The reserves will always be there.

God's guarantee is like that, too.

"But you shall receive power when the Holy Spirit has come upon you."

Power—all the time. It will start me no matter what environment or spiritual climate I'm in.

There's even enough to jump to a brother whose battery is temporarily weak.

Enough to last as long as I do.

Now, that's a real guarantee!

But, I noticed that there is a little added clause to that guarantee. It says, "nontransferable."

The battery is guaranteed only for me. No one else can take it; they're my power cells.

Clever merchants, those battery builders. But it's not hard to figure out where they got their idea.

Someone was reading the Bible.

Prayer: Help me to use the power You have given and show others that they can have it, too.

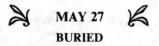

MAY 27
BURIED

> Truly, truly, I say to you, unless a grain of wheat falls into
> the earth and dies, it remains alone; but if it dies, it bears
> much fruit.
>
> John 12:24

Poor kernel of wheat. It falls; it's pushed under the dark, cold earth; it's left, forgotten. What value is it? What good is it doing? Who benefits?

That kernel of wheat is no different from each of us. Have you been thrown aside, pressed into the ground? Are you alone, apparently useless, forgotten day after day? Is life going on around you, and you seem to have no significant part in it?

There's life in a kernel of wheat, and there's life in a child of God. Someday, after the cold, after the rain, it will come to life. Then that kernel will produce thirty or fifty grains of wheat, and each of those will in turn multiply again and again.

Look what God can do with a buried kernel of wheat. It isn't out there in the brightness of the world for all to see, but the results of its quiet work go on and on and on.

Prayer: Dear Lord, let me not measure my value by my place in the sun. I'm willing to be Your buried kernel of wheat.

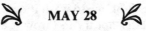

MAY 28

THERE'S A RISK

Whosoever believeth on him shall not be ashamed.

Romans 10:11 KJV

In Arizona there is a place called Slide Rock. It's a water raceway that has smoothed the rock so that it becomes like a sluiceway. Teenagers like to slide down that watercourse. But they have to be careful. More than one enthusiastic slider has lost the seat of his blue jeans or swimsuit on the rocks.

In the slides of life we can leave something behind, too. Slide Rock looks like fun, and it is fun. But there's a risk that it might take something from you and leave you ashamed. Just as more than one teenager has left Slide Rock with his jacket tied around his waist, so there are Christians who, envying the "fun" of the slide that others take, have dared to try it and have had to cover up something rather embarrassing.

The Scripture says that "whosoever believes on Him shall not be ashamed." The reason we'll never be ashamed is that believing in Him means obeying Him, and obeying Him means staying off certain slippery rocks.

Prayer: Lord, keep me from embarrassing myself because I've been doing what obedience says I should not do.

⅍ MAY 29 ⅋

LEAVE MY SHIRT ALONE

... Blessed is he that ... keepeth his garments. ...
Revelation 16:15 KJV

As soon as I come home in the evenings, I reach into the closet for my favorite old shirt. And on Saturday I wear it all day. It has two buttons missing, the collar is frayed, one sleeve is torn, and it's all my wife can do to get it off me to wash it occasionally. It's comfortable, and she had better not try to throw it away! There is even a passage of Scripture that supports my hanging on to this favorite shirt—"Blessed is he that keepeth his garments"—which proves that anybody can find just about any passage of Scripture to support what he already wants to do. I want to keep my shirt, and the Bible tells me it's okay—except that's not what the Bible is saying in this passage.

Jesus is talking about His sudden return. He will come quickly, as a thief, without warning—and we'd better be ready. It's His way of telling us, "Don't get caught unprepared. The Lord is coming soon."

And He is! We have every indication that His coming for His own could be any minute. Certainly today is a strong possibility. Maybe I can refer to my favorite shirt as my "Second Coming shirt" or my "book of Revelation shirt" and quote the passage that I don't want to be found naked when He comes. That ought to convince my wife. Maybe she won't keep eyeing it when the washing machine is running.

Prayer: Lord, may it always be in my consciousness that Your coming is soon—perhaps today.

⅍ MAY 30 ⅋

LOOK OUT!

There will be tribulation and distress for every human being who does evil, the Jew first and also the Greek.
Romans 2:9

That's not a reason to be good; it's a confirmation for good people that God knows who they are. It's also a warning to the evil people; God knows them, too.

"There will be tribulation and distress for every human being who does evil." That's plain language.

To be good is to be of God; He knows what that is and who that is because good is of Himself.

To be evil is the opposite. The point is not for us to be good out of fear, but to be of God—conformed into the image of Christ out of a desire to be God's good people. Christ is God, and He is good; He is the "God example." In Jesus Christ we are the "God ones."

But look around; not many "God ones" left, are there?

Is the world becoming more and more evil?

Probably so.

That's not a surprise or even shocking; it's a reality. In fact, you can deduce that evil will get worse just by the biblical references to the coming judgment.

"Judgment," "distress," "crying out"—horrible words!

How can a loving God use words like that and talk about such things happening to human beings? Yes, why?

Well, why would someone scream, "Look out!" just because a train is coming down the tracks, and you're on the tracks, unless he wants you to jump? And if you don't move, why does he resort to such grizzly statements as: "You'll be smashed"?

God sees the train coming and is yelling, "Look out," "Tribulation," and, "Distress."

Some people have their ears open and hear.

Some don't.

Prayer: Father, I know that sometimes You sound harsh because You love me so much.

MAY 31
BACK DOOR

For we were bondmen; yet our God hath not forsaken us in our bondage, but hath extended mercy unto us in the sight of the kings of Persia, to give us a reviving, to set up the house of our God, and to repair the desolations thereof, and to give us a wall in Judah and in Jerusalem.

Ezra 9:9 KJV

Some people spend Saturday afternoon at the park, having a picnic. Others take their children to the zoo. Still others are out on the golf course. I'm spending my Saturday afternoon in the backseat of my car. I didn't plan to be there, but I have to. A few days ago as I was turning onto the freeway, the back door of my car swung open and stayed open. I had to find a place to stop to slam it shut again. But until I could find a stopping place I was driving down the freeway with one door open like a broken wing. If that was startling to me, I wonder what it looked like to the driver behind me. But I got the door shut. Then later, while turning the corner into my own street, it flew open again.

So now I've got to find out what's wrong. Whatever it is, it will take longer to repair than I want to spend on it. Jobs like that always do.

Ezra wasn't driving down the freeway, but he was aware that the kings of Persia were watching him and his people. He needed God's help to do a repair job. The house of God was desolate, and Jerusalem needed a wall. Scripture says God extended His mercy. God was involved with His people—in their slavery, in their return from slavery, and in their rebuilding of the temple and the city.

If God can lead a nation and move the hearts of kings and help a people when they restore a city and a temple, what can He do for me on a Saturday afternoon? I'm going to be thinking about that as I crawl into the backseat of my car.

Prayer: Lord, repairing a car door isn't going to change the course of history. Yet with all the big things You do, You don't ignore our little things. I want to thank You that You don't.

❧ JUNE 1 ❧
OUTGROWING MY TEDDY BEAR

> I am the Lord thy God. . . . Thou shalt have no other gods before me.
>
>   Exodus 20:2, 3 KJV

She was about three years old, sitting with her legs swinging in one of the big (for her) row seats in the airport waiting area. She was clutching her teddy bear.

I didn't have a teddy bear to hold, but I could see the value of having one. You can talk to a teddy bear on a long flight; you can snuggle with it when you get sleepy; and when the plane hits rough air, a teddy is a nice friend to have.

God isn't a teddy bear. Some people want to make Him one. They like a teddy-bear God because when they lose interest in Him or don't need Him, they can leave Him in the corner, where He'll stay until He is needed or wanted again.

We can depend on God, but we don't hold Him; He holds us. When we talk to Him, it's a conversation, not a monologue; and when we run into turbulence in our lives, He is more than a thing to clutch. But God, unlike a teddy bear, won't be thrown into a corner. We control teddy bears; no one controls God.

The problem with many people is that they have never known God, only a teddy-bear idea of God. Then when they give Him up, they say, "I've outgrown God." But all they've outgrown is their teddy bear. Meanwhile God waits for them to become mature enough to respond to Him. Some do, some don't. Those who don't are so proud of themselves. They think they are grown up as they proudly boast, "I don't need a teddy anymore." But they are still children and don't know it. It's such a shame.

Prayer: Father, help me always to give a reason for my trust in You. There are so many children around me who think they are adults.

⅔ JUNE 2 ⅙
MINUTE BY MINUTE

My times are in thy hand: deliver me from the hand of mine enemies, and from them that persecute me.
Psalm 31:15 KJV

The year holds for each of us about 525,600 minutes, and God is interested in every single one of them. He is interested in what you will be doing with the minute between 3:04 and 3:05 tomorrow afternoon and the time between 10:45 and 11:00 tonight. He is interested in those five- and ten-minute periods of time that you call "mine."

David said, "My times are in thy hand." God sees the times when you are alone or with a friend. He notices the way you watch the clock when a sermon goes too long, or when you calculate that by stretching your work project another twenty minutes you will be able to draw an extra hour's overtime pay. God knows.

He cares about how we use our time because that time is a gift

from Him. It is ours to redeem, commit, waste, or even steal. But it
comes to us from Him. How are you treating your gift?

Time! God's time! It comes in years, months, weeks, days, minutes, and even seconds. Wasted years never start out as wasted
years. Wasted years begin with wasted minutes and seconds. They
can be wasted in so many ways or redeemed profitably even when
napping or going fishing—it all depends on how the time is pre-
sented to Him. God's love, His blessing, His guidance, and His
grace don't just come to us occasionally. His gifts come minute by
minute, like every breath we take. He cares about you—minute by
minute by minute.

*Prayer: Lord, the minutes and hours of the year ahead are given by
You to me. Thank You for those gifts; let me use them well.*

ﾄ   JUNE 3   ﾚ
ONCE TOO OFTEN

And she said, "The Philistines are upon you, Samson!"
And he awoke from his sleep, and said, "I will go out as at
other times, and shake myself free." And he did not know
that the Lord had left him.

Judges 16:20

It was a silly promise, he thought, hard to believe. So Samson
toyed with the sacred wish of God.

And he got away with it, at least he did the first time and the second and the third.

God had told his mother, ". . . No razor shall come upon his
head, for the boy shall be a Nazirite to God from birth; and he shall
begin to deliver Israel from the hand of the Philistines" (Judges
13:5).

But the promise didn't mean much to Samson; the immediate was
more interesting. He was with Delilah, letting her tease him into revealing the secret of his strength—a strength that was his to use so
long as he was committed to using it for the glory of God. But he
stayed with the woman and her temptations too long. It was only a

matter of time until he gave in. And, when he did, nothing happened; so he kept going. Disobedience always seems to work that way.

Samson played with God's trust once too often. In a moment, without his even knowing it, his power was gone.

"And he did not know that the Lord had left him."

Sad words!

The Lord had left him, and Samson didn't even know it.

We usually get by the first time we compromise with sin. Sometimes the second or third time, too. But how long will God let a person toy with His trust and His sacred name?

Which time will be once too often?

Prayer: He didn't know when he was about to go too far. I don't know about me, either—I need Your help.

ᘏ JUNE 4 ᘏ

HELPLESS? NOT AT ALL

And the Lord said, I have surely seen the affliction of my people which are in Egypt, and have heard their cry by reason of their taskmasters; for I know their sorrows.

Exodus 3:7 KJV

Where are you? Where are you going? Are helplessness and hopelessness pressing down on your life? These aren't questions from a television soap opera; rather, television soap operas deal with these questions because so many people are facing them. What the soap operas don't offer is hope. God does.

The children of Israel were exiles in Egypt. Today a lot of faithful believers are, too. They were downtrodden; so are a lot of Christians now. They were under an oppressive government; that's still true in many places. They had no hope, so they thought. Now, looking back, we know better. God knew their sufferings, and He acted. He brought them out. It wasn't an easy trip for them, but God brought them out; He freed them. In a sense He freed them twice—once from the slavery of Egypt and then again for the Promised Land.

Whatever depression or hopelessness you're feeling now, maybe you should look at it with anticipation. Maybe God is getting ready to move you on. God knows where you are now, and He knows what's ahead for you, just as He did for the people in Egypt.

Prayer: Lord, help me to realize that hopelessness and helplessness are not ends, not when I know You. They can be the beginning of something.

❧ JUNE 5 ❧
ONE-UP—FOR GOD

For every one who exalts himself will be humbled, and he who humbles himself will be exalted.

Luke 14:11

But is that realistic?

How will I write my annual Christmas letter and have something to contribute at dinner parties if I don't talk about me?

And how can I talk about me without showing the impressive side?

How else will people be aware of "all that God is doing in my life" so that they can give God the glory?

What Jesus said needed to be said. Self-exaltation is like a disease—spreading, consuming, never satisfied. When it has me, I not only have to one-up my friends, I even have to one-up myself, always finding something more impressive to say about me every time I speak.

There is Only One to be exalted—God.

And if God, by His choice, decides to use one of us in something He is doing, that's not something to brag about; that's something to be awed about. We take off our shoes; we are on holy ground.

No clay pot brags about how he helped the potter form him on the wheel. Before the potter took him, he was a lump. And no clay pot jumps up and down to attract attention; he could break, becoming just another potsherd. But if he waits for the owner's pleasure, he could be used again and again.

We're clay pots—not much to look at in ourselves, functional when He gives us a function, useful as He wishes, content to sit on the shelf when He doesn't need us.

Quietly available.

But not bragging to the other pots.

Prayer: Please don't let me get lured into the sin of showing off.

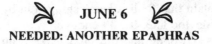

JUNE 6

NEEDED: ANOTHER EPAPHRAS

Epaphras, who is one of yourselves, a servant of Christ
Jesus, greets you, always remembering you earnestly in his
prayers, that you may stand mature and fully assured in all
the will of God.

Colossians 4:12

God in His goodness has sent me an Epaphras; in fact, He has
sent me several. They are men who labor fervently for me in prayer.
I know they are praying every day, lifting me to heaven's gate, in-
terceding on my behalf before the Lord. What a gift!

One of these men has just gone through surgery for cancer. He
can't move very much, but he can pray. He's my Epaphras. He
labors fervently for me in prayer or, as the NIV puts it: "He is always
wrestling in prayer."

The beauty of being an Epaphras is that no matter how weak we
become in other things we do, we can keep getting stronger in
prayer.

Who is your Epaphras? Whose Epaphras are you?

*Prayer: Lord, as I get older, I want more and more to be an
Epaphras. Give me a ministry of prayer; that's where things get done.*

JUNE 7

NOT ENOUGH

. . . And God said unto them, Be fruitful, and multiply, and
replenish the earth, and subdue it: and have dominion over
the fish of the sea, and over the fowl of the air, and over
every living thing that moveth upon the earth.

Genesis 1:28 KJV

It isn't enough.

I was listening to a news broadcast while driving home from
work. I had been anticipating the delicious dinner that would be
waiting for me; then the newscast came on. It was about starvation
in parts of Africa, with thousands dying along the roads and in the
villages, whole villages becoming ghost towns. The commentator

went on to explain that food is being shipped in by caring nations, but it is too little, too late. It isn't enough.

I found myself wondering, did God make a mistake when He made the world? Is there not enough food-growing area? Are there too many people? Or is everything in balance and the only problem is that the few who have more than enough to live on are consuming more than they need? Did God intend for me by accident of my birth to be allowed more, or was I meant to share it?

This isn't so much a matter of food collections; it's not even just a matter of airlifts; it's a matter of a way of thinking: *What am I going to do with what I have?* I have to think about my way of life, because even if I give up the dinner I'm going home to, that won't be enough.

Prayer: Lord, even if I don't know what to do, let me do something. Don't let me become hardened about this. You told us to subdue the earth. You didn't tell us to subdue it only for ourselves. Help me to think this through.

♫ JUNE 8 ♫
REWRITE

> And forgive us our debts, As we also have forgiven our debtors.
>
> Matthew 6:12

That's the Lord's Prayer! I say that every Sunday! I didn't know there was a condition to it.

Forgive. Does He mean in the same way as we forgive others? To the same degree?

"For if you forgive men their trespasses, your heavenly Father also will forgive you; but if you do not forgive men their trespasses, neither will your Father forgive your trespasses" (Matthew 6:14, 15).

That's even worse.

He has made a promise—"your heavenly Father will forgive you"—then qualified it.

Doesn't God understand that there are some people I can't forgive? Doesn't He know how much they've done? The hurt they've caused? The pain?

Oh, no, God, I can't do that. But I'd still like You to forgive me my trespasses against You.

In other words, don't forgive me my trespasses in the same way or to the same degree that I have forgiven others their trespasses against me, because I haven't.

Forgive me my trespasses against You, even though I refuse to forgive those who trespass against me.

There—that version of the prayer is more acceptable to me. I can pray that.

At least I won't be doing what He warned against when He gave us that model prayer—"... heap up empty phrases as the Gentiles do ..." (Matthew 6:7).

My prayers are honest. God will be pleased.

Won't He?

Prayer: Lord, stop me whenever I think I can play games with You. I know that the temptation to qualify Your Word won't let up.

JUNE 9

HE REMEMBERS

And the bow shall be in the cloud; and I will look upon it, that I may remember the everlasting covenant between God and every living creature of all flesh that is upon the earth.

Genesis 9:16 KJV

A rainbow!

Children excitedly point to it, and scientists attempt to explain it. But they aren't the only ones looking.

God promised, "I will look upon it and remember."

He's looking and remembering His covenant, an everlasting covenant.

That covenant isn't going to change or be altered, because He isn't going to change.

And every now and then (we say it's when the conditions are right), another rainbow appears. Sometimes it's only for a few seconds or maybe a minute.

It's His rainbow, not so easily explained after all. There is much more to rainbows than what little children and scientists know.

Prayer: Thank You for your rainbows of promise—the ones I see; the ones I don't see.

➥ JUNE 10 ⬳
NOTHING IFFY

But without faith it is impossible to please him: for he that
cometh to God must believe that he is, and that he is a
rewarder of them that diligently seek him.

Hebrews 11:6 KJV

There is nothing here about "probably," or "it might be a little
difficult," or "we'll manage somehow."

God isn't iffy in His statements, nor does He use bland words that
leave a door ajar for a different way. God states categorically in His
Word, straight out, blunt, that without faith it is impossible to
please Him. Do anything else you want, but without faith it is impossible to please God. Give away your money, work for the
church, do good deeds for the poor, dedicate yourself to missionary
service, but without faith it is impossible to please God.

When I want to get a sense of just how strong that statement is,
and how definite, I go back to it and try substituting other words.
None of them work.

*Prayer: Thank You, Lord, that when it comes to salvation, You are
explicit and clear and never wishy-washy. You demand faith. Lord, I
believe.*

➥ JUNE 11 ⬳
BUT THEN, THERE IS STILL THAT DOG

You did not choose me, but I chose you to go and bear
fruit—fruit that will last. Then the Father will give you
whatever you ask in my name.

John 15:16 NIV

I was enjoying the after-dinner speaker who was telling us how
nice it was for him and his wife to have an empty nest. Freedom! He
said, "You've got it made when the kids all get married and the dog
dies." Then he confided, "Our kids are all married, but the dog is
healthy. I'd like you to make that a matter of prayer."

He wasn't serious, of course—who would ever pray like that? But
I've met some people who get close to it. They pray about which

shoes to wear, call their prayer group when the lawn mower won't start, seek God's counsel about whether they should order the tuna-fish sandwich or the hamburger supreme.

Why not? Aren't we to pray without ceasing, pray about everything? "Let your requests be made known unto God." "If you ask anything in my name. . . ." There is lots of support for that.

I keep wondering if I'm to pray for or pray to. Am I to yield myself and then live with God or make Him some kind of talisman to keep handy? Maybe God doesn't really care which pair of shoes I wear today. Maybe the tuna fish will be just fine so far as He is concerned. Maybe He would like to have a little less of the "quick arrows to heaven" and a little more quality time when He and I can have a good discussion about some of the values and directions of my life. Maybe there is more to me than what goes into my stomach or on my feet.

But then, there is still that healthy dog.

Prayer: Help me to focus on You and Your will more than on me and my stomach and my feet.

☙ JUNE 12 ❧
AN EIGHTY-YEAR-OLD DUCK

Thy word is a lamp unto my feet, and a light unto my path.
Psalm 119:105 KJV

What a description!

She was walking slowly toward me when I asked, "How are you feeling?" The young woman, who was about eight months pregnant, grimaced and said, "I feel like an eighty-year-old duck."

I'm no cynic, so I didn't respond with, "Come on now, how can you know what an eighty-year-old duck feels like?"

Nor did I get logical and reply, "Ducks don't live eighty years." That young woman was being descriptive; no one has to argue with a description. Besides, maybe she does know what an eighty-year-old duck feels like.

Scripture talks to me in pictures sometimes, and I don't argue with it, either. I don't say, as if I could, to the biblical writers, "Now, come on . . . how do you know . . . ?" I read, I feel, I respond to what they are saying. And sometimes, with their picture language, they say it better than they might have said it any other way. The inspiring Holy Spirit does that.

God's Word is a lamp. It is a light for us, and that isn't always something I can define. It is something I use. Lights, like descriptions, help me to see better.

When I read the Word, it doesn't always speak in logic—but it does make itself clear. This young woman had her description. So does God. I took her word for it: I've never felt like an eighty-year-old duck. I take the biblical writers' word for it, too. Some of my best understanding comes that way.

Prayer: You speak, Lord; I'll listen and try to give more attention to understanding.

❧ JUNE 13 ❧
CHECK YOUR ROOTS

He is like a tree planted by streams of water, that yields its fruit in its season, and its leaf does not wither. In all that he does, he prospers.

Psalm 1:3

That's good to know.

It was a warm June afternoon when the storm moved in. Seventy-mile-an-hour winds drove large hailstones into the young vegetable plants in our garden. A few minutes' pounding was enough. The lettuce was pulverized; the tomato plants were naked stalks. The garden was destroyed—or so we thought.

But, as we watched through the summer, we saw plants sprout new leaves and fibrous walls firm up around shredded stems, and before frost came, the harvest was abundant.

The plants had something going for them. They were rooted in rich soil, drawing on the nutriments that first repaired, then strengthened, and finally produced. The plants still had scars, even holes where the hail had torn them, but they bore fruit.

When our personal storms hit, and they do, the difference between destruction and recovery is in our roots. Maybe the scars will stay, even the holes that never fill in, but the promise is there: "Its leaf does not wither. In all that he does, he prospers."

Don't keep checking the weather; check your roots.

Prayer: Help me to go deep into Your truth. I need to be rooted.

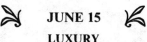

JUNE 14

LOST—AND EATING ICE CREAM

You will seek me and find me; when you seek me with all
your heart, I will be found by you, says the Lord. . . .

Jeremiah 29:13, 14

She wasn't really very far away.

In fact, our two-year-old daughter was over on the next street,
calmly sitting on a front porch, eating ice cream with the family that
had found her and had called the police. We had called the police,
too.

It's a terrible, frantic feeling—not being able to find a lost child.

Searching, calling, questioning each person you meet on the
street, begging every child and adult to help you look.

God's not a child, and He's not lost; we are. But the feeling of
being separated is the same. He has told us that when we are frantic
enough, when we want God as badly as we want to find a lost child,
we'll find Him.

We know the stories in the Bible about the lost coin, the lost
sheep, and the lost renegade son who finally decided to come home
and found his father standing on the road, waiting to hug him. God
wants us found, too, and He wants us home—more than we will
ever know.

But some of us, like children, are calmly eating ice cream—not
even aware that we are lost, not even aware that the Father is looking for us.

*Prayer: Father, I pray for those who still aren't grown up enough to
know they are lost.*

JUNE 15

LUXURY

And I will be a father to you, and you shall be my sons and
daughters, says the Lord Almighty.

2 Corinthians 6:18

We're not slaves, though we could have been.
We're not robots either, and we might have been.

God calls us *sons* and *daughters.*

He is already called *Almighty.* He wants to be called *Father.*

Tell that to one who wonders if he has any value at all. Give that message to the depressed ones and the ones who desperately long to be loved by somebody.

A Father—with strong arms when the weight you are carrying is too much.

A Father—able to give tender care when you don't want to be responsible anymore.

A Father—who will listen to you when no one is around who really understands or even wants to.

A Father—the Provider for always, but especially for those times when you are too sick and too tired to provide anything for anybody.

A Father—a friend when you don't want to have to be anything or pretend anything or say words but just be what you are, even when you are angry and irritable and hurt.

"I will be a father to you, and you shall be my sons and daughters."

That sounds so good.

I'm going to let Him be that for me—you know, what He said.

And I'm going to let Him wrap me up in His love, and I'm going to luxuriate in it.

Prayer: When I don't want to be anything, I'm glad You are still Everything.

❁ **JUNE 16** ❁

GOOD COMPANY

... At that time there was a great persecution against the church. ...

Acts 8:1 KJV

Reading church history is a valuable exercise. There has been a lot of persecution of those who are faithful to God, just as Jesus said there would be. Not all Christians since the days of the early church have suffered persecution, but many have—more than most of us realize. And we need to know that, because none of us can predict the fiery trials that may yet lie ahead.

No one should go around worrying. Our Lord, who went through so much, has promised to be with us. Nor should anyone go around creating circumstances to generate persecution as some way of "proving" His faithfulness. Every believer has to be faithful to God and obedient to biblical truth. But that can bring persecution.

Those who teach that Christianity is a glowing, happy state with the enjoyment of all the pleasures of this world haven't read Paul's words to Timothy: ". . . All that will live godly in Christ Jesus shall suffer persecution" (2 Timothy 3:12 KJV). They haven't read their church history, either.

Prayer: Lord, I don't seek persecution. I certainly don't want it. But at least if it comes, You've made it clear that I'll be in the best company—Yours.

⤺ JUNE 17 ⤻
KNOCK, KNOCK, KNOCK

He, that being often reproved hardeneth his neck, shall suddenly be destroyed, and that without remedy.
Proverbs 29:1 KJV

Try to concentrate on what you're doing if someone is knocking at the door. You can't. Jesus said, "Behold, I stand at the door, and knock: if any man hear my voice, and open the door, I will come in to him, and will sup with him, and he with me" (Revelation 3:20 KJV). We can refuse to open the door, but we can't ignore the knock.

Jesus is knocking. There are men and women who recognize that knock. They have grown up in a Christian home, attended Sunday school and church, have heard the Gospel, know that God wants them for Himself. They know that He wants to give them His love, His peace, His joy—the abundant life—but they've chosen to say no. They have hardened their necks. Believing relatives have prayed and wept, but they've still said no. Friends have talked with them, but they've said no. Still, Jesus is standing at the door knocking. No self-generated distraction can shut out that knocking. A person may say no for many, many years. But every minute of every day of every year he always knows whom he is saying no to.

Prayer: Thank You, Lord Jesus, that You did not give up on me. And You have not given up on those I love who are still saying no.

❧ JUNE 18 ❦
PAPER CLIPS

So God created man in his own image, in the image of God created he him; male and female created he them.

Genesis 1:27 KJV

In a box on my desk is a whole variety of paper clips—different sizes, different colors, different shapes. And I can brighten otherwise tedious desk work by selecting different paper clips for the papers I have to fasten together. They all do what they were meant to do; they're just different, like people.

God created us male and female in His image—some tall, some short, some thin, some heavier, with various color skin or hair or eyes—all designed by Him and for His use.

Sometimes God selects one person for a particular task, sometimes another, just as I do my paper clips. Those clips never stand up and shout or wave and try to draw attention to themselves. They don't fight among themselves, each trying to prove that it is better than another. They are content to wait for my choosing.

Jesus called us friends and said we didn't choose Him, He chose us. God made us for that choosing. We could use the lesson that the paper clips teach us, not only in society, but even in our churches. I wish paper clips could talk.

Prayer: Lord, help me to understand that I'm first made by You, then chosen for a place of service by the One who calls me His friend. When I think I'm better than someone else or better suited to a task, remind me of the box of paper clips.

❧ JUNE 19 ❦
GOD DOESN'T MAKE MISTAKES

Search me, O God, and know my heart: try me, and know my thoughts: And see if there be any wicked way in me, and lead me in the way everlasting.

Psalm 139:23, 24 KJV

I was interviewing an applicant for a job, and afterward I wondered, "Would I pass my own inspection?" I had been asking pointed questions, fishing for the person's ambition, trying to find out his goals, his desires, his commitment. In hiring somebody it's so easy to make a mistake.

But God doesn't make a mistake about us. He doesn't have to hold an interview and look for flaws, He's never surprised at how a person turns out. He's not fooled by the one with the high recommendations who turns out to be a poor worker. He knows, too, about the one who is not so impressive at first glance but turns out to be dedicated, loyal, capable, and a joy to have around. Sometimes those who have the most to say about themselves have the least to offer, and those who say the least have the most to offer. People hiring other people can't always tell. God can.

The psalmist asked God to search him and to know his heart. Well, God does. There's no guesswork with Him. God has searched us; God knows us. That's comforting. He knows if we're trusting Him. If we aren't, He knows that, too, and no well-written résumé and no polished speech touting our capabilities will make any difference at all.

Prayer: I'm glad, Lord, that I don't have to try to convince You of something that may or may not be true. You know me better than I know myself.

⅊ JUNE 20 ⅊
I THINK I'M A SPARE

Before I formed thee in the belly I knew thee; and before thou camest forth out of the womb I sanctified thee, and I ordained thee a prophet unto the nations.

Jeremiah 1:5 KJV

The newlyweds were opening gifts; the bride held up two can openers. A little boy in the corner leaned over to his mother and asked, "Why do they have two of those?"

"Well, if they lose one, or one of them breaks, they have a spare."

The little boy thought about that for a minute and then, brightening, said, "Oh, like twins."

None of us is a spare. I need to know that, because sometimes I feel like one. I assume that there will be a place for me, a special use, and I wait. But whatever I was put here to do, it doesn't seem to be happening. Certainly I don't readily see my use as well as I see the use God makes of my friends. Others seem to find their slots; they seem to fit; they have a sense of value. I keep wondering and waiting, and the years go by.

God says, "Before I formed thee . . . I knew thee; and before thou camest forth out of the womb I sanctified thee, and I ordained thee a prophet unto the nations."

Like can openers, I may look like "just another one." Like a can opener, I may seem to be a spare. But God didn't make me just "another one." He planned for and created a unique me. He says so.

Still, during the long periods in life's "kitchen drawer," waiting to be taken out and used, there are times when I feel sorry for myself. *What is God keeping me in the drawer for?* I wonder. I don't know, but He has His reasons. For all I know, He may be saving me for some big banquet.

Prayer: Father, even while I'm "in the drawer," help me to be an encouragement and comfort to some of the worn-out ones who seem always to be used.

﹏ JUNE 21 ﹏
SOONER OR LATER

Choosing rather to suffer affliction with the people of God, than to enjoy the pleasures of sin for a season.
                                        Hebrews 11:25 KJV

I like ice cream. Especially, I like chocolate ice cream. It's smooth and sweet and enjoyable—like sin. There are no rough edges, it tastes good, and it adds pounds. But it's deceptive, because it doesn't add the pounds right away. I can eat a dish of ice cream, step on the scale, and see no difference. The same can happen the next day, and the next. But a week later that ice cream shows up. What I thought didn't matter did.

The results of sin come like that, too. Moses recognized it. He chose rather to suffer than to enjoy the pleasures of sin for a season. The pleasure of sin, like ice cream, is temporary. It's nice to the taste, but I don't like the results. Most of us don't. What we really want is to enjoy the pleasures of sin and have no aftereffects.

When I step on the scale this week, it reminds me of what I did last week. When I was enjoying the pleasure of ice cream, I wasn't getting by with a thing. Ice cream is an innocent teacher of an ugly truth.

Prayer: Lord, help me to see that everything I do has its consequences.

⊱ JUNE 22 ⊰
IN GOD'S TIME

> If you are willing and obedient, you shall eat the good of
> the land; But if you refuse and rebel, you shall be devoured
> by the sword; for the mouth of the Lord has spoken.
> Isaiah 1:19, 20

God defines the two alternatives quite clearly. There's little chance to misunderstand: "If you are willing and obedient, you shall eat the good of the land; But if you refuse and rebel, you shall be devoured by the sword; for the mouth of the Lord has spoken."

The trouble is, it doesn't seem to work out that way. In fact, my observations are a whole lot different.

The willing and obedient find it costly to be that way; the rebels seem to get all the attention and the nice benefits.

But our time span isn't God's time span; He will do what He says in His own time. He has always kept His word.

Probably the reason He emphasizes this is precisely because our observations about the willing ones and the rebellious ones are different.

If we could see the immediate "good of the land" for the willing and obedient and see the sword for the rebel, God wouldn't have had to make a point of telling us how it will be; it would be obvious.

We are in a different time reference; we live by the promise, not by our observations.

We aren't called to think about the sword for the rebel; that's God's responsibility in His own time.

We aren't called to think about the meaning of "the good of the land" either. That is God's responsibility also.

We're called to hear His word and to believe it.

That's our responsibility.

Prayer: Help me to live by Your promises, not by my own observations.

❧ JUNE 23 ❦
DIRTY WINDOWS

Simon Peter saith unto him, Lord, not my feet only, but
also my hands and my head.

John 13:9 KJV

Twice a year at our house we pull all the windows apart and wash
them. It's a tedious job. But even before I start I know they'll never
really be clean and I'll never be satisfied with the job. A window can
be spotless to my eye; I can stand back and look at it with satisfaction; and then an hour later, when the sun has shifted and shines
through the glass, all the streaks show up.

I can't polish window glass perfectly clean. Spots and streaks
show. I can't polish my life to pass inspection either. No cloth is new
enough or clean enough. On glass, even paper leaves dust. Some
marks seem to be caused by grease or dirt that has eaten right into
the glass. That's the way it is with my soul, too. In fact, the only
time my windows really look good is at night, in the dark. Unfortunately, it's the same for my life.

Peter learned about washing when Jesus told him how to be
really clean; and when he found out, he wanted it. "Not my feet
only, but also my hands and my head." Peter had had enough of life
without being clean. Most of us have. We've all tried on our own to
be clean before God only to see all the streaks later on.

*Prayer: Lord, I can't clean my soul any more than I can clean my
windows, but You can clean my soul.*

❧ JUNE 24 ❦
BUT I'M NOT PACKED YET!

Therefore be ye also ready: for in such an hour as ye think
not the Son of man cometh.

Matthew 24:44 KJV

Is there something about travel that I don't understand? I'm talking about packing a suitcase.

I have a friend who boasts that he has a suitcase always packed
and can leave on a business trip with five minutes' notice. Well, I

can't. How can he know in advance where he is going? Is he going north or south; to meetings where he will be making public presentations or just learning; to a convention or the White House? How can one suitcase always contain exactly what he needs?

I can pack in less than an hour. I know which items fit where in my suitcase, the right tie for each particular suit and shirt, and long ago I got rid of all the brown things so that I only have to take black shoes and a black belt. Shaving gear is easy, too. I shave the same way in New York or Newcastle-on-Tyne, and my toothbrush doesn't require electric current. But other things—well, sorry, but I have to think through my packing.

But last night I dreamt about Jesus coming—suddenly. And waking from my dream, I pondered 1 Thessalonians 4:17 (KJV), when we "shall be caught up together." No one is going to call me ahead of time to give me a little extra time to pack. No one is going to suggest I stop the newspaper and the mail delivery. No one is going to tell me what tie to wear. And no one will boast: "Are you still packing? It only takes me five minutes." None of that is going to happen, because either we are ready or we are not, and our readiness has nothing to do with what is in our suitcases.

Prayer: Lord, I look forward to Your coming for my sake, but I ache at the thought of some I know who aren't ready. They don't even know what's happening.

JUNE 25
NOW? BUT I WAS JUST GETTING SETTLED

Come, I will send you to Pharaoh that you may bring forth my people, the sons of Israel, out of Egypt.

Exodus 3:10

He was about to undergo a terrific change.

Aren't we all?

Nothing is ever really settled or stable. Just as I begin to figure out what's going on around me, the scene changes.

I feel like Moses. It must have been pleasant out there on the west side of the wilderness with the sheep. No one bothered him—no newspapers and no one to introduce new and disconcerting ideas or tell him that all the rules for raising sheep had changed.

He wasn't about to do anything different. He was content to raise sheep his way—that was all.

Oh, he had tried once, back when he was young, to bring about social change, trying to right the system. He killed an Egyptian doing it.

No more getting involved!

Then God came to Moses disturbing his peace and quiet and told him: "You are the one who is going to bring about a revolution." That upset his day.

"Let the younger ones do it, the vocal ones, the ones who understand Egyptian politics. I tried bucking the system once; it doesn't work. I'm going to sit out here in the rural areas and tend sheep."

But God interrupted: ". . . I will be with you . . ." (Exodus 3:12). And God kept His word. He didn't use the young, steamed-up kids; He used the semiretired Moses, who didn't want the job.

For those of us who are like Moses, the "pre-elderlies," that's not a bad lesson. God isn't through with us yet, even when we think we've done enough and want to rest.

When you think that you are ready for a little peace and quiet in the country, just remember, God may have other plans.

You may be the leader of His next revolution.

Prayer: As long as I'm alive, I'll be faithful. Go ahead, Lord; You can use me.

⋙   **JUNE 26**   ⋘

FIRST COMES THE SCRAPING

The beloved of the Lord shall dwell in safety by him; and
the Lord shall cover him all the day long. . . .
                                        Deuteronomy 33:12 KJV

What a job! It looks as if we're going to have to paint the house again this year. It seems as if we just did it.

The worst part about painting is not putting on the paint, it's scraping off all the old paint that is flaking or getting down to the wood where moisture has caused the paint to bubble. But there's no substitute for it. Paint can't be put over cracked, peeling, or chipped places. The surface has to be prepared. If it isn't, the paint won't hold, the covering won't protect, moisture will get into the wood, and it will rot and someday have to be replaced. A good covering is an absolute necessity.

God is a good covering. God called Benjamin His beloved and promised that He would cover him all day long. Talk about protection! With God as a covering, Benjamin could be exposed to any of the harsh or vicious elements, and he would be preserved.

God wants to cover us, too, because He loves us as much as He loved Benjamin. But most of us, before the covering can go on, need a lot of chipping and scraping and peeling. There's too much in our lives that will keep the covering of God from adhering as it ought.

Painting the house gives me some good lessons about my sin and God's covering. Now, where did I put that scraper?

Prayer: Scrape me clean, Lord, and then be my covering. I need Your protection from the elements.

✄ JUNE 27 ✄

HEATHEN PRAY A LOT

> But when ye pray, use not vain repetitions, as the heathen do; for they think that they shall be heard for their much speaking.
>
> Matthew 6:7 KJV

Once I told a class of would-be writers: "Avoid clichés like the plague." No one laughed. I thought they were being polite. Then I realized that no one laughed because no one got it. I had used an old, worn-out cliché to warn against clichés, and my humor fell flat.

We have a lot of clichés that we use when we talk to people about God. Some call it Christian jargon. Like all clichés, these statements started out good and strong. But through overuse they are weak now and don't communicate anymore.

When the disciples asked Jesus to teach them how to pray, it was probably because they had heard the freshness in His own praying and wanted to get away from some of the sterile ritualistic clichés that they had heard from others. So He told them, "Don't use vain repetitions, as the heathen do, but rather in this manner pray." And then He gave them the model prayer that we call the Lord's prayer. I'm not sure how we did it, but we have managed to take that model prayer and make a cliché out of it, too, using it in vain repetition as the heathen do.

There aren't any clichés in the Bible, certainly not in the teachings of Jesus. God is not a cliché nor is anything about Him a cliché. Maybe to teach that we ought to preface our use of the Lord's prayer with the verse that goes before it—"use not vain repetitions, as the heathen do"—and see how long it takes for people to catch on.

Prayer: Help me not to heap up empty phrases when I pray, but to talk to You, person to person, in love.

❧ JUNE 28 ❧
SHUT THE GATE!

But the Lord is faithful; he will strengthen you and guard you from evil.

2 Thessalonians 3:3

As it is with a wall or stockade or fort, we can be inside and safe, or we can be outside, where evil is prowling around. Inside is the better choice.

There's a promise in the Bible about protection: "But the Lord is faithful; he will strengthen you and guard you from evil."

Evil is here; that's certain.

But so is God. And He is "faithful," which is both a description and a name.

Two things are promised: strength and a guard or wall—both are here for us.

Strength is good but can't stand up under constant battering. So we need both strength and the guard around us to keep the pounding enemy from wearing us down.

"The Lord is faithful; he will . . . guard." In other words, He'll put up a high wall where inside we are safe.

There is one problem. Even a high, strong wall won't protect us if we leave the gate open or the drawbridge down.

Prayer: I am going to believe You. Help me to do so totally.

❧ JUNE 29 ❧
NO WONDER GOD DOESN'T GET BORED

... Then Daniel blessed the God of heaven.

Daniel 2:19 KJV

Daniel was singing about God, and since seven is the number of perfection, he listed seven attributes of God (Daniel 2:20–23). He sang:

To God belong wisdom and might;
God changes the times and the seasons;
He removes kings and sets up kings;
He gives wisdom to the wise and gives knowledge to those who have understanding;
He reveals deep and mysterious things;
He knows what is in the darkness;
The light dwells with Him.

Think about that song the next time you feel overwhelmed with what is happening in your life. Look at who God is; look at what God does!

Think about that and be impressed. Think about that and be at peace. Daniel had enough going on in his life that he had to think about it. No wonder he sang.

Prayer: Lord, when I feel overwhelmed, it's probably because I don't know enough about You.

❧ JUNE 30 ❧
THIRSTY?

And he said to me, "It is done! I am the Alpha and the Omega, the beginning and the end. To the thirsty I will give from the fountain of the water of life without payment."

Revelation 21:6

It was a hot afternoon, and we were thirsty, very thirsty. The warm cola that we'd had earlier hadn't helped a bit. Eventually, in a little Swiss village, we found a restaurant.

"Water with ice? Yes, one franc per glass."

Each of us paid gladly. When you want water, you don't want anything else, and cost means very little.

In desert countries it's worse. Sometimes there isn't water to be bought, even if you do have the money.

Thirst! You will do anything to quench it. People can earn great profits by selling water. They can torture with water or even murder by withholding it. When you need water, it's everything. You can't think about anything else.

Jesus said, "To the thirsty I will give from the fountain of the water of life without payment."

We all know what that means physically; some know what that means psychologically. A few know what that means spiritually. Jesus gives living water. He's the Source; we don't even have to bring along a few ounces to prime the pump.

It's sad, but some people still pass Him by, licking their cracked lips.

They still aren't thirsty enough.

Prayer: Thank You for the thirst that drove me to You.

JULY 1
PLASTIC BIBLE

If thou be the Son of God. . . . It is written. . . .
Matthew 4:3, 4 KJV

Satan must like some Bibles. Maybe he likes mine. I once heard a conference speaker refer to a "plastic" Bible, one that we can shape any way we want to.

Satan tried shaping Scripture in the temptation of Eve and quoted Scripture in the temptation of Jesus. Jesus didn't argue with him; He just quoted God's Word right back.

Some of us think Satan would never use Scripture to tempt us, but he will and he does. What scares me is that I can usually see how other people "adjust" their Bibles to what they want their Bibles to say. What I don't always see is how I may be doing the same thing. Or if I do see it, how I am then likely to turn to the commentaries until I find an interpreter of Scripture who supports my view, who interprets it the way I would like to have it interpreted.

The best interpreter of Scripture is more Scripture. Jesus knew that. God's Word proves God's Word. It is its own best commentary. When Satan starts to quote his "plastic" Bible, we can take as our example the Lord Jesus, who came right back with the words, "It is written."

Prayer: Lord, I don't want a "plastic" Bible; I want Your Word.

❧ JULY 2 ❦
IT WASN'T FIRST CLASS

Sirs, I perceive that the voyage will be with injury and much loss, not only of the cargo and the ship, but also of our lives.

Acts 27:10

Paul was a prisoner when he traveled by ship to Rome, so he probably wasn't traveling in the first-class section. Chances are he traveled the way I do—steerage. They don't call it steerage on a jumbo jet, but in a center seat, squeezed between two overweight passengers, it feels that way to me. Mealtime is the worst, trying to manipulate knife and fork with my elbows in front of my chest. I try not to wear a good suit when I travel.

And no matter when I want to get up to go to the back where the toilets are, the person on the aisle is asleep. Then I have to practice gymnastics.

Paul didn't complain, even though they probably had him locked up below with the chickens and the goats. He was glad for where he was going. He was heading for Rome, where he was eager to preach the Gospel. I'm usually glad for where I'm going, too, but I wish I didn't have to travel to get there. Yet it could be worse. Last time I took a flight, the woman on one side of me was holding a baby with a soiled diaper, and the man on the other side was airsick. Maybe Paul was so eager to get to Rome because it meant he would be done with sailing.

I can understand that.

Prayer: You have given me many opportunities to preach the Gospel, Lord. Help me not to complain when there is some minor inconvenience attached to it.

⚮ JULY 3 ⚮

REEDS GET BENT

A bruised reed he will not break, and a dimly burning wick
he will not quench; he will faithfully bring forth justice.

Isaiah 42:3

Think about that promise as you go through the day. And hold
onto it. God doesn't slap us down when we fail or push us into a
corner and say, "That's all for you; no more chances." Isaiah gives
the promise that even if the reed is bruised, God won't snap it off.
Even if the lamp is only flickering, He won't put it out. A bruised
reed can stand again if the roots are strong. A smoking lamp can
flare up again if there is oil reaching it. God is where our roots belong. God is our source of oil.

Life deals some harsh blows. Reeds get bent from trampling feet;
wicks start smoldering when the wind is too strong or the carbon
buildup from the sediment of life is too great. God comes through
the field and sees the bruised reed. He comes into the house and sees
the smoldering lamp. The reed is His. The lamp is His, too. He
won't leave either one the way they were.

*Prayer: Lord, I cling to the belief that no matter how I feel about me,
You will not break or quench.*

⚮ JULY 4 ⚮

FREEDOM

So faith, hope, love abide, these three; but the greatest of
these is love.

1 Corinthians 13:13

Secular individuals tend to smirk at Christian commitment. They
see obedience to God's Word as being just a little bit on the foolish
side. They see discipline and faithfulness and worship as a bit odd,
when we only have one life to live and we might as well take all we
can. If one must believe in God, they say, at least he can be his own
theologian and interpret God using his own good mind. The secular
man doesn't understand that he wouldn't have his freedom to think

as he thinks were it not for those who hold to faith, hope, and love—the three elements that keep what degree of decency and order is left in the world from total upheaval and decay.

People may mock us for holding onto faith, eternal hope, and Christian love. To them it may seem mere silliness. But what they haven't thought through yet is what their world would be like without our faith, hope, and love.

Prayer: Lord, I know that as long as there is one believer in this world the world will be better for it. People try to put us down. Forgive them; they don't know what they are doing.

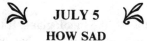

JULY 5
HOW SAD

> Thou didst blow with thy wind, the sea covered them: they sank as lead in the mighty waters.
>
> Exodus 15:10 KJV

If the Egyptians had been able to trade their chariots for submarines when the sea rolled around them, they probably would have been all right. Submarines are very nice. There are many compartments so that even if there is a puncture someplace people can gather in other compartments and seal off the damaged one.

Some Christians, unfortunately, have done that. They've long ago traded in their sailing vessel that catches the wind of God for a submarine with leaks in the hull. But they're safe enough; they just keep moving into other compartments. They close off one part of life and then another part, still saying as they get into narrower and narrower quarters, "But I'm still alive." They aren't free; they don't go anywhere in their vessels lying on the bottom, but "I'm alive," they say. And that's all they are—just alive.

Some of them are in our churches, not doing anything, not going anywhere. We can hear them now and then tapping out a message from inside their sealed-off compartments: "I'm alive." How very sad.

Prayer: Lord, You made me alive to live in all Your fullness. Don't let me be content with just breathing and occasionally announcing, "I'm alive."

❧ JULY 6 ❦

HOW TO LOSE PEOPLE

... And the common people heard him gladly.

Mark 12:37 KJV

Our daughter has spent time in Haiti on two different occasions—a summer, and then a six-month period as part of her college social-science program. Even though French is the national language, she had to learn Creole in order to talk with the people on the street. She said, "If they wanted to talk to me, I could understand them. But if they ever wanted to lose me, they could do it in a hurry."

Those Haitians are a lot like theologians. If they want to, theologians can lose people in a hurry, so that whatever it is they're saying about God most people don't understand. Unfortunately, we can sometimes tell what theologian the local preacher has been reading, because it shows up in his sermons. Like visitors to Haiti, we don't know what he is talking about.

Jesus could have done that, but He came as the revelation of God both in what He did and what He said. The common people heard Him gladly. He didn't try to impress them or confuse them. That wasn't His goal. His goal was communication. He wanted to communicate, and He did.

If theologians and preachers lose their hearers, they didn't learn how to do that from Jesus.

Prayer: Lord Jesus, You communicated in the way You taught. Please help me to do the same.

❧ JULY 7 ❦

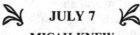

MICAH KNEW

Therefore I will look unto the Lord; I will wait for the God of my salvation: my God will hear me.

Micah 7:7 KJV

Micah knew what submission meant. When you can't trust a friend, when your child is against you, and your worst enemies are living with you in your own house, Micah tells what to do. "I will look unto the Lord; I will wait for the God of my salvation: my God will hear me." Look, wait, and God will.

If I look at my enemies, I will be overwhelmed. If I try to rush ahead and get things settled in my way on my terms, I'll miss the deliverance of God. Look, wait, and God will. That's simple; that's true.

Prayer: Thank You, Lord, for truth that I can grasp when there is so much trouble around me.

⫷ JULY 8 ⫸
LITTLE BOYS CAN GET HURT

Then the men feared the Lord exceedingly, and offered a sacrifice unto the Lord, and made vows.

Jonah 1:16 KJV

It was already dark out when I went for a walk. I was on a fairly busy street when I noticed, about a block ahead of me, two little boys running out into the street and then running back to the curb. As I got closer, my heart began to pound, for I realized that they were engaged in a six-year-old's version of "chicken" with the cars. They'd run out, stand, and at the last minute run back to the curb.

When I got close enough I yelled in my most gruff voice, "Hey, you boys, you can get hurt. What will your mother and father say when they find out?" That frightened them, and off they scampered. I walked on and glanced back, but they were gone. They didn't know that I had no idea who they were, and I certainly didn't know their parents. They had enough guilt inside them already to be afraid of what was going to happen to them when they got home.

Sailors on the ship with Jonah feared God. Everyone, believer or not, has enough awareness of God to be afraid, and that's not bad. That can be a healthy fear if it drives people to call on God. Some people, realizing who God is and the effect of His judgment, are frightened enough to come to Him for forgiveness and salvation, and when they receive it, they never have to be frightened again.

But some people don't learn. They fear God, but only temporarily. Then they forget Him and, like six-year-old boys, they're soon running out into the street again.

Prayer: Father, I thank You that fear and reverence and obedience and love are all bound up together.

❧ JULY 9 ❧

A WORD FOR US IMPORTANT PEOPLE

> I know that whatever God does endures for ever; nothing
> can be added to it, nor anything taken from it; God has
> made it so, in order that men should fear before him.
>
> Ecclesiastes 3:14

God didn't say that; Solomon did!

Whatever God does, it has "for ever" consequences. We can't add to it; we can't take from it. God does it.

That makes us important, influential, prestige-conscious people seem insignificant and inconsequential, doesn't it?

We know (because He told us) that prayer can move mountains, and if we ask anything in His name, He will do it; but that doesn't give me liberty to presume the next step—believing that I can manipulate God.

I don't run God; you don't run God; and none of us ever will run God.

If in awe your mouth drops open and you realize that you are nothing and that God is everything and that all that is or ever will be is because He allows it, then you know what Solomon means: "Men should fear before him."

That'll catch you up short and make you gasp.

Maybe it needs to.

Because our buddy-buddy-with-God relationships that we think we can have, and the casual arm-around-the-shoulder familiarity with God, because He has saved us and has told us we are joint heirs with Christ, goes too far. We need to have more of a realization of just who God is.

That word from Ecclesiastes should put us in our places.

I'm glad Solomon said it.

I'm glad God told him to.

Prayer: Help me to understand that You are not my buddy, but You are God.

❧ JULY 10 ❦

NOAH WASN'T THINKING ABOUT MOSQUITOES

By faith Noah, being warned by God concerning events as yet unseen, took heed and constructed an ark for the saving of his household; by this he condemned the world and became an heir of the righteousness which comes by faith.

Hebrews 11:7

Where we live we refer to the mosquito as the state bird. A sportsman said, "We don't mind the mosquitoes; we filet them."

On a hot summer afternoon with the sun blazing, the mosquitoes still descend like dive-bombers. And the less charitable among us think sourly of Noah, who obviously missed his chance when he only had two mosquitoes to deal with.

But Noah had other things on his mind besides mosquitoes. He was concerned about being obedient. Day after day he worked—jeered and mocked—but he kept on working, every piece of wood prepared, every peg inserted, announcing loud and clear to all those who stood around that God's judgment was coming. Noah could have quit; he didn't. He could have apologized to the neighbors for making so much noise with his hammer and saw, but he didn't. He kept going, they kept watching, and each passing day drew them closer and closer to the coming judgment.

Jesus used the example of Noah to speak of His own coming. "As were the days of Noah, so will be the coming of the Son of man" (Matthew 24:37). God was serious then; God is serious now.

We need to think about Noah and the ark, and God has made sure that we do. He has given us the Old Testament Scriptures, the words of Jesus, and even the buzzing descendants of those ark-preserved mosquitoes.

Prayer: Father, now as then You give plenty of warning; I know You won't keep warning forever.

⇗ JULY 11 ⇖

WHO HAS THE FLASHLIGHT?

But the path of the just is as the shining light, that shineth
more and more unto the perfect day.

Proverbs 4:18 KJV

It was a good experience for me. I was a church camp counselor
responsible for a cabin of eight junior-high boys. One night we decided to pitch tents out in the woods, cook our dinner, and sleep out
all night. We hadn't counted on the weather. About eleven o'clock a
thunderstorm came up, and in a few minutes the driving rain had
soaked through the tents, our sleeping bags, and us. Everything was
wet, and we were all cold. So we decided to make our way back to
the cabins, where we could at least dry out and be warm the rest of
the night.

Then we discovered that only one person had a flashlight that
worked. He became the leader. The rest of us came behind, each
holding onto the fellow in front of him. In the woods at night, during a thunderstorm, the person with the flashlight chooses the path.

God tells us that the just person, the good person, the person who
is God's person, is a shining light. His path is light, only unlike a
flashlight, the light on the path gets brighter and brighter, just like
sunrise, until where the just person is is as noonday, even though
everything else might be dark. God's people are light, and in this
world of darkness, dense underbrush, branches that slap and tear
and pull, and stones that cause us to trip, people are going to turn to
the light. The one who has the light can lead the rest out of the
woods.

*Prayer: Lord, You've given me a light to shine. May others see it and
find their way out of the woods to the warmth and the security of
Yourself.*

JULY 12

THAT'S FOR ME!

If any of you lacks wisdom, let him ask God, who gives to all men generously and without reproaching, and it will be given him.

James 1:5

I do it every time.

When the roadsign points left, I turn right.

When the sign on the door says PUSH, I pull.

And I just now discovered that our Swiss clock winds to the left, but only after I forced it to the right. The stem snapped.

Wisdom—for the everyday, ordinary things as well as for the unusual—that's what I need, and I need it given generously. But could it come without ridicule, please? Usually when I need advice, it's in a public place.

I'm interested: "If any of you lacks wisdom. . . ."

That's for me—I lack.

The thought of asking God bothers me though, always asking, admitting that I don't have enough wisdom myself. At least it used to bother me. Then I met a man who didn't ask.

There he was, pulling on a door marked PUSH. Did he read the sign? No, he just pulled harder.

We're all the same. Some lack wisdom and know it. They're the ones who ask God.

The rest lack wisdom, too, only they don't have enough sense to "ask God, who gives to all men generously."

Apparently the only difference between the wise and the not-so-wise is that the wise know enough to know that they don't know, and they ask God.

That surely beats standing in front of a crowd and pulling on a door that opens the other way.

Prayer: Lord, I don't have the answers; I need You, and I need Your wisdom.

✑ JULY 13 ✑

GARBAGE

But the men of Sodom were wicked and sinners before the
Lord exceedingly.

Genesis 13:13 KJV

Each Sunday night I dutifully put my garbage cans out by the
curb. The man who collects the garbage comes early Monday
morning. He wears gloves to protect himself—he doesn't want to be
contaminated.

My garbage is in metal cans with tight lids to discourage roving
dogs from dragging the garbage all over the street. One night, when
our neighbors were away, their garbage cans were tipped over. My
wife and I put their garbage back into the cans. Our neighbors
would have done the same for us. None of us wants garbage spread
around.

We are careful about garbage. Yet we display on newsstands another form of garbage that people can get into—and we don't even
provide them with gloves.

Some garbage is sent through the mail, purchased by people who
like it, even though observers can see that they are making themselves sick on it. They leave it around where others, especially children, can get sick on it, too.

People take motion pictures of garbage. Some of it is so raw that
it is more sewage than garbage, and people pay to look at that, too.
Now we can even have the sewage sent into our living rooms. We
can gather our families around to watch it flow by on the television
screen, and we can hold enlightened discussions about which type
of sewage is the better art form.

I know that I can't stop my neighbors from wallowing in my garbage cans, if that's what they want to do. But so far nobody has
been curious about looking and tasting. My neighbors are intelligent people; they know the dangers. Maybe someday people will be
just as enlightened about other forms of garbage, too.

People don't argue that the content of my garbage cans is really
tasty food that has just gotten a little old or wasn't properly pro-
tected, even though everyone knows that the garbage, under other
conditions, had been acceptable. Some of the garbage being scraped
out of film cans or peeled out of magazine wrappers is as basic as
food, too. Yet with food we recognize when it becomes garbage and
we get rid of it before anyone gets sick.

Someday maybe people will realize what makes them sick and get rid of the garbage themselves. Until then we need to help them keep their garbage from being spread all over the streets. That would be a neighborly thing to do.

Prayer: Dear Father, to the best of my ability I want to help others by doing what I can to clean up the garbage that makes us all sick.

✑ JULY 14 ✑

WE'RE LOVED

"Blessed be the Lord who has given rest to his people Israel, according to all that he promised; not one word has failed of all his good promise, which he uttered by Moses his servant."

1 Kings 8:56

It isn't easy—this business called living. But look what we've got to go on!

To have His promises is to have the pleasures of God: "Blessed be the Lord who has given rest to his people ... not one word has failed of all his good promise."

That's not wishful thinking; that's truth. And because it is true, every promise yet to be completed stands with the same certainty of being fulfilled.

So we can rest, just as His people have always been able to rest, in what He has promised and what He has already given.

And from rest in Him comes the worship that says with deep feeling: "Blessed be the Lord who has given rest to his people."

From His Word come the promises; from the promises comes the resting; and in the rest are the "blesseds"—the worship.

So much is here in His Word. He didn't just give a few promises scattered now and then among demands or given occasionally to keep us going like rewards or bribes. They are everywhere, an outpouring of Himself—giving, giving, and more giving. We're loved!

We can say in worship, "Blessed be the Lord."

And out of a life lived in Him, overwhelmed by His giving, anyone can join that happy crowd spontaneously singing, "Blessed be the Lord."

It can happen. God invites it.

Don't miss the singing, because you've missed the rest. And don't miss the rest, because you've missed the promises.

Nobody has to.

Prayer: Let me live a life of singing because I live a life of being blessed.

⚘ JULY 15 ⚘
WHERE DID I PUT MY GLASSES?

> . . . And the man whose eyes are open hath said.
>
> Numbers 24:3 KJV

The trouble with eyeglasses is that they are never where they are supposed to be. After angrily stomping around the house, trying to find my glasses, I sat down on a wooden chair to think about where I might have put them—and knew immediately. But then it was too late; I was sitting on them.

Another time, after searching the house for my glasses, I stopped to wash my face and there they were—on my face, covered with soap and water—but at least I'd found them.

Balaam spoke of himself as the man whose eyes are open. They were open because he had heard the word of God. They were open because he saw the vision of the Almighty and even predicted the star that would come out of Jacob, a scepter rising out of Israel. He didn't wear glasses, but he saw very well. He didn't have to stumble around looking to improve his vision. He saw God.

That's spiritual vision, inner insight that comes from the revelation of God. And that can come to me, too, through the indwelling of the Word, through the voice of God in those quiet times of prayer and meditation. He will open my eyes; He will help me to see. And as Balaam, I'll be able to be "the man whose eyes are open," even if I am sitting on my glasses.

Prayer: Father, even with a good pair of bifocals, I know I won't see You until I open my spiritual eyes.

≥ JULY 16 ≤
I'M INTERESTING

Let thine ear now be attentive, and thine eyes open, that thou mayest hear the prayer of thy servant, which I pray before thee now, day and night, for the children of Israel thy servants. . . .

Nehemiah 1:6 KJV

He wasn't really listening to me. The story I was telling was interesting—at least I thought so—because the story was about me. First he frowned, then his eyes started wandering, and I knew I had lost him. Friends, even the best ones, aren't always interested in me, my life, or my opinions.

God is, though.

Nehemiah prayed, "Let thine ear now be attentive, and thine eyes open, that thou mayest hear the prayer of thy servant." And he knew God would hear; the Scriptures make that plain.

While God listens, He doesn't frown. His eyes don't wander as He looks for something more interesting to consider; He doesn't fidget as He wishes I would finish. Not God. And even my small interests are big to Him.

God isn't bored with me. No matter how many more "interesting" people I think there are in the world, to God no one is more interesting than I.

Prayer: I'm glad when we talk together that You aren't bored with me.

≥ JULY 17 ≤
WHICH ISSUE?

The Spirit of the Lord is upon me, because he hath anointed me to preach the gospel to the poor; he hath sent me to heal the brokenhearted, to preach deliverance to the captives, and recovering of sight to the blind, to set at liberty them that are bruised.

Luke 4:18 KJV

It was a discussion of the major issues that editors should be writing about today. And I was interested. Something struck me as I listened to that discussion. Where in all of this is Jesus? We should know, because He is the one constant in the midst of all the changing issues. We can't look at Jesus and ignore the world. Nor do *we* bring Jesus to the world. We go with Jesus into the world. Jesus taught His disciples, but He also experienced the issues of His time while He was teaching them. Israel was under the rule of a colonial power—Rome. The people were not free. There were hungry people around Him. There were sick people who needed help, and there were confused people who needed direction.

He fed the five thousand, yet taught that He Himself is the Bread of Life. His is a "food for all" program, but not the kind we organize. He was directly involved with those who pressed in around Him, yet was able to leave them and go off to pray alone.

There is need occasionally to go back to Luke 4:18, 19 and look again at the passage taken from Isaiah, selected by Jesus as a description of what His ministry is all about. We need to hear those words often. The major issue facing us is not the issues themselves. The major issue is Jesus Christ. To be in Christ is to know far more about our social responsibility than most people realize—because it is a responsibility *to* Him, *from* Him, and *in* Him.

Prayer: Lord, there are so many issues clamoring for attention. Help me to see each through the eyes of Jesus.

From "Decision" magazine, August, 1977; © 1977 Billy Graham Evangelistic Association. Used by permission. All Rights reserved.

ॐ JULY 18 ॐ
HEATING DUCTS

Commit thy works unto the Lord, and thy thoughts shall be established.

Proverbs 16:3 KJV

I remember one hot summer day when I was cleaning dirt out of heating ducts in the warehouse section of the university bookstore where I was working. I was a student then and a new Christian. As I was cleaning, I started whistling. A fellow employee came around behind the stacks and asked me about the tune. Then I realized that I had been whistling a Gospel song, so I explained the words to him. He commented that I was doing a job that nobody else wanted, and he wondered how anybody could enjoy it. Unknown to me, another man was listening to our conversation, and several days later he came to where I was eating lunch to talk about Christ. I wonder if I would have been able to give the reason for the hope in me if I had been grumbling about my work.

That witness probably wouldn't have occurred had I not had that dirty job, nor would I have had a word to say if I had been working only for a paycheck. I wasn't grumbling because of the job I had; it was a part of my day with Christ, therefore I was giving Him my best. There is great satisfaction in doing that. Work is good when God is in it—and He can be, no matter what the job.

Prayer: Father, there is great satisfaction in doing any job at all when I can give it my best for You.

From "Decision" magazine, August, 1979; © 1979 Billy Graham Evangelistic Association. Used by permission. All Rights reserved.

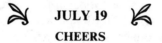

JULY 19

CHEERS

> Wherefore seeing we also are compassed about with so great a cloud of witnesses, let us lay aside every weight, and the sin which doth so easily beset us, and let us run with patience the race that is set before us.
>
> Hebrews 12:1 KJV

We went down to look at the hotel swimming pool, and in five seconds I made my decision. *No, I don't want to swim.* It wasn't the pool that made me decide. All around the sides, sunbathing, were muscular, tanned young men and lithe women. I'm not tanned, I'm not muscular, and when I swim I go through the water like a wounded whale. It would have been like swimming in a fishbowl: everyone around the sides watching the performance. I don't think any of them would have been cheering me on.

But we are cheered on in life by a great cloud of witnesses—those who have gone before, those who see what we are doing for Christ, encouragers in heaven, who are pulling for us, who aren't concerned about muscles and suntans and how we look in a swimsuit. The only question they ask is, "How are you doing with Christ?" And they are encouraging us every step we take.

I suppose it's something like the Special Olympics. Everybody in the crowd is cheering the contender on. And when he finishes, he's a hero.

Prayer: Thank You, Father, for the witnesses who are far more interested in what I am doing than in how I look while I am doing it.

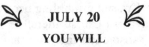

JULY 20

YOU WILL

... And Jesus said to Simon, "Do not be afraid; henceforth you will be catching men."

Luke 5:10

Jesus said what?

Can't you hear Peter's wife when he got home? And the neighbors, too!

He probably had to repeat it again for them.

"Do not be afraid; henceforth you will be catching men."

Could they have known what that meant?

Could Peter have known?

For that matter, do we know?

Catching men for God—that's a sacred task, one made possible by the Spirit of God. It's a holy business.

But right before we can say what we're thinking about that, He says, "Don't be afraid," and with that preface adds, "You will be catching men."

He didn't say, "Maybe," or, "Sometimes," or, "Possibly."

He said, "You *will.*"

Of course He was talking only to Peter. He wasn't talking to you or to me. . . .

Can't dodge it, can we?

He says, "You will."

So, will you?

Prayer: Lord, I know that just as Peter had Your commission, I have it, too.

❧ JULY 21 ❦

WHAT DIFFERENCE DOES IT MAKE?

> . . . First cleanse the inside of the cup and of the plate, that the outside also may be clean.
>
> Matthew 23:26

We don't have a dishwasher at our house. We still do things the old way. We fill a dishpan with hot, sudsy water, put on rubber gloves, and go to work. When our children were younger, they always helped. But we watched. The person drying the dishes also had to serve as inspector.

Some dishes looked clean on the outside but were anything but clean on the inside. Then back they'd go into the dishwater with complaints from the one who had to do the scrubbing. After all, what's a little caked-on food in a pan that's going to be used again anyway? And if the one drying missed a few leftovers in the bottom of a utensil, the one washing wouldn't point it out. If it got by inspection, that was good enough.

There were people like that in Jesus' day, people who were satisfied with themselves. They looked clean and religious and nice on the outside. They weren't interested in being clean; they just wanted to look clean. There are people like that today, too.

Jesus was blunt about it. He described people like that as full of rottenness, decay, dead men's bones—in short, pretty disgusting and capable of making people sick.

They weren't all hypocrites then, and they aren't now, either. Some just don't think it matters that the inside isn't washed properly. They're just like children trying to get by inspection and feeling pretty good about themselves if people don't notice. They don't realize that God does.

Prayer: Lord, You know what corruption inside can do. Here I am. Make me truly clean.

ૐ JULY 22 ৼ

OH, NO, NOT AGAIN!

But the day of the Lord will come like a thief, and then the heavens will pass away with a loud noise, and the elements will be dissolved with fire, and the earth and the works that are upon it will be burned up.

2 Peter 3:10

But I've already read that!

Old Testament, New Testament—the same words keep turning up. Peter, Isaiah, Paul, John—they're all saying it. Jesus, too, for that matter.

God keeps putting the same theme in different places in the Bible. It offends my preference for "selected" Bible readings—the kind more suited to my personal tastes.

What Peter wrote is an unwelcome subject.

I prefer more comforting words.

Who wants to hear about earthquakes, fervent heat, Christ coming like a thief, skies rolled up like a scroll, new heaven, new earth, judgment?

And it's everywhere I look. The Bible is full of it. It's as if God is saying, "Don't miss what I'm saying." Well, who could miss it?

But I'll keep looking.

Ahh, now here's an obscure book, seven little chapters, right toward the end of the minor prophets. I'll read Micah. There isn't enough here to carry all that doomsday, new-order stuff—just comfort, the type of thing I want to find in my Bible. . . .

Oops!

I just started reading Micah.

Prayer: I'm glad You kept saying it, so I would pay attention.

❧ JULY 23 ❧
KEEP THE INSECURITIES OUTSIDE

Jude, a servant of Jesus Christ and a brother of James, To those who have been called, who are loved by God the Father and kept by Jesus Christ: Mercy, peace and love be yours in abundance.

Jude 1, 2 NIV

I need neat packages of truth that I can sort out, bundle up, and tuck into my brain. Six words have done a lot for my insecurity.

For those times when I look at myself and wonder who I am and what I have going for me, Jude comes to my rescue. He makes it plain that because I am called, loved, and kept, I have mercy, peace, and love, and I have them in abundance. I can remember that—I'm called, I'm loved, I'm kept. And as a result of that I have mercy, I have peace, I have love.

Nail that to the doorpost of your heart. It'll keep the insecurities outside.

Prayer: Thank You, Lord, that in such a little bit of Scripture there is so much for me.

❧ JULY 24 ❧
JUST LIKE A CAT

Be sober, be vigilant; because your adversary the devil, as a roaring lion, walketh about, seeking whom he may devour.

1 Peter 5:8 KJV

I've never met a roaring lion, at least not where he could get at me. There have always been the bars of cages between us. But I met a Siamese cat once, and I think I know what Peter was talking about.

One evening when we were newly married, my wife and I took a baby-sitting job together on a Saturday night. She was putting the children to bed; I was stretched out on the sofa, sleeping. Suddenly I felt a weight on my chest. I came awake, opened my eyes, and there, standing on my chest, staring me right in the face, was a Siamese cat. His eyes weren't two inches from mine. I was rigid with fear until my senses came back enough for me to ease the cat off and sit up.

He had been prowling around the house, had seen me, and I suspect knew exactly what he was doing when he landed on my chest. If his intention was to scare me, he must have been a very satisfied cat!

We think when we are doing nothing, lying around, Satan won't bother us. After all, we aren't getting into anything. But he prowls, looking, looking. Some people think that Satan is a made-up figure. Others think he's a joke. And some think that if he's real he's quite harmless. I'll take God's warning and believe it. I don't want to wake up sometime and find Satan standing on my chest.

Prayer: Thank You, Lord Jesus, that when I'm with You I'm with One who has overcome the power of Satan.

⚮ JULY 25 ⚮
I'LL SETTLE FOR THE TEN-WORD VERSION

And this is what he has promised us, eternal life.

1 John 2:25

Friday afternoon: Theology 437—Yawn!
Subject: Eternal Life. Dr. I. M. Boring, lecturer.
Professor Boring understands eternal life—sort of. At least for two hours he expounds on it. He draws fine distinctions like the difference between *eternal* and *everlasting*.

"*Eternal*—that's what God is."

"Got it!"

"*Everlasting*—that's what we get through Christ."

"Ah, excuse me, I don't think I fully comprehend the distinctive nuances between *eternal* and *everlasting*. As a matter of fact, to be truthful, I don't get it at all."

"Well, *eternal*—God is eternal, no beginning, no end."

"Yes, that's the part I understand."

"But we humans all have a beginning; we are born within time and space."

"Yes."

"But when we are saved through faith in Jesus Christ, we are given new life in Him; it's His life, a 'postgrave' life, eternal life. We move into life eternal because we move into Christ."

"Yes."

"So, we had a beginning, but we won't have an ending. We have new life now, and that life will continue; we will live forever. Though it is not eternal for us from our birth, it is eternal for us from our new birth, when we receive the gift of life from the Eternal Life Giver. Thus it lasts from now on—forever. That's life everlasting."

"Great. Now what about. . . ."

"Of course there is much, much more that could be said about all of this."

"Uh, I'd rather not. . . ."

"But between us, I'll tell you something. Just tell everyone what John said: 'And this is what he has promised us, eternal life' (1 John 2:25)."

You can say it in ten words, and everyone will understand—even seminary professors.

Prayer: Even when I can't grasp all of You, Lord, I'm thankful for what I do understand and can lay claim to.

JULY 26
TRICKY SQUIRRELS

> . . . But all things are naked and opened unto the eyes of him with whom we have to do.
>
> Hebrews 4:13 KJV

We have a pair of gray squirrels living in a tree in our backyard. My brother-in-law told his children that they are really elderly brown squirrels that have come to our yard to live out their retirement. But I don't think so. I think God made them gray.

They're clever, those squirrels. At least they think they are. They have a nest high up in an ash tree. I know it's there; I've seen it many times. And it's quite visible in the winter when the leaves are gone. But they don't think I can see it. Nearby is a maple whose branches stretch out and touch the ash. So when the squirrels leave their nest, instead of coming down the ash, they go up to the highest branches, then out on an extended limb, leap to the maple, and go down the maple to the ground. When it's time to return to the nest, they go up the maple, out on a limb, jump to the ash, and then go down to their nest. As I watch them do that, I chuckle. They don't know that I know where they're going. They aren't fooling me. But I think sometimes I'm like those squirrels. God watches me go in and out, and I'm human enough to think He doesn't know where I'm going or where I'm coming from. But He does. The Scripture says that everything is open before Him. We can't outsmart God. That's true whether we're gray-haired squirrels or gray-haired men.

Prayer: Keep me, Father, from being so foolish as to think that I could ever fool You. Help me not to want to.

 JULY 27

CONTRACT TIME

Ask, and it will be given you; seek, and you will find; knock, and it will be opened to you. For every one who asks receives, and he who seeks finds, and to him who knocks it will be opened.

Matthew 7:7, 8

Okay, God, let's negotiate.

We come ready for bargaining. Maybe there's no oval table, maybe no ashtrays or ice water, but the system is the same: You propose; I'll counterpropose. You compromise a little, and I'll compromise a little.

But then, just when I think I'm ready for the bargaining table, Jesus breaks in, ignores the rules, and pleads a different way: "Ask, and it will be given you; seek, and you will find; knock, and it will be opened to you. For every one who asks receives, and he who seeks finds, and to him who knocks it will be opened."

Now what?

If I'd won a contract like that, I'd brag about it everywhere and take all that's coming to me.

But how do you brag and how do you grab with this?

I know what most people do. They ignore the offer and keep on bargaining. But that's mostly to hear themselves talk and to impress themselves with their own concept of one-to-one equality with God. I wonder what would happen if they just accepted His offer.

There is one little clause in this contract. It's in John 15:7: "If you abide."

That's the kicker. He does expect something.

Abide? All the time? As if I belong to Him? No contingencies, no outs, no escape clauses?

Okay, God, let's negotiate.

Prayer: Please stop me when I take it into my head that I can bargain with You. Show me the joy of accepting.

⚜ JULY 28 ⚜

SERMON PREPARATION

And at his appointed season he brought his word to light through the preaching entrusted to me by the command of God our Savior.

Titus 1:3 NIV

Last Sunday's sermon was a flop. It wasn't coherent, it didn't communicate the Scriptures, it wasn't well thought out, and it was poorly delivered. I've failed again. Oh, I wasn't preaching; I was in the pew.

Paul told Timothy to preach the Word, and he meant the Word. He didn't mean to preach opinions; he didn't say preach political viewpoints or topical items, but preach the Word. Preachers are to preach with authority, to preach exhaustively, to preach winsomely, and to preach all the Scriptures. The preacher is to preach so that the doubter may be convinced, the sinner may be converted, the fearful may be encouraged. And if that doesn't happen, it may not be the preacher's fault. It may be mine. Listening makes the preaching; a praying congregation makes an effective preacher.

If I'm really hungry, I'll demand a good meal. If I don't care, I'll settle for junk food. Going to morning worship is the same. If I want solid preaching, I'll seek it. I'll pray, I'll bring the messenger to the Lord, not only just before he preaches but weeks before as he studies and prepares.

But I haven't been doing that. I've been sliding into the pew, greeting those around me, exchanging a joke or two with the ushers, and then slouching down with my arms folded, just as I do in front of my television set when I want to be entertained or let my mind slow down before bed.

Good preaching is my responsibility, every day of the week. So, if you'll excuse me, I've got to go get ready for next Sunday's sermon.

Prayer: Lord, I know that there is a far better chance that I'll be blessed and fed when I want to be. Help me to want to be.

৯ৄ   JULY 29   ৵
THAT'S NOT EVEN A GAMBLE

Commit your way to the Lord; trust in him, and he will act.

Psalm 37:5

It's like a formula or a code:
"Commit," "Trust," "He Will."
Simple. "Commit your way to the Lord; trust in him, and he will act."
Sounds easy. Something must be wrong with a formula like that. If I knew which way I was going, then I could commit my way to Him. And if I knew more about the circumstances surrounding my life, I would be able to decide better whether or not I could trust Him. But that formula, that's asking a lot.
God didn't have to make that promise, but He did. And if He will act, that would certainly put an end to a lot of my worry and struggling with doubt.
But what if I commit, trust, and He won't?
Then I'd be . . . right where I am now.
Put it that way, and it isn't even a gamble. All I have to do is take Him at His word.
Commit, trust, and He will.
That's nice.

Prayer: Father, I seem to think my gamble is more certain than Your promise. Forgive me.

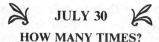

JULY 30

HOW MANY TIMES?

> How precious also are thy thoughts unto me, O God! how
> great is the sum of them!
>
> Psalm 139:17 KJV

Quick! How many times did God think about you today? Would
your pocket calculator help? Maybe if you plugged into one of
NASA's computers. David knew. "How precious also are thy
thoughts unto me, O God! how great is the sum of them!" He had
them added up. He had a total. Or did he? "If I should count them,
they are more in number than the sand . . ." (v. 18 KJV). So he didn't
know the sum of them. That's an exclamation! That's a statement of
awe. How great is the sum of them!

Maybe you're thinking, *Well, the Lord may think about other
people—the rich, the famous, the talented, the gifted, His special servants; but not about me.* If you think that, you don't know what
David knew. "But I am poor and needy; yet the Lord thinketh upon
me . . ." (Psalm 40:17 KJV).

How many times does the Lord think of me? David knew, and he
didn't have access to a computer. You can start calculating if you
want to, or you can sit back, shut your eyes, think for a little bit, and
then exclaim with David, "How great is the sum of them."

*Prayer: O God, until I read this verse I had absolutely no idea how
many times You think of me and how much You love me.*

JULY 31

OPPORTUNITY

> . . . Indeed, you have been concerned, but you had no op-
> portunity to show it.
>
> Philippians 4:10 NIV

When ideas that demand to be written down come to mind, I tend
to forget everything else, including food. I was on a trip, eating
alone in a restaurant, and my head was full of ideas that needed to
be put on paper. So while I was supposed to be eating my salad, I
had papers spread out on the table, where I was writing furiously.

The waitress came once with my entrée in her hand and, not knowing what to do, asked if she should return it to the kitchen. I thanked her, said "Yes," and promised, "I'll try to eat this salad right now." But then I forgot again and got involved in my writing. Finally I looked up, and there was the waitress, watching me. I realized she was looking for an opportunity to serve me my food. She was waiting for me to eat the salad and clear my papers off the table so she could bring me the rest of my meal. She was concerned but had no opportunity to show it.

Paul thanked the Christians for the same thing. They were concerned for him but didn't have an opportunity to show it. They wanted to provide for his needs. Paul understood that they needed to. "Not that I am looking for a gift, but I am looking for what may be credited to your account" (v. 17). They needed to give for their own sakes. Paul knew that the kindest thing he could do was to give them opportunity to give to him.

That's a hard lesson for many Christians to learn. Being good givers, many haven't yet understood that being a good receiver helps others who want to give.

When I saw the waitress staring at me, I gathered up my papers, shoved them on the floor by my feet, moved the salad plate in front of me, and concentrated on it. When I finished, I looked up, smiled, and she brought me the rest of my meal. I owed her that opportunity to serve me, and I knew it.

Prayer: Lord, I welcome opportunities to give to others. Help me to be alert to opportunities to help others have the joy of giving, too.

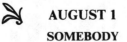 AUGUST 1

SOMEBODY

. . . Faith apart from works is dead.

James 2:26

Summers in the northern climes of the Western hemisphere are short, so as soon as the warmth comes, I'm quick to put up the hammock that my daughter bought for me when she was serving in Haiti with Teen Missions International.

The rustle of leaves, the birds singing, the Sunday newspaper on my chest, and I have the makings of an idyllic afternoon—except for one thing: the mosquitoes like me.

We joke in Minnesota about the mosquito being the state bird. The mosquitoes come in by squadrons, even in the heat of the afternoon sun, and attack while others swarm in holding patterns, waiting their turn to swoop down after the first wave has had its lunch. And I fret, "Why doesn't the state or some government agency do something about these mosquitoes?"

I open the pages of the newspaper and read stories about people starving—millions throughout the world—and I think as I slap another mosquito, *Why doesn't somebody do something?* I turn the page and read that hundreds of millions of people will die in the first nuclear conflagration and think, *Somebody should do something.* I read of elderly people needing medical care, and families without paychecks, and I mutter, "Somebody should do something"—as I slap at two more mosquitoes.

It is too much. I pick up my newspaper and run for the house where the mosquitoes can't get me. As I pull tight the screen door and stand there a minute looking through, it occurs to me that those dying of malnutrition can't run away from starvation; a screen door won't keep out a nuclear blast; and where does one go to hide from inflation, unemployment, and sickness? *Somebody needs to do something,* I think to myself as I sit in a comfortable chair to finish reading the newspaper.

Perhaps millions of others are doing what I am doing; they are wondering, *Why doesn't somebody do something?* And maybe—as God points to my neighbor who is out of work, to the elderly woman down the street who is hungry, the international foster programs for starving children, other Christian relief organizations that minister to the needs of people, the voice and vote that are given to me to use—He is replying: "That's right, somebody ought to do something."

And then He adds what by then is so obvious:

"Why don't you?"

Prayer: Father, open my eyes to the needs around me. I know I am saved to serve.

⅍ AUGUST 2 ⅋
GOD WANTED THAT

> And no longer shall each man teach his neighbor and each
> his brother, saying, "Know the Lord," for they shall all
> know me, from the least of them to the greatest, says the
> Lord. . . .
>
> Jeremiah 31:34

It has come true!

People are like that now.

". . . I will put my law within them, and I will write it upon their hearts; and I will be their God, and they shall be my people" (Jeremiah 31:33).

There are people, like a new race or new family, who no longer obey the law of God just because it is written down on tablets of stone and must be slavishly followed, but they follow the law because it is inside; it's in their hearts. Their souls have God's law.

God wanted that. More than twenty-five hundred years ago He wanted that. And now it has come.

The law has moved from the outside—a cold formal thing—to the inside—a warm living system.

It takes more than a new resolve for that to happen; it takes a new birth.

The law is in people's hearts when the Lawgiver is in people's hearts.

That's God's way.

Prayer: Come into my heart, dear Lord, with Your law and Your love.

⅍ AUGUST 3 ⅋
NEW

> What has been is what will be, and what has been done is
> what will be done; and there is nothing new under the sun.
>
> Ecclesiastes 1:9

Ho hum, we have been through it all before. Christians make commitments, the same commitments they have made before: to have a daily quiet time, to join a Bible study, to stick to a diet, to reexamine their priorities, to be better fathers or mothers, husbands or wives. But they have done that before.

Except—you have never lived tomorrow before. You have never been your present age before. Social, political, economic, religious affairs have never lined up before in quite the same way that they are now lining up. Never before has your family faced what is now ahead. New people, new events, will touch your life in ways that they have not touched your life before.

"Nothing changes," you say. No! Everything does. There is no "déjà vu" with God; He is the unchanging One to be sure, but He is also the only true dynamic One, the nonstatic, omnipotent, efficacious One who is the only true "life." To be in life with Him is never ordinary or dull or the same. It is never anything as it ever was before.

Prayer: Thank You, Lord, that with You nothing is ever as it was before. You are the dynamic One.

❧ AUGUST 4 ☙
LAUGHTER

A merry heart doeth good like a medicine: but a broken spirit drieth the bones.

Proverbs 17:22 KJV

We laughed a lot last night; we were with friends. And then we slept well because we'd laughed so much. Cares slip away when we're laughing with friends in a way that doesn't usually happen while watching television or reading. That's because friends enjoy each other, and if they're Christian friends, they enjoy God.

Probably Christians have more good times than any other people. Why? They can laugh out of their wholeness. They can laugh out of the freedom of being redeemed, forgiven people. They can laugh because they can put themselves into perspective as children of God. They don't have to take themselves so seriously, because God takes them seriously. A pure heart can be a merry heart because it isn't a heavy heart; it isn't dragged down.

If a merry heart doeth good like a medicine, and it does, I can't wait for my friends to come visiting again. I look forward to my medicine.

Prayer: Thank You, Lord, for providing friends and laughter and the spiritual health to enjoy them and You.

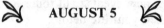

AUGUST 5
ESSENTIALS

> But we will give ourselves continually to prayer, and to the ministry of the word.
>
> Acts 6:4 KJV

When a young seminary student moved to his first church, an older minister in town came by the house to meet him. He was shown the room that was to be the minister's study, and it was completely empty except for a television set. The young minister explained, "Well, I only had time to move the essentials."

Think about the birth of the Church. Would the early disciples have done so much if they were like that young minister? Acts 6:4 doesn't read: "They gave themselves continually to prayer, during commercial breaks."

"They postponed the ministry of the Word until their books arrived and they had time to shelve them."

The difference isn't in the availability of entertainment; there was plenty of that for them, too. The difference is in attitude.

Prayer: O Lord, in the early disciples You gave me a good example to follow, and to the best of my ability, I will.

AUGUST 6
WHAT'S BEHIND THE CURTAIN?

> Having therefore, brethren, boldness to enter into the holiest by the blood of Jesus, By a new and living way, which he hath consecrated for us, through the veil, that is to say, his flesh.
>
> Hebrews 10:19, 20 KJV

I've always wondered what they do in the first-class section of an airplane. I can't tell, because they always draw the curtain. Those of us who travel coach will probably never know what mysteries lie hidden up there, unless we pay the extra fare to be upgraded. If we don't, whatever goes on up there will never be learned, because if we pull back the curtain and try to take a peek, we will be met by a frowning cabin attendant who will make it clear that what is in front is reserved for the privileged few.

The ancient Jews must have had a similar feeling about the curtained area of the temple. Only priests could go there. And when it came to the most holy place, only the high priest could go there, and then only once a year. That added to the mystery.

God chose to reveal Himself, but not in a wholesale manner. The priests were intercessors for the people. That all changed when Jesus Christ died on the cross, offering once for all the perfect sacrifice for our sins. At that moment, the temple veil was rent from top to bottom. Now all who come by faith in the finished work of Christ can approach the holy place. Now all can go "beyond the curtain." God is no longer off limits. God has opened to us the holy place.

Even though the first-class-cabin attendant on an airplane isn't approachable, God is.

Prayer: You opened the way to Yourself through the price paid by Jesus. Thank You that He is my high priest and I don't have to be an outsider anymore.

AUGUST 7
REBUKE

> But even the archangel Michael, when he was disputing with the devil about the body of Moses, did not dare to bring a slanderous accusation against him, but said. "The Lord rebuke you!"
>
> Jude 9 NIV

Bible memorization can be dangerous. I was in a group where people were being asked to give a verse of Scripture that had recently spoken to them in a personal way. It so happened that that morning I had been impressed by Jude 9. "The Lord rebuke you" was lodged in my mind. When it came time for me to give a verse, I had to give something else. How could I stand up before that group and say, "The Lord rebuke you"?

But that verse did grab me, because by nature I'm a person who wants to retaliate. When I'm upset with someone who is trying to cause damage to Christian work, instead of lashing out, I know I need to keep quiet and let God do what He's going to do. My old nature wants to get in the way and let me be the rebuker, but that's God's work.

And when I face such an individual, I find myself saying, "The Lord rebuke you." He doesn't hear it, because I don't say it aloud, but I hear it in my own mind. It keeps me from lashing out, criticizing, and being nasty. I don't say it in my mind as a curse. I say it as a reminder to myself that I am not to interfere in God's business. God will rebuke, and He doesn't need any help from me.

Prayer: Father, help me to remember that You have the authority to rebuke. I do not.

❧ AUGUST 8 ❧

MAYBE YOUR COMPASS IS OFF

Thou dost keep him in perfect peace, whose mind is stayed on thee, because he trusts in thee.

Isaiah 26:3

What is *perfect* peace, anyway?

Is it a peace that satisfies me?

A peace that is constant—no variations?

Actually, peace can be checked only against the ultimate standard of peace—God. It's like finding true north.

God is the fixed point of peace.

"Thou dost keep him in perfect peace, whose mind is stayed on thee." (Isaiah 26:3).

The two go together—the fix on God and the peace of God. When a person's mind is stayed, fixed, locked into God, then the promise follows—that person will be kept, preserved, guarded in perfect peace.

There are no variables, no options.

No one says, "I'll forget the compass, but I'd like always to find north."

And no one says, "I'll take the peace of God, but I'd like the luxury of a drifting mind." Perfect peace goes with the "staying."

A lot of people say, "I don't have peace," or, "Peace comes and goes; I fluctuate."

The problem isn't in the source of peace. That's always constant. God is willing to give perfect peace. The problem is in the focus of the mind.

Minds that are fixed on God have perfect peace.

Check the compass of your mind.

Prayer: I want my mind on You, Lord, because I know that's how I'll have peace.

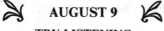

AUGUST 9

TRY LISTENING

For the Son of man is come to seek and to save that which was lost.

Luke 19:10 KJV

We talked about it in the Sunday-school class that I teach. And we wondered.

Why is it that new Christians are usually far more burdened for the lost than those who have been in Christ and in the church for a long time?

I think we realized the answer: new Christians remember what it is like to be separated from God; older Christians don't. New Christians know what people are struggling with when they are unsaved. The believer of many years either doesn't remember, doesn't know very many non-Christians, or assumes that unsaved people are quite comfortable in their unbelief.

We read magazines and watch television programs and from them make the assumption that people outside Christ have it all together. The emptiness, agony, and restlessness of a soul adrift from God are not seen, or if they are, they're overlooked.

Somebody in our class said, "Maybe older Christians need to go to a few cocktail parties and listen to the conversations—they would see then how bored people are and how empty their lives are, and maybe they would be far more eager to share Christ."

As it is, Christians tend to talk only to other Christians and aren't aware of the total lostness, the sense of separation of those who are trying desperately to make some meaning out of their existence.

We believe theologically that people without Christ are lost, and we believe the Great Commission, but many of us do not have that heavy burden that comes from knowing how lost "lost" is. We haven't listened to the lost ones.

If you think somebody without Christ has life worked out and has inner peace, you probably haven't been listening to him. Read the Bible; it will tell you about the emptiness of being lost. Or just listen to people for a few minutes. They can tell you, too.

Prayer: Help me to see people the way You do and to care about them.

ᕦ AUGUST 10 ᕤ
INDIGESTION

> A man shall eat good by the fruit of his mouth: but the soul
> of the transgressors shall eat violence.
>
> Proverbs 13:2 KJV

Eating can be hazardous to your health. Several years ago in a restaurant I was eating a salad when I crunched down on a piece of glass. That spoiled my appetite. A few years later, while having lunch with friends in another city, I was again eating a salad and began to tell them my "glass in the salad" story. Just then I bit down on another piece of glass. My friends didn't believe me until I showed it to them.

What we eat can hurt us and cause a whole lot more than a mild case of indigestion. Scripture tells us that transgressors (those who violate God's laws) make a meal of what is harmful.

"The soul of the transgressors shall eat violence." Does this mean we take it in, digest it—that violence is our food?

Obviously there is a whole lot more to obeying God's commands than just avoiding the "thou shalt nots." Transgression can give an appetite for violence, and violence can do a lot of harm—like glass in the salad.

Unlike glass, though, violence doesn't come as a surprise to the eater. As a transgressor of God's ways, he wants it in his diet. His appetite is for violence. Satan is a good cook; he knows what our appetites want, and he serves it.

Prayer: Father, Your laws are a protection for me and everyone around me. Help me to want to keep them.

AUGUST 11

WHAT A WASTE!

But the meek shall possess the land, and delight themselves
in abundant prosperity.

Psalm 37:11

He clawed his way to the top.

Some admired him for it, called him a go-getter.

Others—the ones who knew him best—saw what he was.

His wife and children hardly knew him; they didn't respect him,
and his colleagues learned that their kindnesses to him were taken
only as weaknesses. He used his colleagues and elbowed them aside.

It's painful to be stepped on when all you want is to be sensitive
and to care for others. It hurts to be taken when you wanted to do
some kindness.

Kind people don't want retaliation. So it isn't with any sense of
glee or you'll-get-yours pleasure that the kind ones read: "Yet a little while, and the wicked will be no more; though you look well at
his place, he will not be there. But the meek shall possess the land,
and delight themselves in abundant prosperity" (Psalm 37:10, 11).

The meek and the kind aren't particularly interested in the
"abundant prosperity" either. If that's what they wanted, they
would have adopted the behavior of the wicked.

Instead, it's a point of sorrow that they alone will have all the
abundant prosperity of God and the wicked will miss it. They watch
the wicked grasping and taking and hurting, and think, "You're
causing hurt now, and you will be hurt later"—losers in both
worlds.

The kind people will hurt later, too, when they see the wicked go
down in pain, screaming at their loss and cursing God, not understanding that they brought it all upon themselves.

Good people know the pain that's coming, even though it will be
happening to others, not to themselves.

The wicked don't know and keep on clawing and grabbing now.

What a waste!

*Prayer: Lord, I know I can't escape seeing the wicked hurt themselves.
Help me to show them Your way.*

➷ AUGUST 12 ໕

GNATS IN THE TEETH

> ... And there came a grievous swarm of flies into the house
> of Pharaoh, and into his servants' houses, and into all the
> land of Egypt: the land was corrupted by reason of the
> swarm of flies.
>
> Exodus 8:24 KJV

Wherever I go on warm summer nights, gnats go with me. They
swarm around my head, crawl into my nose and ears and mouth,
and I find myself spitting them out. One evening as the sun was
going down, we were visiting with a group of neighbors in their
yard. There were six of us, three couples, having a good time chat-
ting, except for one thing—the plague of gnats that were all over
and around our heads.

Then someone mentioned hearing that gnats always go for the
head, because it's the highest part of the body and that if something
is higher than the head, that's where they'll go. So we experimented
by holding one hand up over our heads. It worked. There we stood
in a circle on the grass, six people, each with a hand up over his or
her head. A man driving by in his car almost drove up over the curb
when he saw this sight!

If gnats bother us, what must it have been like in Egypt with the
plague of flies? Flies in the food, flies crawling down the back, flies
in the hair, ears, nose, mouth—and no way for people to get away
from them, even if they put their hands up in the air. God was
showing His power, and He did it in a way that would be most real
to them. It was certain that nobody thought about anything except
those flies, where they came from, and why they were there.

God had a reason for sending that plague, and it's a story worth
reading. It was a plague that could have been avoided. Pharaoh
must have been a sight to see, stubbornly proclaiming that he alone
was king and ruler, while all the time spitting out flies.

*Prayer: Lord, though there are some shocking, even somewhat dis-
gusting stories in Scripture, I'm not sorry that they're there. I need
things I can identify with to learn the lesson You're teaching.*

❧ AUGUST 13 ❦

BALD AND CUTE

Woe unto you, scribes and Pharisees, hypocrites! for ye are like unto whited sepulchres, which indeed appear beautiful outward, but are within full of dead men's bones, and of all uncleanness.

Matthew 23:27 KJV

A friend told me recently that she thinks bald men are cute. So I take comfort in the knowledge that I'm getting cuter every day. But this morning I noticed one of the tires on the car. It's beginning to look like the top of my head; that's not cute, that's dangerous. A bald tire endangers me, my passengers, and anyone who is around me on the highway.

When I get the car washed, they scrub the white sidewalls on that tire, along with the rest of the car, and the tire looks good until I get close. But no matter how nice it looks from the side, it is still dangerous.

Jesus talked about religious leaders who had outward religion but inside were corrupt. People in those days whitewashed the tombs, because to touch a body or a grave would leave a person ceremonially unclean. So to protect people, tombs were painted white. There were people who tried to look religious, act religious, talk religiously, but inside, Jesus said, they were full of corruption and death. That's dangerous. Just to follow a person like that leads us to where they are going—not to life, but to death.

It takes more than religious language to be a safe spiritual leader, just as it takes more than a clean white sidewall to make a tire safe. Checking the depth of a tire tread is not difficult. Checking the depth of a religious leader is more difficult but just as necessary. Drive on a bald tire and you might not arrive home safely. Follow the wrong religious leader and you might not arrive home safely either. Religious hypocrites, like bald tires, are dangerous. We need to be careful of them.

Bald heads are still okay!

Prayer: Lord, no matter how spiritual someone appears, give me discernment about whether he has the depth that comes from knowing You.

❧ AUGUST 14 ❧
AN EASY RUN

> But they that wait upon the Lord shall renew their strength;
> they shall mount up with wings as eagles; they shall run,
> and not be weary; and they shall walk, and not faint.
>
> Isaiah 40:31 KJV

Twenty-seven laps to a mile on the downtown YMCA track. Some days I can hardly make it; other days it's easy. The pleasure of running comes on those "other" days.

There's a difference. When the running is smooth and easy, the laps roll by, and I enjoy the rhythm, the lubricated feeling. It's like a celebration of the physical.

But when it's hard, it's a labor, and to push on seems as if I have no air left to breathe, and my legs won't agree with each other.

God promised, "They shall run, and not be weary." It was His word to people who needed to be reminded about the difference between idols and the holy God.

I know what He means. I've tried to run with idols.

But with God, it's like those "other" days—the whole twenty-seven laps.

Prayer: There is exhilaration and joy in running with You, Lord.

❧ AUGUST 15 ❧
DRIED UP

> As for man, his days are as grass: as a flower of the field, so
> he flourisheth.
>
> Psalm 103:15 KJV

Hot prairie winds are tough on lawns. It seems no matter how much water we pour on the grass, it quickly turns brown anyway.

David could see that, too. He needed good green grass for his sheep. Most of the places he went we would call desert. It was hot, dry, and the winds took all but the hardiest weeds. But God, speaking through the pen of David, makes a simple application from all that and lets us know that we're like grass, too. The wind comes, those hot, dry winds of adversity—the winds of the years, the winds of time—and we're gone, no matter how flourishing and promising we seemed to be in the springtime.

But two things don't dry up—God's loving-kindness and His righteousness. He offers us both, but not as a blanket promise. He offers both to those who will fear Him, meaning those who respect Him, stand in awe of Him, honor Him, and worship Him.

I have to go move the sprinkler in the yard again. I'm glad I don't have to move God's loving-kindness around; it reaches everywhere.

Prayer: I don't even have to add an extra length of hose to reach the driest corners of my life. You alone, Lord, are the water of life. I'd be dried up and dead if it weren't for You.

⅀ AUGUST 16 ⅄

THAT'S LONELY!

Let this mind be in you, which was also in Christ Jesus: Who, being in the form of God, thought it not robbery to be equal with God: But made himself of no reputation, and took upon him the form of a servant, and was made in the likeness of men.

Philippians 2:5–7 KJV

College women tell me that Saturday night is a terribly lonely time when they are in their dormitory rooms and all their friends are out on dates. I have sensed something of that loneliness when I have been miles from home on a trip and am alone in a hotel room on a Saturday night, thinking about home and family and wishing I were there. No amount of busyness can dilute the pain.

When Jesus came to this earth, He left the Father. Scripture says He did not think that His equality or oneness with the Father was something to hang onto, but took upon Himself the form of a servant. He left behind everything that was good and holy and just and pure to come into a world that was the opposite. Talk about loneliness! Who could even begin to understand what He left behind? How many lonely nights must Jesus have had thinking about home and the Father, wanting to be there yet in faithfulness staying because He had a ministry to perform, redemption to bring, and a price to pay for our sins.

It's a big, lonely city when it's Saturday night and you're miles from home. For Jesus, it must have been a big, lonely earth to have come here and be so far from Home. I marvel that He thought we were worth it.

Prayer: Thank You, Jesus, for coming to this earth and staying here long enough to pay the penalty for my sins.

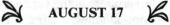 **AUGUST 17**
BECAUSE HE WANTS TO

I myself will be the shepherd of my sheep, and I will make them lie down, says the Lord God.

Ezekiel 34:15

There's that shepherd picture again.

You never have to go far in Scripture to find it. And you probably noticed how God talks about it—all positives.

There's not a negative, punitive, judgmental, critical statement in the whole passage.

"I myself will be the shepherd of my sheep, and I will make them lie down, says the Lord God. I will seek the lost, and I will bring back the strayed, and I will bind up the crippled, and I will strengthen the weak, and the fat and the strong I will watch over; I will feed them in justice" (Ezekiel 34:15, 16).

He's bringing the strayed sheep back. They don't have to find their way home on their own. They just call.

And He's doing the mending and the binding of whatever it is that's crippled.

For the weak He gives new strength. That's good news when we have no reserves of our own left.

Even when everything is just right, and all is well, and we are contented, He's standing there watching.

We don't have to stay on our feet, tense, ready to run or fight. "Lie down," He says, and we can.

He promises all that to us, just because He wants to.

Prayer: Your loving heart is open to us—those who are Your sheep. Thank You for bringing me into Your sheepfold.

❧ AUGUST 18 ☙

HE'S A GOOD TEACHER

When the Spirit of truth comes, he will guide you into all the truth; for he will not speak on his own authority, but whatever he hears he will speak, and he will declare to you the things that are to come.

John 16:13

Teaching stretches the teacher—or it should. The stretching is not necessarily academic. The tough part about teaching is not simply having too little content to disperse; the tough part about teaching is communicating the material so that students learn.

I like to teach. I serve as a visiting faculty member at a college and a theological seminary, teach at schools of Christian writing, and give lectures at the Billy Graham Schools of Evangelism. I also like to teach Sunday school and am committed to a college-and-career class when I am not traveling.

Sometimes students have to tell me, "Don't be academic." What they are really saying is, "Stop trying to impress us with all that you know. Help us to learn as much as we can from you."

Jesus offered the Holy Spirit, who would lead and guide into all truth. That's an interesting teaching position—not talking at or lecturing to, but leading, guiding, directing. The Holy Spirit doesn't have to impress us with all that He knows. The Holy Spirit is God, therefore all-knowing. He is deeply concerned about you and me and our growth. That's what makes Him such a good teacher.

Prayer: Thank You, Father, for the Holy Spirit, who not only is my teacher but an example of what a teacher ought to be.

❧ AUGUST 19 ☙

YOKEMATE

Take my yoke upon you, and learn from me; for I am gentle and lowly in heart, and you will find rest for your souls. For my yoke is easy, and my burden is light.

Matthew 11:29, 30

"Take *my* yoke."
It doesn't chafe or rub—no irritation there.

And like most yokes, it's designed for a team. Jesus fits; so does His yoke.

You don't have to pull too hard with Jesus or strain to keep up. In fact, if you do, it might be counterproductive. Imagine pushing or pulling against Him! That's real opposition. What a contrast to the easy moving along with Him—the gentle walk in the balanced harmony of His grace. And during our walk together, He tells us that teaching will take place—teaching about Himself—and with the teaching His "soulrest."

Some yoke!
Some Yokemate!
Some promise!

Prayer: Lord Jesus, everything fits together and works when I'm yoked with You.

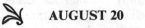

AUGUST 20

SURE AND STEADY

Dear friend, I pray that you may enjoy good health and that all may go well with you, even as your soul is getting along well.

3 John 2 NIV

My soul isn't always soaring. I'm not always on the upper planes spiritually. But John doesn't suggest that anyway. What is normal, it seems, is a soul that "is getting along well."

A soul that is getting along well is steady, not racing ahead or falling back, but progressing at a regular pace. The saved soul is the moving-along soul. This is possible because of what he says in verse 3 (NIV), our "faithfulness to the truth" and our continuing "to walk in the truth." If we stay faithful to the truth, walk in the truth, our souls will get along well.

Maybe when we meet one another in the street we shouldn't just be asking, "How do you feel?" or "How's business?" or "How are the children?" Instead, maybe we need to be asking, "How is it with your soul? Is your soul getting along well?"

Prayer: Lord, instead of my always trying to be in a race, then dropping like an exhausted runner, give me that steady, ground-consuming walk that goes the distance.

❧ AUGUST 21 ☙

I FALL DOWN A LOT

For a righteous man falls seven times, and rises again; but
the wicked are overthrown by calamity.

Proverbs 24:16

"If you really loved the Lord, that wouldn't happen." "If you
were walking with God, you wouldn't have tripped."

When I fall down, I don't need someone heaping guilt on me; I
need help to get back up. I'm glad that God gives that help. The
Scripture says that a good man, a righteous man, may fall seven
times. That's a total number (in other words, again and again); he
can fall and fall and fall, but he also gets up again. The Scripture
never tells us the good won't fall. The history of the saints proves
that's not true. Scripture does say that God's people will get up
again. Not so for the wicked.

There are a lot of snares, rocks, and pitfalls in this life trail that I
walk. But God walks with me. I may stumble and fall again and
again, but He is there, and His strong arm lifts me up again and
again. The wicked person, the one who rejects God, doesn't have
that strong hand.

So don't heap guilt on me when I fall down. I may fall a lot because I don't walk very well. But I'm trying, and when I'm walking
with God, He helps me up again.

*Prayer: Thank You, Lord, that even though I go through this life with
skinned knees and scraped hands, I can reach out to You and You pull
me up again.*

❧ AUGUST 22 ☙

RIGHT IN THE MIDDLE OF MY BATTLEFIELD

Peace I leave with you; my peace I give to you; not as the
world gives do I give to you. Let not your hearts be troubled, neither let them be afraid.

John 14:27

"Peace in our time."
But it didn't last, did it?

Peace missions, peace plans, peace councils—name some more, any number—they won't last either.

People talk a lot about peace, and sometimes even arrange peace treaties. But they are just temporary pauses in hostility. Peace can last only so long as everybody is happy with his lot in life and nobody ever starts to want what somebody else has.

Peace—the real kind that lasts—will have to come from a different direction.

It can!

And when it does, it doesn't matter what kind of wars are going around. It's His peace in spite of wars. That's different!

"Peace I leave with you; my peace I give to you; not as the world gives do I give to you" (John 14:27).

Jesus said that not out of ignorance about the way people are made but out of a perfect awareness of how we are made. He said it because He knows us and He knows Himself. He alone can give that kind of peace; the world with all of its councils and programs can't produce it.

Some people say, "Ah, peace—that's what I want. No struggles, no problems, perfect tranquillity."

They're in for a shock. Because it doesn't come that way, and the tranquil scene they anticipate turns out to be a battlefield.

Jesus wasn't kidding us though, because right in the middle of that battlefield (even living is sometimes a battlefield) is peace. It's His peace—inside; the world can't give it, but then neither can the world take it away.

Peace! It's generated from a different direction. It comes from the One who is above and beyond the turmoil.

And it lasts.

But then, why shouldn't it last? The Source does.

Prayer: Thank You for peace. It comes from You, so it is always there, no matter what battles are raging.

❧ AUGUST 23 ❦
HERE'S YOUR CHANGE

... Am I my brother's keeper?

Genesis 4:9 KJV

As I started to turn the key in the ignition of my car, I realized, "That man gave me too much change." So back I went.

I had pumped my own gas, gave the attendant a bill that required change, and was already back in the car before it hit me that he had cheated himself.

It was obvious that math wasn't his strong subject. First I had to explain his mistake, then go to his adding machine to prove that I owed him another ninety cents. Finally he just took my word for it, because the figures were troubling to him.

When I told my wife what had happened, she said, "He short-changed me ten cents last time, but it wasn't intentional; he just can't handle figures."

I wondered how long he would last on his job and found myself wishing either that he could do only the physical work and not be obliged to make transactions or else that everyone who came there for gasoline would give him the correct amount.

That man was trying hard. I admire that in a person. He was giving his best and would probably be hurt if he lost his job because he couldn't handle one part of it.

Then I thought about me. Why am I able to figure change? What right do I have to the ability that made possible the education that in turn gave me the skills to make change or to do a lot of other things? *Why me, God?* I wondered. And, of course, there is no answer except that, because some can do some things that others can't do, we are responsible for each other.

I am my brother's keeper. If I have more ability in some area, then that skill isn't just for me, but for him, too. God expects that of me. He gives us all the opportunity to help, for the other person's blessing and for our own. If we don't help each other, we all lose.

Prayer: Father, make me sensitive to others, to help them when and where I can, because I know I need help, too.

⚮ AUGUST 24 ⚮
ANGER IN THE FAMILY

... First be reconciled to thy brother, and then come and offer thy gift.
Matthew 5:24 KJV

Growing up can be painful. Before we come to faith in Christ we watch people get angry with one another, and it seems to be the way people are. Then we transfer our trust from ourselves to Jesus

Christ and move into the family of God and understand why the heathen rage. But then there comes that growing up, that discovery that there is sometimes anger among brothers in Christ also. Jesus had to speak plainly about trying to worship if there is anger with a brother. The writers of the epistles had to warn: ". . . Let not the sun go down upon your wrath" (Ephesians 4:26 KJV); "If it be possible . . . live peaceably with all men" (Romans 12:18 KJV); ". . . Let us love one another: for love is of God . . ." (1 John 4:7 KJV).

That's too bad. There shouldn't have to be that kind of teaching if the One who is Himself love really moves into an individual's life through trust. But we don't have to be around fellow believers very long before we find distrust, anger, even what seems to be hatred. Jesus went so far as to say that anger can bring us into danger of judgment (*see* Matthew 5:22).

Some people enjoy being angry. It gives them a sense of overpowering other people. They don't think of their own anger as being dangerous. They may run over loving people with their anger, but I wonder if they think they are going to run over God with their anger, when they stand before Him at the Judgment.

Prayer: Help me to realize that You mean what You say about anger. Please control my mind and my tongue.

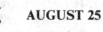

AUGUST 25

NOBODY

> Now therefore, if you will obey my voice and keep my covenant, you shall be my own possession among all peoples; for all the earth is mine.
>
> Exodus 19:5

"This one is mine!"

She was standing in front of a group of entering freshmen and was letting the new girls know that among all the fellows there, one belonged to her.

He did, too; later on she married him.

We smile at that. But still all of us are possessive. No one else has claim to what is mine, because it is mine.

God feels that way too; He may feel that way about you.

"Now therefore, if you will obey my voice and keep my covenant, you shall be my own possession among all peoples."

No matter how many people there are in the world, God knows
His own and says to those who obey His voice and keep His covenant: "You shall be my own possession."

"You're mine."

"My own."

"Nobody else's"

Try that on when you're in a nobody-loves-me mood. You can't
say, "Nobody loves me."

God isn't a "nobody."

Prayer: Lord, You are really Somebody, and You love me.

❧ AUGUST 26 ❧

GOD IS NOT TOO POLITE

Come now, and let us reason together, saith the Lord:
though your sins be as scarlet, they shall be as white as
snow; though they be red like crimson, they shall be as
wool.

Isaiah 1:18 KJV

There are two kinds of readers in my world; it's probably so for
most writers. There are those who are so polite they won't criticize
anything that I write, which means there could be misspelled words,
poor grammar, syntax that's not correct; but they'll smile politely
and say, "That's very good." They don't help me at all.

But there are those who want to help me and aren't afraid to say,
"This is poorly written," or "You've done better." They aren't polite, but they make me a better writer. And if I want help, I'd better
not be defensive or stubborn about making changes.

When God corrects me, He's not necessarily polite about it, but
He does it lovingly. He says, "Come now, and let us reason together." "Let's put our minds to this," God says. "Your sins are
scarlet, but they can be as white as snow." If He were being polite
he'd say, "That's all right; your sins aren't so scarlet. I know many
whose sins are far more scarlet than yours." And if I were defensive,
I would say, "Don't tell me my sins are scarlet. I know my sins;
they're not so scarlet."

But almost as if He's putting His arm around my shoulder, God
says, "Come and look at your sins. Though they be as scarlet, they

can be white as snow." God is not too polite to be helpful, and I'd better not be too stubborn to be helped.

Prayer: Lord, I'd rather You be the one to correct me than anybody else. Please go ahead.

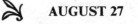

AUGUST 27
WE CAN WAIT

Therefore, wait ye upon me, saith the Lord. . . .
                                    Zephaniah 3:8 KJV

For the vision is yet for an appointed time, but at the end it shall speak, and not lie: though it tarry, wait for it; because it will surely come, it will not tarry.
                                    Habakkuk 2:3 KJV

High on my list of life's most miserable experiences is having a center seat on a jumbo jet that is packed full of people while the plane waits on the ground. That happened recently, and the pilot came on the intercom about every fifteen or twenty minutes to tell us that we would be departing momentarily. We were never allowed to leave the plane, because we were going to take off any minute. We sat there for four and a half hours.

All of us have waited for a letter that we hoped would come any day. Most of us have paced the floor, waiting for a surgeon to come out of the operating theater to tell us about our loved one. Waiting can be painful, especially because of the uncertainty. We don't know when something is going to happen, how it will happen, and what it's going to mean to our lives when it does happen.

Habakkuk waited in the tower for an answer from God. God gave it, and there was no uncertainty about it, nothing to wonder over. It was clear because God supported it with His own promise. "Though it tarry, wait for it; because it will surely come, it will not tarry."

Though it tarry, it will not tarry. God is saying that though the answer isn't here yet, it's already on its way. The letter has been sent, the messenger is coming down the hall. When we know that, we can wait.

God is the great I Am, always present tense, not future. His word is on its way now. His promise is in the process of being carried out now. What we wait for is already happening.

With God we don't have to wait for the next announcement: "Only a few minutes more." We'll never have to groan, saying, "We've heard that before."

Prayer: Lord, teach me the meaning of waiting when I am waiting for You.

 AUGUST 28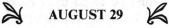

ARE YOU SURE HE SAID THAT?

I will not leave you comfortless. . . .

John 14:18 KJV

Straight out—that's the way it came.

No secret code, no need to trace the source, no documentation or special verification required. This message came right from the Lord Himself. No one ever has to ask, "Are you sure He said that?"

"I will not leave you comfortless."

What does that mean?

Ask the crippled old man who sits alone in his room all day, wondering what he's worth.

Ask the young widow.

Ask the twelve-year-old boy whom no one wants to adopt.

There's a lot of pain around; our Lord knows that. And from His loving heart He says, "I will not leave you."

He's not sending some temporary representative who will telephone once a day—if it doesn't take too long.

"I will not leave you." That's for now and that's forever.

Prayer: You Yourself are here with me. Thank You for making that promise and keeping it.

 AUGUST 29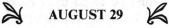

GOOD MORNING

. . . And as soon as ye be up early in the morning, and have light, depart.

1 Samuel 29:10 KJV

Author George MacDonald once wrote about getting up early to "watch God make a morning." There is something revitalizing, fresh, new—a reminder of God's mercies and goodness—that late sleepers miss. It's a visual experience of the awesomeness of the renewing of God.

My wife and I once spent the night in a tent, camping on the eastern shore of Florida, right up against the Atlantic Ocean. We woke early and watched the sun just as it began to come up, seemingly out of the water, changing by the second, the rays lighting up the sky and the sea. We watched God make a morning, and though I do not recall many other things about that particular trip, I can still see that morning and relive it.

Scripture tells us that Abraham got up early in the morning. So did Abimelech, Jacob, Laban, Moses, Joshua, Gideon, Samuel, David, and Job. Through the Scriptures we're told about those who rose early in the morning. They may have done it to take advantage of first light, because when darkness came they could do no more. We, with electricity, have the benefit of late-night light. But that also steals from us the experience of watching God make a morning.

We get much more than an early start on our day when we rise early. We get the lesson of God's renewing, the freshness of His gifts, the splendor of His beauty. To do that may mean changing our habits and going to bed earlier, but something special happens when we watch God make a morning.

Prayer: Lord, in the changing colors of the light breaking up the night, I see more than a sunrise. I see Your promises.

✒ AUGUST 30 ✒

GOD HAS A GOOD EYE AND A SHARP SAW

> I am the true vine, and my Father is the vinedresser. Every branch of mine that bears no fruit, he takes away, and every branch that does bear fruit he prunes, that it may bear more fruit.
>
> John 15:1, 2

"Let's just trim that one branch that's hanging down." When my wife says that, I know I'm in for a full day's work. Has anybody ever gotten by with trimming only one branch? Most of us are lucky if, when we finish shaping the whole tree, we don't have to trim all the other trees in the yard as well.

Sometimes in what I think are my great moments of spiritual commitment I've said to the Lord, "You may trim this unsightly part of my life. It doesn't glorify You; it makes me unattractive as a Christian. . . ." But before I can finish, He reminds me, "I am the vinedresser." In other words, He knows far better than I do what needs trimming in my life, and if I'm going to invite Him to beautify me, I'd better expect a lot of pruning.

If you open your life to God, He won't stop with one unsightly branch; He knows what attractive is, and He intends to make us beautiful. Don't try to tell Him, "This is the only problem branch," because He's likely to say, "That's minor. The bigger problem is this branch over here."

The decision for each of us to make is not what will I have God trim out of my life; rather, the decision is whether I will allow God to make me as fruitful as He alone can, because only He understands fruitfulness. Once we open the garden gate and invite the vinedresser in, nothing is going to stay the same.

Prayer: Lord, You shape my life the way it ought to be, even though sometimes I know it's going to hurt.

⋈ AUGUST 31 ⋉
LIST THE PROMISES

But upon mount Zion shall be deliverance, and there shall be holiness; and the house of Jacob shall possess their possessions.

Obadiah 17 KJV

Go ahead, try it. Take a sheet of paper and start listing the possessions of the child of God. List the promises. List what is ours in Christ Jesus: eternal life, peace, fellowship with the Holy Spirit. The list will get longer and longer and longer, limited only by your vocabulary and your awareness of what God says in His Word. But wherever you stop on the sheet of paper, or however many sheets of paper it takes to make the list, when you're finished, put your hand on those promises and realize that all of them are your possessions if you are trusting in Christ Jesus.

Prayer: Thank You, Lord, for all that I have in Christ. The more I think about it, the more I stand in awe before You.

❧ SEPTEMBER 1 ❦

LOOK WHO'S WEARING THE HAT

And thou shalt make a plate of pure gold, and grave upon
it, like the engravings of a signet, HOLINESS TO THE
LORD. . . . and it shall be upon Aaron's forehead. . . .

Exodus 28:36, 38 KJV

Some hat! The high priest wore it, and because he did, not only
was he conscious of what was on his head but the people were, too.
They couldn't look at him without reading what was engraved
there: HOLINESS TO THE LORD.

We do not have high priests today as such, and yet in another
sense we do, because all of us who are redeemed, sanctified by the
cleansing blood of Christ, are priests of God. This is not a bragging
point; this is something that makes us tremble and stand in awe. As
priests we have free entrance to the Holy of Holies, the very throne
of God.

If we had a hat like Aaron's, we'd be very careful about the way
we lived. We couldn't wear a hat saying HOLINESS TO THE LORD and
do some of the things we do or say some of the things we say.
Would I wear a hat like that to the office or to the bowling alley or
when I'm out of town? Would I even wear it to church? Somebody
might say, "Look who's wearing the hat."

Aaron knew when he wore it that he was making an announcement to other people, but he also knew when he wore it that the
people were looking not only at the inscription; they were looking at
him. There aren't very many of us who could preen in front of
others and ask, "How do you like my hat?" Wearing such a hat
would revolutionize our behavior. Aaron wore that hat with its inscription and was conscious that he was doing it.

As priests of God, every believer wears that inscription, too. Unfortunately some of us have forgotten that we're wearing it.

Prayer: O God, engrave HOLINESS TO THE LORD *on my heart so that,
unlike a hat, I can't put it off and on.*

ঽ SEPTEMBER 2 ৬

IT HAPPENED AGAIN

Yet his sons did not walk in his ways, but turned aside after gain; they took bribes and perverted justice.

1 Samuel 8:3

It happened again! The checkbook is unbalanced. I thought my subtraction was wrong, but it wasn't. I thought there would be fewer bills this month; there weren't.

This is when temptation starts. There are all kinds of schemes I hear about for getting some money. They're legal, but they push greed. I'm asked by promoters of this program or that one if I would like to increase my income to meet my wants. No one has ever asked me if I would like to reduce my wants to match my income. I get brochures in the mail, telling me that if I'm not taking advantage of this tax break or that loophole, or if I don't attend a certain lecture on finances, investments, and so on, I'm losing money.

Samuel's sons must have had similar temptations. They were judges in Israel; their paychecks should have been adequate. But apparently their wants were greater than their salaries, so they "turned aside after gain." Aside from what? They turned aside from the ways of discipline, the ways of obedience, the ways of faithfulness to God. They turned from all that their father had taught them, and they went after money. They turned aside.

It is a simple thing to turn aside. I can do it while hardly knowing I have made a turn. It doesn't have to be a sharp turn, or even a gradual curve, just a little bit at a time. For Samuel's sons, it probably started simply enough. Maybe, like me, they looked at their checkbooks and exclaimed, "It happened again!"

Prayer: Lord, in my head I know the danger of the love of money. Keep me from turning aside to go after it.

❧ SEPTEMBER 3 ❧

BAGELS AND CREAM CHEESE

Therefore let us keep the feast, not with old leaven, neither
with the leaven of malice and wickedness; but with the un-
leavened bread of sincerity and truth.

1 Corinthians 5:8 KJV

What I wanted, really had a craving for, was a cheese omelet. Instead I got one bagel and a small package of cream cheese. But I
couldn't call for a waiter or complain to the cook. I was 32,000 feet
in the air, on a flight to Chicago. I had two choices: eat the bagel or
don't eat the bagel. And as my mother always taught me, "If you're
hungry, you'll eat it."

Mother was right. And God says the same thing about His truth.
"If you are hungry, you'll eat it."

Sounds like His truth is food, doesn't it? It is!

It's needed—you can't live without it.

It's good to the taste—a pleasant experience.

It's easy on the digestion—unless you are angry with God.

It supplies all the essential daily requirements for health.

But if a person doesn't want God's truth, he doesn't have to take
it. No one will force it down his throat. He can go without. But if he
does refuse, he'll be weak, then sick, and eventually starve to death.

I ate the bagel.

*Prayer: Lord, Your Word is enjoyable every day, and Your truth feeds
me.*

❧ SEPTEMBER 4 ❧

GOOD-BYE

So therefore, whoever of you does not renounce all that he
has cannot be my disciple.

Luke 14:33

Farewells are hard. It's difficult to say good-bye. We prolong it—
a few more loving words, one last hug, another backward glance
even as we walk away.

That's also the way it is when we do what Jesus said: "So therefore, whoever of you does not renounce [literally, "say farewell to"] all that he has cannot be my disciple."

That's difficult to do. The possessions that we hug closest are hardest to let go. And even when we make up our minds that we have to leave them behind, we still take one or two more backward glances, trying by sheer willpower to pull our hearts away.

Jesus said that treasure and heart are always in the same place (*see* Matthew 6:21). Discipleship is a love matter as much as a mind matter. If my mind is on my possessions, it won't be on Jesus. God and mammon don't go together.

But it's the farewell that is so hard. It's wrenching. And most of the time it isn't until we've moved on down the road that our thoughts begin to move from what we left behind to what is ahead.

Sooner or later everyone who is serious about Jesus will have to look at his watch and announce to himself as much as to anyone else: "It's getting late, and I've got to get going. I guess it's time to say good-bye."

Prayer: Lord, there are things that come between us. Please help me to do what I know I must do—say farewell.

SEPTEMBER 5

SING OF IT

... A pleasant vineyard, sing of it! I, the Lord, am its keeper; every moment I water it. Lest any one harm it, I guard it night and day.

Isaiah 27:2, 3

Sometimes only a song will express what God is doing and giving.

He has a pleasant vineyard in mind, and like a concerned vinedresser, He tenderly cares for the plants in that vineyard, helping them to grow and flourish.

They don't have to struggle for water, like plants in a desert. He waters them.

No one will come in and pull them up and throw them on the mulch pile or tread them down. It's His vineyard, and He guards it day and night.

It isn't hard to make the mental jump from vines and vineyards to what He is really talking about. He has used the illustration of vines, vineyards, and vinedressers in other places in the Bible.

We know what He means; He's talking about us.
And because we know, we don't need a reminder to "sing of it."
We will!

*Prayer: When You say You will keep Your vineyard, I'm so glad You
are speaking about me.*

❧ SEPTEMBER 6 ❧
GOD'S BATTLE

If, when evil cometh upon us, as the sword, judgment, or
pestilence, or famine, we stand before this house, and in
thy presence, (for thy name is in this house,) and cry unto
thee in our affliction, then thou wilt hear and help.

2 Chronicles 20:9 KJV

Jehoshaphat and the people of Judah were in trouble. They were
facing their enemy.

All the people gathered with Jehoshaphat to pray. They stood,
and Jehoshaphat did the praying. Even the children were there,
perhaps not understanding, but knowing that their parents were
trusting God.

Jehoshaphat rehearsed the power of God—that He is the God of
heaven, that He rules all nations, that He had driven out people before—and on the basis of that was able to say, "We stand before
You, respecting Your name and Your presence, and cry to You, for
You will hear and You will help."

He wasn't pleading so much as he was making a statement. Why?
Because his wasn't a "hope so" religion. He knew God, and he
knew what God had promised. He knew what God had done before. His was a statement based on trust.

The answer came. They didn't have to fight; it was God's battle.
They could stand still and see the salvation of the Lord.

It may be that a lot of our personal and corporate fear is due to
our not understanding who God is, what He has done in the past,
and what He is able to do now.

*Prayer: Lord, I know that You don't want me to be fearful and dis-
mayed. You want me to have the courage and boldness of a Jehoshaphat. Thank You for these Old Testament leaders who knew what
following and obeying You means.*

SEPTEMBER 7
CLEVER!

Then the devil took him to the holy city, and set him on the pinnacle of the temple, and said to him, "If you are the Son of God, throw yourself down; for it is written, 'He will give his angels charge of you,' and 'On their hands they will bear you up, lest you strike your foot against a stone.' "

Matthew 4:5, 6

Satan was with Jesus when he quoted God's promise, and he may do the same when he is with us. He may use the Bible, particularly an obscure text, if it will appeal to our wants. It doesn't have to sway others—just us. He's good at "customizing" the Word.

But Jesus knew what was going on. This ruse of Satan's doesn't work when someone pays attention to all of Scripture. Jesus wasn't caught; we don't have to be caught either.

One nice thing about this whole business—the pledge of God must be pretty special. Why else would Satan point it out?

He can't change God's promises, and if we stay with the declarations as God gives them, we won't be lured away from either the promise or the Promise Giver.

Satan must be counting on my being a little weak or careless with God's Word.

He's clever!

Prayer: Help me to stay with Your declarations. Even Satan must know how powerful they are; he keeps trying to twist them in my mind.

SEPTEMBER 8
ACCOMMODATION

Demas hath forsaken me, having loved this present world. . . .

2 Timothy 4:10 KJV

I've thought about it constantly; it has played like a recording, over and over in my brain. Dr. Francis A. Schaeffer ended a challenging message with the words, "Accommodation leads to accommodation, which leads to accommodation." I haven't been able to escape those words. A gradual giving in, a little bit of surrender, leads to more and more of the same. It happens in the accommodation of morals, ethics, trust, human relationships, responsibility, faithfulness, discipline ... it happens in every dimension of life.

We can all talk to other people about their accommodations, the problem they have of adjusting, adapting, making to fit. But other people are not where the problem lies. The way to overcome accommodation is for each of us to overcome accommodation in our own lives. For me to do that means I have to work at stopping the accommodation of what is already obvious to me, what I already know about, what doesn't have to be pointed out, what my heart and mind tell me are already accommodations in my life. Then, yielding that accommodation to God and promising to stand firm by His strength given, I can depend on God not only to help me with that accommodation, but reveal other accommodations that are crippling as well. He will show them to me one at a time as I prove by my actions that I am serious about doing something about them.

The rest of the world, even the Christian world, may or may not follow my actions. Some will, many will not. But that doesn't matter. In my life, accommodation started with me; and if it is ever to be broken, it has to be broken in me. That's where accommodation has to stop—with me. Before God I am responsible for me—and you are responsible for you.

Accommodation leads to accommodation, which leads to accommodation, but only because a first accommodation was permitted. It started sometime, someplace. It can end that way, too.

Prayer: Dear Father, I know where the problem of accommodation begins, and You do, too. Help me to stop it when it first starts.

 SEPTEMBER 9

HEADLINES

He who is steadfast in righteousness will live, but he who pursues evil will die.

Proverbs 11:19

Maybe God hasn't been reading the newspapers!
Because if He has, why does He say some of those things in the

Bible: "He who is steadfast in righteousness will live, but he who pursues evil will die"?

If it were my Bible, I'd have phrased it the other way around: Crime pays; honesty doesn't.

At least it seems that way.

Of course the verse does look a little different when I look at it in context. Verse 18 says, "A wicked man earns deceptive wages, but one who sows righteousness gets a sure reward."

"Deceptive wages"—they look good, feel good in the hand, but they won't buy anything. I can work for wicked wages, and they are deceptive, or I can be given "a sure reward."

No wonder God is so definite about His statements. I guess since the rewards are His to give, He has a right to be.

Maybe He has been reading the newspapers. Maybe He does know about those who seem to be getting the riches.

Maybe it doesn't matter.

He knows a whole lot more than today's newspaper headlines. He knows tomorrow's.

Prayer: Thank You, Father, that my world and the headlines I read don't limit You. You know much more.

☙ SEPTEMBER 10 ☙

MY NAME ISN'T MARTHA, BUT ...

"Martha, Martha, you are anxious and troubled about many things; one thing is needful. Mary has chosen the good portion, which shall not be taken away from her."
Luke 10:41, 42

One of my employees wanted a few minutes to talk with me. I started to ask, "Can it wait?" when I caught myself and stopped what I was doing to listen.

It was a busy day, with work piling up faster than I could deal with it. It seems to be that way a lot lately.

Later, I thought of Martha and Mary and the comments of Jesus. "Martha, Martha, you are anxious and troubled about many things." Me too!

I need two things—quiet time with God and quality time with people. If Martha had made a wrong priority choice by putting her work first, so do I when I put my work ahead of people and God.

I've found that if I work a little later after employees leave, I start to catch up; and by getting up a little earlier each morning, I can have the time with God I need so desperately.

My name isn't Martha, but as usually happens when I read Scripture, my name goes in. And when it does, I can hear Jesus calling me by name and saying, "You are anxious and troubled about many things."

Being troubled wasn't good for Martha, and it isn't good for me.

Prayer: Please, Lord, help me today to get my priorities straight.

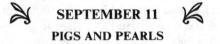

SEPTEMBER 11

PIGS AND PEARLS

Give not that which is holy unto the dogs, neither cast ye your pearls before swine, lest they trample them under their feet, and turn again and rend you.

Matthew 7:6 KJV

Pigs don't always appreciate having company. After church one Sunday we were invited to a farm family's home for dinner. While we were waiting for dinner, one of the youngsters asked us to go out and look at his pigs, so we did. As we stood along by the fence, a big old sow came wallowing over to the side of the fence and let out a terrific sneeze, all over my wife's leg. There she stood in her Sunday dress, with pig sneeze from ankle to knee. We decided the pig wasn't happy about our visit.

Jesus understood something about pigs, and He warned about throwing pearls to pigs. We want everyone to have the Gospel and will go anyplace with the good news, no matter how dangerous or shabby or evil. But discernment says that not everyone is receptive, nor will everyone know how to handle what we offer. If a pig doesn't know what a pearl is, he won't know what he's being offered. If a person doesn't know what a pearl is, there's no point in offering him one either. We need to go, we need to ask, no one should be ignored; all are of value to God. But there's no point in having them trample the pearl or sneeze on you. There are too many others longing to have the pearl.

Prayer: This is hard for me, Lord. I want everyone to hear, yet I know that there are good and bad investments to be made for the Gospel. Help me to know what I must do.

SEPTEMBER 12

DRIFT

... For what fellowship hath righteousness with unrighteousness? and what communion hath light with darkness?

2 Corinthians 6:14 KJV

The house was beautiful to look at, but it had a problem. When the main structure was built, the contractor gave it a double foundation, sending the footers down to rock. He did it because the land sloped away into a swampy area. It was reclaimed drainage land. Later, when a garage was added, it was given only a normal depth of footers, not down to rock. Then an attractive breezeway was built, connecting the house and garage. It looked very nice.

But as the years went by the garage slowly began to drift inch by inch toward the backyard, pulling the breezeway with it, separating it with ever-widening cracks from the house. Finally, a contractor had to be called in to take out the breezeway, separating the house from the garage, so that the slipping garage wouldn't pull the house with it.

There are people who look good, attractive, attached to the church with its foundation—but they don't have a foundation. They don't go down to the Rock. When they start slipping backwards, they can pull us with them. Sooner or later, unless the slippage stops, the part without foundation is going to have to be cut loose. Separation is painful, but sometimes it has to be.

Prayer: Lord, help me to encourage my friends to build their lives not just on morality and goodness but on the Rock, Christ Jesus.

SEPTEMBER 13

THERE'S HIS FLAG

So shall they fear the name of the Lord from the west, and his glory from the rising of the sun. When the enemy shall come in like a flood, the Spirit of the Lord shall lift up a standard against him.

Isaiah 59:19 KJV

And I thought I was alone!
"When the enemy shall come in like a flood, the Spirit of the Lord shall lift up a standard against him."

That's exactly what Satan is like, too—an enemy who comes in like a flood. He's like a wall of water pouring down, inundating. Sometimes it's all I can do to grab for air; survival is everything. It's a victory just to make it.

But the standard of God—over against the enemy—tells me a whole lot more than that God will erect a wall or dike or dam against Satan or even provide a boat to escape. God Himself is there, right in the middle of the whole struggle.

Like the admiral's flag above a churning, pitched battle, the standard is up where I can see it—over against my enemy.

What is God planning? What force is He marshaling, what maneuver?

I don't know. But I can see the flag.

And I know that Satan can see it, too.

Prayer: Your standard is always there. Help me to keep my eye on it, even in the battles.

 SEPTEMBER 14

ALONE?

I watch, and am as a sparrow alone upon the house top.
                                                Psalm 102:7 KJV

She was completing her studies at the University of British Columbia, preparing to go home to China, when she attended the Billy Graham Crusade in Vancouver. She heard the Gospel message, opened her heart to Christ, and by faith received Jesus as her personal Savior. She told the counselor who explained the way of salvation, "So far as I know, when I go home I will be the only one in my community who is a Christian."

She is going to be lonely. Many people are. They can identify with the prayer of the overwhelmed, the afflicted, the one pouring out his heart before God: "I watch, and am as a sparrow alone upon the house top." God may lead that young woman to other Christians. The Gospel is spreading throughout China. But it may be years, because there are so many people. Until she finds others, she'll struggle alone, surrounded by millions who do not understand.

But in another sense she is not alone even now, anymore than we are. She has the Holy Spirit—her Comforter, her Guide. She has the assurance, "I will never leave you or forsake you." And sooner or later she will find this verse about the sparrow alone, and she'll find another about the sparrow that Jesus described. She'll discover what Ethel Waters discovered and sang about with deep conviction—"His Eye Is on the Sparrow"—and she'll learn to depend on that.

Prayer: Father, when I think that I am all alone, help me to understand that I'm not.

 SEPTEMBER 15

HE KNEW THAT

But seek first his kingdom and his righteousness, and all these things shall be yours as well.

Matthew 6:33

I like "things"—the things He warned us not to be anxious about: the eat-and-drink things, the what-you-shall-put-on things.
Maybe that's why He made a point of talking about it.
Clothes get frayed—or even worse, they go out of style.
Food spoils, and ready or not, my stomach won't retain it.
But the Kingdom doesn't fray or spoil. Neither does His righteousness.
He doesn't want me to go hungry or naked. He'll give those things if I need them. But I'd better not be seeking them first, because when I'm through grabbing, I won't have anything anyway.
He wants me to have what lasts—forever. That's His Kingdom and His righteousness.
"Seek first."
If I do, there won't be any time left to seek the seconds, which is all right because that's the part He adds anyway—the "all these things."
It works out when I seek the "first." He knew it would.
And there's a plus; I'm happiest doing it His way.
He knew that, too.

Prayer: Thank You for knowing more about me than I do, and adding "all these things."

SEPTEMBER 16

BUT I'M DIFFERENT

If any one says, "I love God," and hates his brother, he is a
liar; for he who does not love his brother whom he has
seen, cannot love God whom he has not seen.

1 John 4:20

People!

They pull at me, push at me, make demands—little people, old
people, neighbor people, people who are associates in business—all
made in the image of God.

Interrupting people—made in the image of God.

Incapable people—made in the image of God.

Whining people—made in the image of God.

Boorish people—made in the image of God.

Lazy people—made in the image of God.

Snappish, argumentative, critical, nasty people—made in the
image of God.

John had them around him, too, and makes a statement that I'd
prefer to avoid. "He who does not love his brother whom he has
seen, cannot love God whom he has not seen."

John's statement has me cornered. But I'm glad other people
don't face the dilemma I face, because surely I am easy for others to
love. I can't think of any reason why they wouldn't.

*Prayer: Lord, it is so easy to be a hypocrite and so hard to obey You.
Please help me.*

SEPTEMBER 17

HELPERS

Jesus saith unto them, Bring of the fish which ye have now
caught.

John 21:10 KJV

It always takes longer to cut the grass or wash the car when you
have a four-year-old helping you. But at times like that speed is not
important. What is important is that the four-year-old gets to be a
helper.

In a way Jesus must have had that in mind when He called to the disciples in the boat, "Children, have you any meat?" (*see* v. 5). When they replied, "No," He told them where to cast their net. They did, and brought in more fish than their nets could hold. When they got to shore, Jesus already had fish cooking for them. But He invited them to bring their fish, too. He didn't need their fish; He was inviting them to participate even though He had already provided enough fish for them, too. The disciples shared in both the hauling in and the meal. They had pride in helping.

Jesus does that. He doesn't really need our help, but like four-year-olds helping with the lawnmower, He knows what we need.

Prayer: Lord, You could do it all Yourself, yet You've invited me to participate with You in life and ministry.

❧ SEPTEMBER 18 ❧
GOLD DOESN'T JUST HAPPEN

"And I will put this third into the fire, and refine them as one refines silver, and test them as gold is tested. They will call on my name, and I will answer them. I will say, 'They are my people'; and they will say, 'The Lord is my God.' "

Zechariah 13:9

This promise isn't for everyone.

But there is no guesswork about it; the promise is for exactly one-third. The other two-thirds will be cut off. They will perish. The Prophet Zechariah says so.

And there are reasons.

But even for the one-third remaining, what happens won't be easy. It won't be pleasant.

"And I will put this third into the fire, and refine them as one refines silver, and test them as gold is tested. . . ."

It seems to be necessary that this happen. Maybe people tend to brag: "I'm among the select one-third."

Or maybe some impurities need burning off. That's what God says will happen.

But, after refining and testing: "They will call on my name, and I will answer them. I will say, 'They are my people'; and they will say, 'The Lord is my God.' "

Not many people say, "The Lord is my God," and even among that one-third there will have to be some refining before they do. Refined silver and pure gold don't just happen. That's why they are so precious. There isn't a lot of either.

Prayer: Lord, I'd rather be put through the fire, if that's what it takes to make me pure.

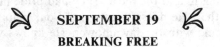

SEPTEMBER 19

BREAKING FREE

Behold, I am weighted down beneath you As a wagon is weighted down when filled with sheaves.

Amos 2:13 NAS

We all know the feeling. We've experienced it. I've felt it most when riding buses and trains in Asia: the masses of people pushing and crowding in so that there is hardly space to breathe. I've felt the growing pressure of wanting to get out, to stretch, to run.

That's a feeling that unbelievers have about belonging to God: they feel it will be so confining, oppressive. What they don't realize is that the oppression they feel is the oppression of their own guilt and sin.

Salvation is just the opposite to what the unbeliever thinks. Salvation is liberation. It is a breaking free from the bondage and the confinements and the oppression, the claustrophobic sin that grips the mind, the soul. It is a breaking free as one is free when he runs with arms outstretched along a beach, with the breeze blowing in off the ocean. That's salvation—to be liberated. It is becoming all that God designed us to be—free in the openness of God.

There are so many who are pressed down as a cart full of sheaves. And to understand, all we need do is think about the times when we have felt suffocated. Then we eagerly want to go to them, throw open the windows, fold back the doors, seek to open up their lives to God's redeeming life, and say to them, "Come out into the openness of Christ and live!"

Prayer: Lord, when I feel suffocated temporarily, give me compassion for those who are suffocating all the time and don't yet know how to get their windows open.

❧ SEPTEMBER 20 ❧

BEGGARS BY THE SIDE OF THE ROAD

... Lord, that I may receive my sight.

Luke 18:41 KJV

The Greek text is more emphatic. "Pity me ... that I may see again."

Here was a man who sometime in his life must have had sight, and wanted it again. So Jesus did what only Jesus can do—He gave him back his sight.

I've met people like that, people who have the same condition, only they have it spiritually. They start out with spiritual sight, trusting Christ by faith, seeing Him. Then something happens. They slowly lose their sight. Self interests take them away from Christian fellowship, from learning the Word; prayer becomes occasional. Then one day, like the man who couldn't see anymore, they find themselves spiritually poverty stricken, sitting by the road, beggars without any means of sustaining themselves, their spiritual eye muscles not working anymore.

For some reason, this loss of spiritual eyesight often starts to happen in the late teens, with realization of blindness coming only after twenty or thirty years of stumbling around. Finally, in mid-life, many start to realize what is wrong and, like the man by the roadside, at last cry out in desperation, "Pity me ... that I may see again."

But not all. There are people who continue to see with their physical eyes but not with their spiritual eyes. They sit by the road, poor beggars missing life. Though they have memories of the sight they once had, they take pride that they aren't "seeing" as they did when they were children. They boast that they outgrew what they had in their youth.

The roads are littered with sophisticated, adult, proud, blind beggars.

Prayer: Lord, may I be alert to those who may be ready to cry out to see again so I may help bring them back to You.

SEPTEMBER 21

I'D BE EMBARRASSED!

For it stands in scripture: "Behold, I am laying in Zion a stone, a cornerstone chosen and precious, and he who believes in him will not be put to shame."

1 Peter 2:6

No shame?

None at all?

Not even a little bit embarrassed?

People embarrass me sometimes, Often I embarrass myself.

How come God is never embarrassed like that? "Take a look," He says. "Go ahead and examine the cornerstone that I'm laying."

There are no soft spots to crumble, no pits or breaks, no offhand, "Oh, well, that's close enough."

There's no sliding by the code on this one.

God has a selected, chosen Cornerstone, examined and graded. And He says if I use His cornerstone to build on (build what I am, what I feel, what I think, what I am becoming), I will not be put to shame.

But what will I do with this patched and slightly crumbled building that I've got already?

Start over?

I'd be embarrassed!

Prayer: Give me the courage to admit that what I've built myself won't last, so that I'll start again, building on You.

SEPTEMBER 22

LIFE IS ORDINARY

Ye stand this day all of you before the Lord your God; your captains of your tribes, your elders, and your officers, with all the men of Israel.

Deuteronomy 29:10 KJV

It was an unusual week. On Saturday a geologist in Alaska took me in his small plane to see the glaciers. He would drop the plane down along those icy cliffs into the valleys, where he would point out moose and occasionally a trapper's cabin tucked away in the tree line. But mostly there was nothing but ice and snow and the reflecting sun. Then he put the plane down on a frozen lake. It was absolutely still, not a sound, and the air was crystal clear. It was indeed virgin land, practically untouched since creation.

One week later my wife and I were in Israel on a twenty-fifth-wedding-anniversary trip. Saturday found us on top of Masada, overlooking the Dead Sea. Behind us was barren desert, hot—the opposite to the Alaskan glaciers. We stood there remembering people who had been there many, many centuries before. Here was a land where history was being written before most of the known world was even discovered.

That was an unusual week, not ordinary. But most of life is ordinary. The days move into weeks, the weeks into months, then years, with nothing new or different or exciting happening. We get up in the morning, not really expecting the day to be much different from all the days that have gone before. Life is, as one writer put it, so everyday.

But just as it was true for God's people in Israel, it is true for us now: "Ye stand this day all of you before the Lord your God." We stand every day before God. He sees everything that we do; we are accountable to Him; we walk with Him, even if the most exciting thing we do is make a weekly trip to the corner Laundromat.

Prayer: Lord, help me to understand that my days are measured not by what I do, see, or experience, but by the fact that every day I stand before You.

SEPTEMBER 23

MISTAKE?

"And I will set up over them one shepherd, my servant David, and he shall feed them: he shall feed them and be their shepherd. And I, the Lord, will be their God, and my servant David shall be prince among them; I, the Lord, have spoken."

Ezekiel 34:23, 24

There must be some mistake in the Bible. Ezekiel talks about David, but David had been dead for centuries.

He speaks of one shepherd, but that means one flock. The kingdoms were divided after the time of David's son Solomon. Everybody knows that.

It has to be a mistake.

You have to give Ezekiel high marks for boldness, though. Either that or he was confused. Poor Ezekiel. He attributes these statements to a direct speech of God—that takes nerve. Ezekiel should have known he couldn't get away with that.

David was God's man; God knew David and knew when he died. Ezekiel might be able to tell us some story about David, but he can't tell that same story to God.

Unless he means more than that—like maybe a picture statement about another David.

But that's hard to believe.

One shepherd?

A prince?

Standing in such a position that the Lord God could be God of those sheep while the shepherd is right there feeding them, close enough to the sheep to feed them, yet also close enough to Almighty God to be His servant shepherd?

If not David, then who is it?

Ezekiel must be mixed up.

Prayer: O Lord, how wonderful your truths are. Thank You for prophecy that points to Christ.

SEPTEMBER 24

COOKING IS A HIGH CALLING

And Samuel said to the cook, "Bring the portion I gave you, of which I said to you, 'Put it aside.'"
1 Samuel 9:23

Cooking is not one of my strengths. If I didn't have a wife to look after me, I'd probably starve to death. I can make toast in the morning, and this morning the toast actually popped up out of the toaster before the smoke alarm went off.

Jesus must have been a good cook. He prepared fish and bread for the disciples along the Sea of Galilee. I've eaten fish there several times and thought about Jesus being a good cook. He must have learned from his mother, which is a good thing for every young boy to do.

Samuel had a cook, too, the right person to prepare the leg (probably a leg of lamb) as one of the events preceding Saul's anointing as king. The leg was especially set aside, probably specially cooked.

Cooking is a high calling, a sacred work in the Old Testament, a work practiced by Jesus in the New Testament, and today those who are able to cook have a way of bringing happiness to others.

Someday I'm going to expand my culinary expertise beyond the making of toast, but first I have to figure out how to disengage the smoke detector.

Prayer: Father, I know that nothing is mundane or ordinary or everyday. Thank You for those who know how to express their love through cooking.

❧ SEPTEMBER 25 ❧

SCARY!

> For my thoughts are not your thoughts, neither are your ways my ways, says the Lord.
>
> Isaiah 55:8

It has always been that way.

In creation God spoke, and it was; the word became the fact.

In redemption the Word became flesh. The Logos, the manifestation of God, became Jesus.

And when God speaks His message to us, it's more than words written; life is there in the words themselves.

Scary?

It is to us who are used to saying things that people only half listen to. The word we speak has nothing in itself, only in what it stimulates in the hearer.

We have no human measure of the "God speaks" reality. We don't understand. We never will.

"For my thoughts are not your thoughts, neither are your ways my ways, says the Lord. For as the heavens are higher than the earth, so are my ways higher than your ways and my thoughts than your thoughts.

"For as the rain and the snow come down from heaven, and return not thither but water the earth, making it bring forth and sprout, giving seed to the sower and bread to the eater, so shall my word be that goes forth from my mouth; it shall not return to me empty, but it shall accomplish that which I purpose, and prosper in the thing for which I sent it" (Isaiah 55:8–11).

When God speaks, His word has permanence. What He says will be, will, in fact, *be.*

Whether it's a blessing or a judgment, a command or a promise, when He speaks, that Word will not return empty. His Word will have its intended effect.

That's not scary.

That's exciting!

Prayer: You will do exactly as You say. Now help me to build my life on Your Word.

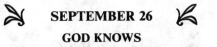

SEPTEMBER 26
GOD KNOWS

But the very hairs of your head are all numbered.

Matthew 10:30 KJV

Jesus said the very hairs of our heads are all numbered, indicating God's concern and care for us. It's getting easier and easier for God to measure His care for me; there are fewer hairs to count.

The point is, He knows me. He knows every hair, even the ones I've lost. He knows everything inside my mind, my heart, what's happening to me. He knows everything that happens to me. There are no events, circumstances, surprises in my life that are unanticipated or unknown to Him. That's a comfort. I can face each day knowing that He knows what that day holds for me. I can go into the day with peace.

So each morning as I pick up my hairbrush and look in the mirror, I'm reminded "God cares about you. He knows everything there is to know about you"—even the hairs that stay on the brush.

Prayer: Thank You, Lord, for caring about me so much. There isn't a detail in my life or a hair on my head that You don't know about.

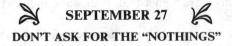

SEPTEMBER 27
DON'T ASK FOR THE "NOTHINGS"

Take delight in the Lord, and he will give you the desires of your heart.

Psalm 37:4

Backward!

That's my problem. I've been doing it backward.

God says in the Bible, "Take delight in the Lord and he will give you the desires of your heart" (Psalm 37:4).

My "corrected" version reads: "Take delight in the desires of your heart and try to have God, too."

That's more than a perversion of Scripture; that's blasphemy!

For most people it's the same. Things that I buy are a delight, for a couple of days; work is a delight, if the promotion comes; and even church is a delight, if I can come away with that nice warm glow that a preacher or a choir is able to generate in me.

And then there's God. He's God not because He does something for me, or promises anything in the future, but just because He is God!

"Take delight in the Lord," not in what He offers, not in what He does, not for His miracles, not even for some nice "religious" feeling, but because He *is*, and to know Him is to live in delight of Him.

"Take delight in the Lord, and he will give you the desires of your heart." Well, the desire of my heart is a new car. I've been praying about it for a long time, and surely God knows that I need it. Mine is the cheapest model in the church parking lot, and I am uncomfortable about going to church in it, and God knows that I can't honor and praise His holy name in church if I'm uncomfortable. . . .

Hold it, there's more!

"And he will give you the desires of your heart." To know Him is to delight in Him and to delight in Him is to desire more of Him. He will give you the desire of your heart—more of Himself.

Delight gives more desire, and desire fulfilled is more to delight in. Don't mess that up by breaking in with the "gimmes." What if just once God did what you asked and instead of Himself, He gave you things?

See!

A lot of nothing, isn't it?

Prayer: Lord, what I really want and really need is more of You.

SEPTEMBER 28
FOLLOW THE MAP

He that followeth after righteousness and mercy findeth
life, righteousness, and honour.

Proverbs 21:21 KJV

Stories about buried treasure make exciting reading. There is that
lure—where will the spot be? What will the cache reveal? To get
there, the hero or heroine has to follow details, markings on paper,
find huge boulders or trees or a river. But it's worth following the
map.

It's worth following the map in the Christian life, too, because
life, righteousness, and honor are there to be found. God said so.
There's a map, and the map to follow is righteousness and mercy.

Righteousness is available. Jesus Christ makes us "right" with
God. Scripture tells us that we can be clothed in His righteousness—not our own, His. If we follow the righteousness in Christ and
exhibit the mercy in Christ, both of which are possible because ". . .
not I, but Christ liveth in me . . ." (Galatians 2:20 KJV), there is
waiting for us life, righteousness, and honor. Life, abundant life,
eternal life. Righteousness, ". . . the measure of the stature of the
fulness of Christ" (Ephesians 4:13 KJV). And honor, "If any man
serve me, . . . him will my Father honour" (John 12:26 KJV).

God gives us the map, and He gives us the treasure.

*Prayer: Thank You, Lord, for offering life, righteousness, and honor
for me to find and keep and enjoy.*

SEPTEMBER 29
FIVE O'CLOCK SHADOW

Thrice was I beaten with rods, once was I stoned, thrice I
suffered shipwreck, a night and a day I have been in the
deep.

2 Corinthians 11:25 KJV

Every morning I stand looking blurry eyed into the mirror, then
put my razor to my face and start working on the stubble. What a
boring job! And I know it's going to be the same the next morning,

and the same the next. If I'm going out in the evening, I will have to do it again, because my five o'clock shadow can't tell time and usually shows up shortly after noon. So I mumble as I shave, lamenting about how much I "suffer."

But then my mind drifts to a man I met whose face had been burned. He doesn't have to shave. There is no hair on his face. In fact, the doctors had to replace his eyebrows to give him as much of a normal appearance as they could. And I think of a man I saw in the hospital. He was suffering from a paralyzing stroke. People came in from time to time to shave him; he couldn't do it himself. And there is a blind man I know who always shaves but doesn't look in the mirror to see what he's doing. Any of these men would, I think, gladly exchange their lot in life for my "burden." All three would like to stand in front of the mirror every morning and shave. I think for each of them it would be a time of rejoicing and praising God.

Prayer: Father, I've had an easy life, and I take it for granted. Help me to stop feeling sorry for myself.

⨖ SEPTEMBER 30 ⨖
HE'S RAKING MY YARD

O God, thou knowest my foolishness; and my sins are not hid from thee.

Psalm 69:5 KJV

First there is one; that's easy to take care of. Then two and three. Still no problem. Then seemingly all at once the falling autumn leaves cover my yard.

God says sin is like that, and it is. Sin is hardly noticeable at first, not too hard to "pick up," removing it from sight. Even more sin, if I move fast enough, can be kept from littering my life. But not for long. Soon I'm inundated, and everyone sees what is in my life, which, like what is in my yard, can't be hidden.

"My sins are not hid from thee." The psalmist knew it. We know it, too. Like leaves on the ground, every sin is spread out before Him. That's why David also prayed, "Hide thy face from my sins, and blot out all mine iniquities" (Psalm 51:9 KJV). God can do that, and God will, turning His face and seeing sin no more. David asked one more thing: "Create in me a clean heart, O God; and renew a right spirit within me" (Psalm 51:10 KJV).

Christ came from the Father to do that, and He does do it for any who will ask.

David knew how much sin he had, and even if he didn't know, someone would have told him. Sin, like leaves, can't be disguised. And as in raking leaves, no rake of mine will ever get all the sin. When God hides His face from sin, He isn't pretending it's gone; He is weeping for the One who is raking my yard in my place.

Prayer: Thank You for providing Another to do for me what I could not do for myself.

❧ OCTOBER 1 ❧
WE'RE ADOPTED

For all who are led by the Spirit of God are sons of God.
Romans 8:14

Politicians are good at it; so are other public speakers.

They wind up and proclaim with great authority and a touch of religious fervor: "After all, we're all God's children."

The only thing wrong with that is it isn't true.

God wants us as children, and through Jesus Christ it is possible to be adopted as children, but we are not all God's children: "For all who are led by the Spirit of God are sons of God. For you did not receive the spirit of slavery to fall back into fear, but you have received the spirit of sonship. When we cry, 'Abba! Father!' it is the Spirit himself bearing witness with our spirit that we are children of God" (Romans 8:14–16).

And when we become children by adoption, we also become heirs: "So through God you are no longer a slave but a son, and if a son then an heir" (Galatians 4:7).

Why do speakers say things that aren't true when they could just as easily tell the truth? Think of the response.

What they mean to say, of course, is, "We are all God's creation," and that's true. We are created by God and breathed into by God (made a living soul), so we are all equal, which is the point that they want to make.

But to be children, well, John explains that: "But to all who received him, who believed in his name, he gave power to become children of God" (John 1:12).

Instead of saying, "We are all God's children," which is not what

God says, think what it would mean to people if we said: "We are all adoptable, and God wants us in His family."

But it seems that there will always be those who will go on saying, "We're all God's children."

Imagine telling God who His children are.

He's the Father; He ought to know.

Prayer: You provided the way into Your family, Lord. Help me to show that way to others.

OCTOBER 2

SECURITY

For when they shall say, Peace and safety; then sudden destruction cometh upon them, as travail upon a woman with child; and they shall not escape.

1 Thessalonians 5:3 KJV

As I turned onto the freeway, I thought I noticed smoke or steam coming out from under the hood. It couldn't be. But it was! And as I drove along, more and more of what appeared to be smoke came billowing out around the car. I had just had a gasket replaced, and my first thought was that oil was spilling out; the car was on fire!

I headed for the next exit on the freeway, thinking I'd never get there, but I did get off, with traffic parting around to let me through. I pulled into a gasoline station and jumped out of the car. It wasn't oil; it was a broken hose, spilling antifreeze all over the hot motor. I never expected that, because just the week before a mechanic had checked all the hoses and pronounced them sound. I thought I was secure, that all was well.

But I realized, as the mechanic replaced the hose and the fluid, that nothing is certain. Whether with a car or in life, we rest in our own idea of security; then suddenly destruction comes upon us.

There is only one security, and that's the security of knowing and belonging to the One who is Himself the Source of all security. Nothing else is certain, no matter what mechanics or other people say.

Prayer: Thank You, Lord, that You are my security. Nothing else in this life is certain.

❧ OCTOBER 3 ❧
WANT ADS

And the glory of the Lord shall be revealed. . . .

Isaiah 40:5

It came to him like a job description.

Isaiah had explained it, and John the Baptist knew with the spiritual insight that God gives that this was exactly what he was to do for Jesus.

"In the wilderness prepare the way of the Lord, make straight in the desert a highway for our God. Every valley shall be lifted up, and every mountain and hill be made low; the uneven ground shall become level, and the rough places a plain. And the glory of the Lord shall be revealed . . ."(Isaiah 40:3–5).

Maybe it's a job description for you, too?

When was the last time you asked about it?

There are spiritual roads that need straightening, valleys of confusion that need filling in, heights of conflict that need grading, to prepare a people for the Savior and the revealed "glory of the Lord."

We think of ourselves as generating a witness; yet the witness to Christ that we have comes from the gentle prodding of God's Spirit in the inner soul. Our calling, like John's, is to be "way preparers."

John had a specific job to do and died a horrible death for his faithfulness in doing it. Our job description—leveling, building up, filling in for Jesus—may also end in an inglorious, even painful way.

But that doesn't matter if Jesus can change just one life because we were faithful.

It's a holy calling.

Prayer: Help me to be faithful to the calling You have given me, no matter where it leads.

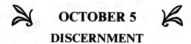

OCTOBER 4

THERE IT IS AGAIN

He entered once for all into the Holy Place, taking not the blood of goats and calves but his own blood, thus securing an eternal redemption.

Hebrews 9:12

Every year it shows up again.

Where we live we have an annual block party as a way for neighbors to meet each other. It's financed by a white-elephant auction. People have fun bidding on ugly objects from other people's garages and attics.

One item that defies description shows up every year, and every year someone buys it. Then, the next year, it shows up again. Nobody wants it, yet somebody always takes it home. Bidding on it brings laughs.

When Jesus came—the great High Priest—it is made plain in Scripture that He entered the holy place once for all, paying the final price for our redemption. And because He paid the price, no one can add to it. No matter who is auctioneer, no one can pay more than Jesus paid.

No one wants sin, yet so many of us won't let Christ do what He came to do about it. Instead, like a white elephant, we try to get rid of sin our way, but it doesn't work. Like that ugly object at our block parties, dealing with sin our way is a joke. It can't work. It is going to stay with us year after year, no matter how many times we try to get rid of it.

Prayer: Help me to see that my way of "redemption" is a bad joke. You came and paid the price for my sin once for all.

OCTOBER 5

DISCERNMENT

. . . Be ye therefore wise as serpents, and harmless as doves.

Matthew 10:16 KJV

"Are you a Christian?"
I replied, "Yes, I am."

"Are you a believing Christian?"

Again I said, "Yes."

Though there can be no such thing as an "unbelieving Christian," that man had discernment. He knew the difference between those who merely wear a label and those who genuinely believe. Do we have that kind of discernment about the persons and beliefs circulating around us? Can we recognize the difference between rhetoric and real conviction, between social pressure and social need, between right and wrong when those who call wrong "right" and right "wrong" believe what they are saying? Are we as wise as serpents in our understanding of what is happening around us, aware because we know God and know that some things are not negotiable and neither the means nor the ends are justified, if they are contrary to God's Word?

Are we able to discern, even when others can't or won't, the logical outcome of a slide in morals or ethical behavior? Are we able to stand firm, to give stability where otherwise there would be none? Do we depend on God's discerning Word to serve as a nonvacillating guide? Do we stand on that, remaining steady even when our own words are twisted or our pronouncements are taken out of context, or we are thought to agree with persons or groups in all of their teachings, because we agree with them on one point?

The Lord said to the church at Philadelphia, "I know thy works: behold, I have set before thee an open door, and no man can shut it: for thou hast a little strength, and hast kept my word, and hast not denied my name" (Revelation 3:8 KJV). Maybe we have little strength, but we can exercise with discernment what strength we have. We can keep God's Word and vow never to deny God's name—for any reason.

Prayer: Lord, give me discernment with people and teachings. I want to be obedient to You.

OCTOBER 6

WELL, WHERE IS IT THEN?

Therefore, since we are justified by faith, we have peace with God through our Lord Jesus Christ.

Romans 5:1

That's it.

That's what everybody is looking for, and we have it.

Peace.

Then why do I feel so miserable? Churning stomach, jangled nerves, headaches, ready to fight all the time.

And there's the Bible telling me I have peace.

Well, something is wrong. I'll recheck the requirements.

"Justified by faith." I am trusting Jesus Christ as my Savior. I've claimed His promise to forgive my sin; I've committed my life to Him as my Lord. Therefore I am justified by faith according to His terms.

So where's the peace that I'm supposed to have?

Maybe it's there, but I don't have it yet. Fulfilling the requirements for it and "picking it up at the front desk" are two different things.

Or maybe it's like a peace treaty at the end of a war. When the peace treaty is signed, peace has come. But even so there are always a few still running around shooting up the countryside, struggling to capture something that they think is strategic.

And somebody has to find them and say, "Look, it's over. Put down your gun. Relax."

God's peace has come. It's peace with God for those who are justified by faith.

Still, here I stand, wearing my combat boots and dragging my gun. I haven't even realized how peaceful *peace* is. It's quiet; it's beautiful—like a meadow on a June afternoon.

Silly, isn't it! I'm all set for battle, and God has arranged for peace—His life-changing peace.

I guess it's time to realize that I don't have a war to fight anymore. It will seem strange—this peace—a little hard to get used to.

I'll take off my boots—the clover does feel good—and throw away my gun and go join the picnickers.

Prayer: You bring the very peace I've been struggling to find. Help me to relax and receive what You brought.

❧ OCTOBER 7 ❦
GET-RICH SCHEMES

Go to now, ye that say, To day or to morrow we will go into such a city, and continue there a year, and buy and sell, and get gain: Whereas ye know not what shall be on the morrow. For what is your life? It is even a vapour, that appeareth for a little time, and then vanisheth away.

James 4:13, 14 KJV

If there is some new way to earn money, someone will discover the way to do it. The human mind is masterful at thinking of money-making schemes.

I thought of one. My wife and I have bicycles that are identical, except hers is a girl's bike and mine is a boy's. The color is the same, the stripes are the same, everything is exactly the same. As I was putting them away for the winter and covering them to keep the dust off, I thought: too bad we can't mate them and sell the offspring. It wouldn't work, of course, but if there were any way it could be done, someone would figure how to do it.

We have an inbuilt tendency to keep planning and thinking and organizing and arranging, which isn't bad so long as we remember that God controls the days ahead. We have no idea what's coming. So even if we come up with a get-rich scheme, God will have the final word. The greatest gain is not money anyway; the greatest gain is knowing God. No matter how much we're earning or spending, God holds tomorrow and eternity.

Prayer: Lord, help me to keep in perspective who You are and who I am. Don't ever let me switch my allegiance from You to some profit-making scheme.

❧ OCTOBER 8 ❦
HERESIES HAVE STRONG TEETH

The foxes have holes, and the birds of the air have nests; but the Son of man hath not where to lay his head.

Matthew 8:20 KJV

Raking the yard isn't a hard job. It's even fun sometimes, except when I have to rake along the chain link fence. Then the rake likes to grab hold of the fence, and I have to pry it loose tooth by tooth. Some things are tenacious. The rake holding onto the fence is one. A penchant for holding onto an idea is another. Ideas have teeth; they don't let go. For example, take the idea that God helps those who help themselves. There are a lot of people, even Christians, who think God is on the side of the aggressive and rich capitalist in the West, not on the side of a poor peasant in an underdeveloped country in the East. Yet that peasant, struggling to put a little bread on the table, perhaps subject to a political situation he can't help, may be more faithful to God than the man who is fortunate enough to be in a country where he can invest and get gain and invest again.

Jesus described Himself as one who "had no place to lay his head." He contrasted His "homelessness" with foxes who have holes and birds who have nests. Pilate had a nice home; Jesus didn't. But we don't preach that God was pro-Pilate and anti-Jesus.

God helps people who are faithful to Him, but it may not be in the terms we like to measure. We can never say that God is helping the rich man make his wealth but is not helping the poor man, or else he wouldn't be poor. If we did that, we'd be teaching heresy. Someone must be teaching it though, because that heresy, like my yard rake, is tenacious.

Prayer: Lord, You look not on the outward appearance but on the heart. Help me to do that, too.

OCTOBER 9
DO MORE!

> For God is at work in you, both to will and to work for his good pleasure.
>
> Philippians 2:13

It's a beautiful thing to watch.

God can take a person with all the rough edges and residue from his days before he knew Jesus and bring about a transformation.

People grow and mature and expand in Jesus and open up as a flower to the sun, giving a beauty and fragrance that is so very attractive, because God does supernatural things in people's lives.

It's His pleasure to take someone and do the miraculous. He wills it, and then He works it.

To see it happen is so indescribably wonderful that there can be no jealousy about what God is doing.

To see Him work in someone else and bless someone else's life is too good to want to meddle in.

He may be willing and working for His good pleasure in me, and that's good, and I'm glad; best of all, I know that you are glad.

But because we are brothers and sisters, I'm happy as I watch God at work in you, willing and working to do His good pleasure in you.

And I pray, "Lord, make him even happier; do more!"

Prayer: Thank You, Lord, for the joy of seeing what You are doing in the lives of others.

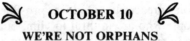

OCTOBER 10

WE'RE NOT ORPHANS

For the Lord will not cast off his people, neither will he forsake his inheritance.

Psalm 94:14 KJV

It's easy to come to a wrong conclusion. Life is hard, nothing seems to be going right, problems are compounded one upon another, and the thought begins to creep in: *Has God forsaken me?* He hasn't.

Do you feel you're being chastened by God? That's what a father does. He loves his children too much not to chasten them. The psalmist said that in verse 12, then makes the definite statement in verse 14: "The Lord will not cast off his people." He will not do it. His people are His people—the redeemed people, the people He loves, still part of the suffering of this world, still subject to all the difficulties that sin and corruption impose, but nevertheless His people.

We are His inheritance. He will not forsake His inheritance. Whether you are a poor child, a sickly child, a child picked upon by others, you are not an abandoned child. You have a home to go to. Your heavenly Father loves you. The Scripture is clear on that, whether you're reading in the Old Testament or the New.

Many a father has had his child crawl up in his lap and cry. The father can't take away the pain, though he wishes he could; his heart goes out to the child, and he puts his arms around him and hugs him until the tears stop. There are times when each of us needs to do that. The Father has big arms and a lot of love.

Prayer: Father, there have been days when I've wondered if I was an orphan, but then when I've cried to You, You have loved me.

❧ OCTOBER 11 ❧
IF NECESSARY

When the poor and needy seek water, and there is none, and their tongue is parched with thirst, I the Lord will answer them.

Isaiah 41:17

When the time is right and it is necessary, God will do the impossible.

He is a God of order, with universal laws and systems.

But those can be changed.

Not all the time, or we would worship the miracle instead of Him. We would look for the dramatic event and miss the quiet, ongoing, day-by-day involvement of God in the lives of His people.

So He will stick to His created order—most of the time.

But because He is God, He can change anything—at any time. "When the poor and needy seek water, and there is none, and their tongue is parched with thirst, I the Lord will answer them, I the God of Israel will not forsake them. I will open rivers on the bare heights, and fountains in the midst of the valleys; I will make the wilderness a pool of water, and the dry land springs of water" (Isaiah 41:17, 18).

When we are seeking, He will answer.

Even if He has to act in a way that is contrary to all that we have ever known or understood. If He has to break laws that He has established, He will do it.

When it is necessary, He will do something.

Sometimes, in desperation, a person will say, "I've tried everything."

"There is no way out."

But there is!

Because God will not be limited by what limits us.

He said, "I . . . will not forsake them."
He will keep that promise. He can be trusted.

Prayer: I'm so thankful, Lord, that You are never limited by what limits me.

⤞ OCTOBER 12 ⤝
FORTY-FIVE YEARS TO WAIT

And Caleb stilled the people before Moses, and said, Let us go up at once, and possess it; for we are well able to overcome it.

Numbers 13:30 KJV

Caleb wasn't afraid. He knew what God could do. The name *Caleb* means "bold" or "wholehearted." When the spies were sent out to bring back a report on the land of Canaan, some told Moses it was impossible to take the land. Caleb said, "We can do it." He was right; they could do it. But because of the murmurings, the dissension, Moses spent all those frustrating years wandering in the wilderness with those people. They weren't yet ready to possess the land.

But old "wholehearted" was always ready, and at age eighty-five he saw the results of his readiness. Judges 1:20 (KJV) says, "They gave Hebron unto Caleb, as Moses said. . . ." If Caleb was like me, he might have said at age forty, "Well, nothing's going to happen; these people aren't going to move. Even God can't work with this crowd." But he held to his vision, and forty-five years later he saw the results.

What happens at age forty isn't the end of any matter. It can all be turned around by age eighty-five, if God is in it.

Prayer: Lord, help me not to determine everything by what I see happening around me today.

OCTOBER 13

A GIFT FOR YOU

For the wages of sin is death; but the gift of God is eternal life through Jesus Christ our Lord.

Romans 6:23 KJV

Payday is a popular day in most offices and factories. Few people get sick on payday. The day after payday a cold may take hold and oblige the worker to stay home—but not on payday.

And it's not likely on payday that many employees stand around praising the boss saying, "Look what he gave me!" Most people would laugh at that. "He didn't give me anything; I earned it. I worked hard for this. This is mine. I have a right to it."

There is another payday coming, sadly. Scripture says, "The wages of sin is death." We don't like that. There will be people on that day who will say, "Why was this given to me? How could God do this to me?" What they don't realize is that wages aren't a gift. Wages are earned. The wages of sin is death. We hire out for our wages, we punch in on the time clock, we roll up our sleeves, and we work. Then we get paid. When payday comes, no one can say he didn't earn his wages.

There is a gift, but we can't earn it. If we could earn it, it wouldn't be a gift. "The gift of God is eternal life through Jesus Christ our Lord." We can't earn a gift, it's free; we reach out and take it. It seems surprising that so many people are confused about that.

God made the difference plain enough in Scripture, but some people refuse the gift, reject the Giver, work as hard as they can for the wages of sin, and then wonder why the paycheck is marked "death." Yet all the time God is saying, "I have a gift for you."

Prayer: Lord, I don't know why this is so hard to explain to people, but with Your help I'll keep on trying to do it.

❧ OCTOBER 14 ❧

BOOKS, BOOKS, AND MORE BOOKS

... Of making many books there is no end; and much study
is a weariness of the flesh. Let us hear the conclusion of the
whole matter: Fear God, and keep his commandments: for
this is the whole duty of man.

Ecclesiastes 12:12, 13 KJV

Book companies send me their latest releases, and I divide them
into two groups—those I don't want to read and those I do want to
read. The trouble with those I do want to read is that I don't have
the time to read them all, and I find myself sorting and resorting,
hating to get rid of them but not having time to read them either.
Sometimes I envy those who just turn on their television sets and
forget the whole business.

Add to the books the magazines that are published, and there is a
real dilemma. There are about 450 Christian publications in the
English language. I try to read about forty of them a month. Every
month I fail at my goal, so I skim books, skim magazines, trying to
catch the most important parts, then hoping to be able to retain
what I've skimmed.

Had I not read Ecclesiastes, I would have thought that I was becoming a cynic, because after hours of this I do become weary in the
flesh, as the writer said would happen. At least he has a summary or
rule to follow. He calls it the end of the matter. When everything
has been heard, no matter what else we read or what we remember
or don't remember, read and remember this: "Fear God, and keep
his commandments: for this is the whole duty of man." Now,
knowing that, I can relax and peruse this new book that just arrived.

*Prayer: Thank You, Father, that amidst all the writings and compli-
cated answers given by man, there is one basic writing—Your Word.
And there is one clear truth—Yours.*

~ OCTOBER 15 ~

GRUBBY CHRISTIANS

And the armies which were in heaven followed him upon
white horses, clothed in fine linen, white and clean.
Revelation 19:14 KJV

Not very far from where we live is a house with Christians in it. I
know Christians live there because there's a big sign on the front
door that says, JESUS SAVES. That's one reason the house stands out.
The other reason is that the house and the yard are filthy. The house
hasn't been painted in years, the doors and windows are shabby, the
roof has broken shingles, the yard is overgrown with weeds and littered with junk. On either side and across the street the neighbors
have immaculate yards and houses. They get to look at the mess in
the middle belonging to the Christians.

Probably the people who live in that dirty house are thinking that
they're too busy serving the Lord to bother with things that are only
temporal anyway. Maybe they want to show that their neighbors
put too much emphasis on what isn't going to last, and they want to
be an example of the deterioration that's going to come to everybody. If so, they've made their point. Maybe instead of cleaning up
their yard they're passing out tracts to their neighbors, ready to
pounce on any neighbor who comes out to cut the grass, ready to
tell him about Jesus.

God has an army dressed in fine linen, which Revelation 19:8
says stands for the righteous acts of the saints. So our Lord's army is
made up of saints who have done righteous acts. There is one other
description about this army that the Christians down the street seem
to have missed. God's army is clean.

*Prayer: Lord, don't let me get caught in this idea that sloppiness is
next to godliness. I know it isn't.*

❧ OCTOBER 16 ❦

BOSS

Then Moses led Israel onward. . . .

Exodus 15:22

There it was, on my desk. The card, signed by the staff, said, "Happy Boss's Day." That was nice, and a surprise. I'd forgotten that it was Boss's Day.

I forget Boss's Day because I tend to forget I'm a "boss." I think of myself as a colleague. The others don't feel that way, though. As soon as my promotion came, they started treating me in a different way. I wonder why? Did I change? Or did they recognize something that had to be?

I once saw a sign: THE BOSS ISN'T ALWAYS RIGHT, BUT HE IS ALWAYS THE BOSS. Someone put it on my boss's desk, and he wrote underneath, "A fortunate arrangement." And it is.

Someone has to lead. God, in orderliness, had leaders among His people. Moses led but got helpers at the insistence of his father-in-law. His army had captains to lead. Leadership carries authority with it, because it also carries responsibility. One doesn't come without the other.

God is our leader, and He has full authority. But He also has responsibility. When He leads and I follow, and it appears to be a "wrong direction," I'd better keep going, just as a soldier keeps going with his captain. The captain has the authority and the responsibility. He also has the map. So does God.

Prayer: Be my Captain; I'll trust You. I'm grateful that none who have trusted You have ever gone wrong.

❧ OCTOBER 17 ❦

CLEAR AND FINAL

"You shall know that I am in the midst of Israel, and that I, the Lord, am your God and there is none else. And my people shall never again be put to shame."

Joel 2:27

Never again!

It's clear, and it's final. God says: "I am in the midst of Israel . . . my people shall never again be put to shame" (Joel 2:27).

Israel has had hard times. There may be more hard times to come. The people of Israel are not naive; they know. But the promise of God is there; they know that, too.

When God makes a promise like that, woe to the person or nation that takes it lightly.

God is in the midst of Israel.

We can spiritualize it—"the new Israel," or we can qualify it—"only those who know Yahweh," but God's statement doesn't make those distinctions.

Any who go against Israel should know what God says: "I am in the midst of Israel."

Interesting choice of words He uses.

God not only says He will be in their midst, He uses "I am" to say it.

There's much more to God's Word than just words.

Prayer: O God, You are greater and more involved than I ever thought You were.

❧ OCTOBER 18 ❦

SOMEDAY WE'LL SEE IT

There failed not ought of any good thing which the Lord had spoken unto the house of Israel; all came to pass.

Joshua 21:45 KJV

God is going to do His work in His way in His time, and no matter how we fill in our calendars and project our plans and set our goals, His timetable is His timetable. Not that we shouldn't be organized. Joshua was. He could not have taken the Promised Land if he hadn't been extremely organized, militarily correct, properly equipped, carefully disciplined. We have to be, too, if God is going to use us to fulfill His plan.

Then when everything else is in order, God will fulfill His promise to the letter. Not one good thing that God spoke failed to come to pass. What a testimony to God. And someday people are going to look back on our day and say the same. We may not see it all. Moses didn't; he was dead. But when the pilgrimage is over, we're all going to be able to say what Joshua said: "All that God promised, He has accomplished."

Prayer: Father, I thank You that You do as You say. You don't tell lies, and You don't make empty promises.

 OCTOBER 19

SOMEDAY

So that you are not lacking in any spiritual gift, as you wait for the revealing of our Lord Jesus Christ; who will sustain you to the end, guiltless in the day of our Lord Jesus Christ.

1 Corinthians 1:7

To the end.

No quitting in the last quarter, no "I'm too tired," no wondering aloud, "How much longer do I have to keep doing this?"

That's not God's way.

His way is to stay with us and sustain us right to the end.

"God will sustain you to the end, guiltless in the day of our Lord Jesus Christ."

Someday Jesus is coming back; someday there will be no more sorrow, no more pain; and someday He will establish a new heaven, a new earth.

Someday.

That will be the day of our Lord Jesus Christ.

But until then, even though everything around us is crumbling, and pressures are unbearable, and the temptations to let go and slide are almost too much to withstand, there will still be His promise, as firm as the day it was given.

He won't renege—no matter how long until someday.

Prayer: Until that day comes, Lord Jesus, when You return, thank You for the promise to sustain me.

⌇ OCTOBER 20 ⌇

HE'S OUTSIDE THE DOOR NOW

. . . Behold, the judge standeth before the door.

James 5:9 KJV

I've been reading the newspaper, and the reports are awful. I don't find much good news there. And when I read about people who have committed an unusually sick criminal act, I tend to want to judge them. I become judge and jury. If the person claims to be a church leader, then I really judge. And I find myself saying, "This all points to the end times. Things are going to get worse; the wheat and the tares are going to grow together. This proves it."

But then I read James, who had thoughts about the coming of Christ. He told us to be patient, firm up our hearts, the Second Coming is right around the corner. Then he told us not to murmur against one another, that the Judge Himself is standing before the door. So if things are going to get worse and worse before the Lord returns—and the Bible indicates they will, and the newspaper seems to prove that they are—the tendency to judge is going to get greater and greater.

James, led by the Holy Spirit, anticipated that. He called for patience and the remembrance that the Lord who judges is just about to step across the threshold.

We all need to know that. If the coming Lord is on the threshold, that's all the more reason to be calm, patient, and to keep our mouths shut about who's to blame and who isn't. No one in the courtroom passes judgment just before the Judge enters the room. When He enters, all will rise in deference to the One who alone has the right to judge.

So I read my newspaper with my feet on the floor. I'm ready to jump up. The Judge is just outside and starting to come in.

Prayer: You alone are Judge, O Lord, and I know it won't be long before judgment begins. Keep me from trying to rush You or take Your place.

OCTOBER 21

THAT CLOGGED DRAIN

> Honor your father and your mother, that your days may be
> long in the land which the Lord your God gives you.
>
> Exodus 20:12

It happened again. My mother-in-law's sink drain was blocked
and my wife was trying to clear it. She tried hot water. That didn't
work. Then she tried drain cleaner. That didn't work, either. She
tried more drain cleaner and had to wait fifteen minutes to see what
would happen. What was hard about the waiting was that she was
already behind schedule for an appointment that she had to keep.
She couldn't leave her mother with a clogged drain, but in staying
she couldn't make her appointment on time.

Sometimes it's not easy to honor parents. We want to, but the responsibility of caring for them often hits at the most inopportune
times. Drains don't block up during free hours. They only block up
when we're already late for something else. But honoring parents is
an obligation, a commitment, not a choice; it is what we are to do,
not what we would like to do. Honor your father and mother, God
says. That means even when you have an appointment and her
kitchen drain is stopped up.

*Prayer: Father, may I obey my responsibilities not with resentment but
with a sense of obedience and joy.*

 OCTOBER 22

A FULL SOUL

> The full soul loatheth an honeycomb; but to the hungry
> soul every bitter thing is sweet.
>
> Proverbs 27:7 KJV

It's time to go to the grocery store. How do I know it's time? I just
had a big dinner. If I go to the store before I eat, I'm seduced by
every impulse item the store manager puts on display. But if I wait
until after I've had a big meal, I buy only the things on my list.

My soul and my body are a lot alike. When my soul is full of the
good things of God, very little is tempting. But when I've strayed or

lost interest or grown cold, then even the bitter things that have a bite to them taste sweet to me. A full stomach is good for grocery shopping. A full soul is good for all the time.

Prayer: Lord, I want to be full of You so that I really don't have a desire for all the impulse sins that are put out there for me to take.

OCTOBER 23

MORE HAPPINESS

You love what is good And hate what is wrong. Therefore God, your God, Has given you more gladness Than anyone else.

Psalm 45:7 TLB

This sort of sneaked up on me. I wasn't ready for it when I found it. God knows that I want gladness. Now He tells me about the availability not only of gladness but of more gladness than anyone else has.

How? I ask.

Then, working backward, I figure it out. "God, your God, has given you more gladness than anyone else" because—and the rest follows—"you love what is good and hate what is wrong."

Now that's something to ponder, because if I do not love what is good, or worse, hate what is good and instead love what is wrong, or at least put up with it, God will not give me gladness.

I can't create gladness. If I could create it or package it, I'd have what everyone wants. I could sell it.

But gladness is a gift. A gift like this comes from God and follows what He establishes as a way of living. So I have to decide on my way of living. What am I going to love, and what am I going to hate? After I work that out and do it, the happiness will come. God says so.

Prayer: Father, You have offered the gift of happiness. Help me to stop trying to produce it my way and receive it on Your terms, as You meant for me to do.

❧ OCTOBER 24 ❧

NO FINGER DRUMMING

And the world passes away, and the lust of it; but he who does the will of God abides for ever.

1 John 2:17

Forever.

Like a whole ham for just two people?

Like a layover at London's Heathrow Airport for a flight to one of the little countries in Africa?

Like the last few days before the wedding—for the groom?

If that's what God is saying, forever is going to be a drag—waiting, wishing, and fighting the monotony.

But take a closer look; read all the words: "And the world passes away, and the lust of it; but he who does the will of God abides for ever."

The hams, the airports, the weddings will all pass away; the drag part will be gone. What will be forever is the abiding part, the "with God" part.

We won't be killing time; the no-waiting sign will always be posted. Forever free, we'll come and go and enjoy Him. There won't be any finger drumming, no wrangling, lusting, pushing, grabbing, wishing—just lots of enjoying.

The world will pass away; the boring part will be gone. And free of that, I'll be able to enjoy forever what I could only sample before.

Total liberation, total fulfillment, total happiness, and total variety—that's God, and that's mine for the abiding, and it's yours, too, if you are in the will of God.

Until then, just keep trying to think of another way to serve the ham.

Prayer: Forever with You, Lord, doesn't sound dull to me. It's exciting.

❧ OCTOBER 25 ❦

REAL WORLD

And I will set up shepherds over them which shall feed them. . . .

Jeremiah 23:4 KJV

There is probably no more demanding or rewarding ministry than that of being a clergyman—the shepherd of a flock. God established shepherds over Israel. He still calls shepherds to care for His own. In many ways the shepherding or pastoral ministry is a lonely vocation. One is called away from his family in the evening, awakened in the night; the clergyman works with those who are distressed and troubled, people whose lives are falling apart. But he rarely is honored or respected for it. In fact, some think he lives in another world.

In public, a businessman once said to his pastor, "Pastor, you need to get out into the real world." Everyone sort of sniffed and laughed, but what that audience didn't know and what that pastor didn't say was that the man who was boasting of knowing the real world and chiding the pastor for not being out in it was at the same time privately being counseled by that pastor because his own life was falling apart.

A pastor is probably one of the few people in the community who does know the real world. He knows what people are struggling with; he counsels men and women when they're trying to put their lives together; he sees them in their honest times, when they are looking at their marriage, their children, their vocation, their walk with God. He sees life in all of its rawness. Yet no matter how hard he works, no matter how much of "life" he encounters, he can't tell anybody about it. He bears much of his real-world ministry alone.

Prayer: Father, help me to remember to be supportive and to pray for those shepherds You have placed over Your flocks.

❧ OCTOBER 26 ❦

AN IMPORTANT CONVERSATION

And it came to pass, that, as he was praying in a certain
place, when he ceased, one of his disciples said unto him,
Lord, teach us to pray. . . .

Luke 11:1 KJV

Prayer meetings are interesting. There is stream-of-consciousness
praying, in which whatever comes to mind is said. There is emotional praying, in which the person talking to God starts out in a
normal tone of voice and soon accelerates, getting higher and
higher, until he's at a fever pitch. There is limited-vocabulary praying, in which a person ties together well-worn clichés and manages
to put them all in before he says, "Amen."

That's not to fault our praying, but Scripture is quite clear. We
are to be self-controlled and clear minded in our praying. It is not
that our praying is to sound like a legal contract, but it is to be
carefully thought out and logically expressed. We are conversing
with our heavenly Father.

If I were invited to have an important conversation with my em-
ployer or senator or the president of the United States, I would not
ramble, I would not sail up on an emotional high pitch. I would
seek to be as logical and clear as I could to communicate with that
person.

We have an audience—the living God who tells us to enter into
that audience with Him clear minded and self-controlled. The disciples knew that when they asked Jesus to teach them to pray. He
gave them some clear directions. He didn't tell them just to ramble.

Prayer: Lord, help me when I pray to show proper respect for You.

❧ OCTOBER 27 ❧

AN EXAMPLE—WHO? ME?

But the natural man receiveth not the things of the Spirit of God: for they are foolishness unto him: neither can he know them, because they are spiritually discerned.

1 Corinthians 2:14 KJV

They surely don't know us very well, do they? Have you noticed that news magazines, newspapers, and books have all been analyzing the evangelicals?

"What does it mean to be born again?"

"Who are the evangelicals?"

"What is neofundamentalism?"

By and large, the reporting can't be faulted. Most of the articles have been well researched, interviews carefully taken, people quoted accurately. But still at the end there is that feeling that they don't truly understand—that reporters aren't really capturing the essence of the Christan faith.

Most of the time it isn't that reporters don't want to understand. A good reporter tries to do a thorough piece of writing. And of course, it's true that "the natural man receiveth not the things of the Spirit of God: for they are foolishness unto him: neither can he know them, because they are spiritually discerned" (1 Corinthians 2:14 KJV). It is also true that "the preaching of the cross is to them that perish foolishness" (1 Corinthians 1:18 KJV). Thus the secular writer is hindered by an inability to grasp spiritual truth.

But even with those Scriptures in mind there could still be another reason. Somebody made an interesting observation to me. He said, "If the articles written appear to lack a grasp of what it means to be an evangelical Christian, it may not be that the reporters are inaccurately reflecting what they see, but rather that they are accurately reflecting what they see. Maybe they are carefully reporting what we are—and that's the problem!"

If a journalist looks at me, what will he see? There will always be the occasional reporter who writes a poor story, regardless of what we say or do. Maybe he is blind to spiritual things. Maybe he has a personal ax to grind. Maybe he doesn't want to get a true picture.

But each of us needs to ask, "What if he does? If he comes to me in search of true Christianity, will he find it?"

Prayer: Help me to live what I say I am so that others looking will be able to say, "There's a Christian."

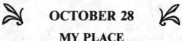

OCTOBER 28

MY PLACE

> "In my Father's house are many rooms; if it were not so, would I have told you that I go to prepare a place for you?"
>
> John 14:2

He's talking about heaven and all the rooms there.

I'm glad He told us; it is comforting. The best part of all is that last line; I can't get over that. He tells about a place for me.

A place for me!

It's being made ready for me.

I don't know if that means my favorite wall covering, or furniture style, or carpeting. I don't know if it has the view from the window that I've always wanted. But I know I will like it, because He says it's a place for me.

He knows me. He loves me. He knows who I am, how I'm made, what I like; He knows what is comfortable for me, and feels right.

He knows!

And He's preparing that place—that special place—just for me. If it were an ordinary place, He wouldn't have added the "for you."

So it's obviously no dormitory—institutional and functional.

It's no stock-plan apartment (beige everything, NOTHING ON THE WALLS, PLEASE, AND NO NOISE—signed "The Management"), but it's my place, prepared by the Lord for me. And it will be all ready when I get there.

Going home will be very pleasant.

Living at home will be fun.

I don't even have to fret about the decorating being finished on time or the furniture being arranged before I move in.

When it's ready, He'll call me.

Prayer: You are preparing a place for me. Thank You, Lord.

OCTOBER 29
SUPERMOM

And Deborah, a prophetess, the wife of Lapidoth, she
judged Israel at the time.

Judges 4:4 KJV

She was the ultimate "supermom." We don't know anything
about her husband Lapidoth; maybe he stayed home and did the
cooking, drove the kids to Little League games, hung out the laun-
dry. In any event, if he had any image problems or problems with
role modeling, it doesn't show up in Scripture.

Israel needed leadership, and God appointed Deborah, a prophetess, a judge, the one who went with Barak and encouraged him on
a military expedition that overwhelmed a superpower and brought
peace to the land for forty years. But when she sang her song of rejoicing at the victory, she didn't refer to herself as a prophetess or a
judge or even as a great military person; she just called herself a
mother (Judges 5:7). There aren't a lot of supermoms around, but
when God needs one, He knows where to look.

*Prayer: Thank You, Father, that when You need someone to do a job,
sex isn't an issue. For Israel, one of Your best men was a woman.*

OCTOBER 30
DECAY

For the creation waits with eager longing for the revealing
of the sons of God.

Romans 8:19

That's true.

Creation, all of it, has been groaning. There is decay. It's in us, in
nature, and even in our most noble achievements.

We are waiting to be set free.

"For the creation waits with eager longing for the revealing of the
sons of God; for the creation was subjected to futility, not of its own
will but by the will of him who subjected it in hope; because the
creation itself will be set free from its bondage to decay and obtain
the glorious liberty of the children of God. We know that the whole

creation has been groaning in travail together until now; and not only the creation, but we ourselves, who have the first fruits of the Spirit, groan inwardly as we wait for adoption as sons, the redemption of our bodies" (Romans 8:19–23).

There is an indicator of what those words mean: "liberty, redemption, adoption." That indicator is the Holy Spirit—already resident in the "Christ ones."

He's a glorious sample of the peace, security, wholeness, comfort—a reservoir of gifts and fruits.

But it isn't all ours—not yet.

Because we are still in bondage to time, space, and all of the rest of creation that is marred by sin and is decaying.

It's like living on a garbage heap—not pleasant by a long shot, but tolerable because our food and drink is supplied from another Source, a pure one.

Someday we'll no longer have to live on top of the garbage heap. We'll have our residence with the Pure Source.

We wait.

Some groan.

But we have hope.

Those without hope are those who have no Pure Source, either as a Provider now or as a promised total experience later.

All they have is the garbage.

Prayer: Please, Lord, keep reminding me that someday all that is pure and good will be mine.

❧ OCTOBER 31 ❧
PERSISTENCE

And Asa cried unto the Lord his God, and said, Lord, it is nothing with thee to help, whether with many, or with them that have no power: help us, O Lord our God; for we rest on thee, and in thy name we go against this multitude. O Lord, thou art our God; let not man prevail against thee.

2 Chronicles 14:11 KJV

Asa knew the truth, and while he was obeying the truth and doing right in the eyes of God, God had His hand on his life. But then it all fell apart for him. What happened? How could a man who had so much going for him lose it all? How could someone who understood God so well turn against God and die so far from God that he wouldn't even seek Him for His help? ". . . Yet in his disease he sought not the Lord . . ." (2 Chronicles 16:12 KJV).

That has happened other times to men and women of faith. That's why Peter told the elders, ". . . God resisteth the proud, and giveth grace to the humble" (1 Peter 5:5 KJV). Asa experienced that. He came up against the resistance of God. For that reason Peter urged, "Humble yourselves therefore under the mighty hand of God . . ." (v. 6 KJV). Asa didn't, Asa wouldn't; and Asa is a clear example to us of what happens to a person who turns his back on God. God sent Hanani the seer to warn him, but Asa wouldn't be warned and threw Hanani into prison. His own pride took him all the way from the top to the bottom. And apparently he never cried again unto the Lord. He never again said, "Lord, it is nothing with thee to help." Never again did he pray, "O Lord our God, we rest on thee."

That's a sad story in history. It is sadder yet today when people who should know better follow Asa's path.

Prayer: Lord, help me to learn from this and to remain faithful to You.

NOVEMBER 1

THE REST OF IT FOLLOWS

If we confess our sins, he is faithful and just, and will forgive our sins and cleanse us from all unrighteousness.

1 John 1:9

That's the good news about the good news. It's all-inclusive: "If we confess our sins, he is faithful and just, and will forgive our sins and cleanse us from all unrighteousness."

God, who is the Forgiver, is also faithful to forgive.

What if He weren't?

What if He could forgive, but wouldn't do it? What if He left a part of our sins untouched? It would spread and grow like mold in a petri dish.

But He is serious about what He does, and He's complete in the way He does it.

His forgiveness offer is total; it covers everything.

Unless we think that we can bypass the first part of His statement—the "if-we-confess" part.

Because if we think that, then His promise isn't inclusive anymore. In fact, it doesn't include anything.

We don't have to confess our sins, either part or all. That's the prerogative of the offer taker.

But when we do, well, that's the reason it starts the promise. The rest follows.

Prayer: Please help me not to try to take Your Word apart.

 NOVEMBER 2

WINTER IS COMING

> When you come, bring the cloak that I left with Carpus at
> Troas, also the books, and above all the parchments. . . .
> Do your best to come before winter. . . .
>
> 2 Timothy 4:13, 21

In the autumn, when the leaves are falling, I'm caught by two emotions—pleasure at the beauty of the season and sadness that winter is coming.

But winter is coming; I can't stop it. Everything will be more difficult for me; the sun won't shine as much, and I'll be more irritable. Winter is coming, and life will no longer be as it was last summer.

Yet winter isn't the end. Winter is something we go through. We endure the difficulties, but there is enjoyment, too. There are things to do and enjoy in winter that are not possible any other time. There is a new kind of beauty, and winter enjoyments that the "try-to-hang-on-till-summertime" people never get to know.

Paul urged Timothy to come before winter. He was speaking of his need for books, parchments, and a cloak—a personal visit that wouldn't be possible once winter descended.

Some of us aren't ready yet for winter. We are trying to hang onto the summertime of life. But we can't; we are aging. If we aren't ready for winter, we won't be ready for God's springtime either.

Paul was giving more than instructions to Timothy; he was giving us a message about life. We need to come to God before winter.

Prayer: Father, before winter comes, as best I know how, I come to You in faith believing. I receive Jesus Christ as my Savior.

⊱ NOVEMBER 3 ⊰
HOW DO THEY KNOW HOW TO DO THAT?

And he said unto them, Come ye yourselves apart into a
desert place, and rest a while.

Mark 6:31 KJV

My forty-two friends came back this week. I'm always glad to see
them. They are forty-two Canada geese who stop for a few days, or
sometimes a week, at a small lake near our home. Whether they are
heading north or south, that's their regular resting place.

Actually, I know they're coming or going before I see them, because early in the morning, or just before dark, I hear them coming
over the house. They talk a lot. I can hear their honking even before
they get close. If I'm outside, I can hear the swishing of their wings.

But what I've always wondered about is how they know how to
divide into flying groups and how they know when to rotate leaders.
One is always in front of the V-shaped formation. When he gets
tired, he drops back and another moves up to keep that tight formation that cuts the wind. And they never seem to argue over it.

I've been in churches where people won't give up leadership, and
they burn out. Jesus told His disciples after a hectic day with people
coming and going, when they didn't even have time to eat: "Come
apart and rest a while." But some people in our churches won't do
that. They don't know how to fall back and take a position behind
some other leader. You'd think if they weren't willing to follow the
suggestion of Jesus, they would at least have enough sense to follow
the example of a goose!

*Prayer: Father, help me to realize that the Kingdom isn't going to
come by my efforts alone. Keep me from the ego trip of trying to be a
"super-Christian."*

⊱ NOVEMBER 4 ⊰
A TOUCH OF GOD

... Inasmuch as ye have done it unto one of the least of
these my brethren, ye have done it unto me.

Matthew 25:40 KJV

They were together in the same voting booth when I took my
ballot into an adjacent one. The woman was saying to the man who

was mentally handicapped, "Do you remember the ballot?" He did. "Do you want to vote for this candidate [she named him] or that one [and named him]?" There was a long pause, then came his answer. And she kindly showed him what to do to cast his ballot. When he was finished, she took another handicapped person into the booth with her, and I noticed that there were others waiting in line, eager to cast their votes. I don't know who she was; she deserves praise. That's an example of caring.

In churches, too, there are people deserving of praise, for they're starting programs for the handicapped, for hurting people, for alcoholics, the divorced, parents of crippled children. There is a real caring among people. These people are doing more and more.

But not everybody; there are still many who "visit" the church to see if there is anything there for them. There will always be those selfish ones—the takers, the shoppers—who give nothing to others, even in church. They wouldn't care for the handicapped; they are too busy looking out for themselves.

But I'm seeing more and more dedicated ones who love and give and care. They are the ones Jesus was talking about, I think, when He said, "Inasmuch as ye have done it unto one of the least of these my brethren, ye have done it unto me."

As I left the voting booth, I thought, *That woman probably knows Jesus.* Her kindness had the kindness of Jesus in it. There was a touch of God in that voting place.

Prayer: Lord, thank You for those who truly love and care. Bless them and encourage them.

❧ NOVEMBER 5 ❧
I DON'T WANT TO

> ... I am come that they might have life, and that they might have it more abundantly.
>
> John 10:10 KJV

It's time to visit my dental hygienist again. I think she pumps iron. When she goes to work on my teeth and bears down, muscles rippling, she draws blood from every part of my mouth. Then while I'm still in pain, she sweetly sits back and gives me the toothbrush lesson. I don't mind the toothbrush lesson; I always promise to obey. But I don't like the flossing lesson. For that I make no promises.

It's easy for her; she gets the floss in both hands, reaches into my mouth clear to her elbows, and starts pushing hard until the floss gets in between my teeth. My teeth are set close together, so she gets a good workout. But I can't do that myself, because I'm not coming at it from the same direction she is. So I can't do it, I won't do it, and I'm certainly not going to visit her every morning and let her do it for me. She means well; she doesn't want me to lose my teeth.

Her ways are painful but necessary. It is so with God, too. He wants me to live, not die; to be whole, not weak; happy, not sorrowful; and He offers the way to that fullness. Jesus said, "I am come that they might have life, and that they might have it more abundantly." He wants us to have it; there's health if we will take it. But unfortunately, some people are just as stubborn with God as I am with my flossing hygienist. There are going to be a lot of people gumming at God their famous last words: "I don't want to."

Prayer: Lord, wherever I go there are lessons that point to You, Your grace, Your goodness, and Your help for me, even when I go to the dentist's office.

❧ NOVEMBER 6 ☙
COLD SATURDAY

> . . . I have learned, in whatsoever state I am, therewith to be content.
>
> Philippians 4:11 KJV

It isn't fair!

All day long people were telling me, "It's so beautiful outside. This is probably the last nice day of the fall season." Then they added, "A winter storm is coming." So I would grind my teeth, turn my back on the window, and try to concentrate on my work.

It's hard being inside on the "last nice day of the season." It's no fun looking forward to Saturday, when the weatherman predicts cold and snow. What I'd really like, of course, is to be inside working on the snowy cold days and have the sunshiny days free. But I don't run the weather or the universe; God does.

The Apostle Paul said, "I have learned, in whatsoever state I am, therewith to be content." He said it after having been beaten, shipwrecked, hungry, imprisoned, lonely—and he didn't complain about any of those things.

Paul didn't complain about the weather either. Nor did he spend time daydreaming about what the weather was going to be like on Saturday. He was too busy living every day for Jesus, no matter what the day was like.

Prayer: Thank You, Lord, for giving us the Apostle Paul to help us put some things into perspective. It's so easy to get turned around.

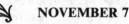

NOVEMBER 7

EXCELLENCE

So that you may approve what is excellent. . . .

Philippians 1:10

Excellence is not easy to find, mostly because we tend to look for it in the wrong places. It's interesting how we often trade off gifted people for celebrities. We look for big names, we look for the headliners, but these aren't necessarily the ones who strive for excellence. Listen sometime to the movie stars on talk shows. Notice how often they give evidence of shallow and weak thinking.

Gifted people are often the quiet ones, quiet because they are seeking not acclaim but excellence. Those are the people to be around, because they pull us along; they force us to be more disciplined, to stretch. People who are impressed with themselves soon get smaller. Those who stretch and reach out to be the best they can be are the real giants.

I've learned that if I'm going to find excellence, I'm more likely to find it by being close to people who are themselves seeking excellence. And most of the time excellence isn't on the television or movie screen; it's in the church down the street.

Prayer: Help me, Lord, to approve what is excellent and seek what is excellent. Help me to know where to look for it.

❧ NOVEMBER 8 ❧

HE'S RIGHT!

" 'A little while, and you will not see me, and again a little
while, and you will see me.' "

John 16:19

What did He say?

First He says it one way, and then He says it the other.

Well, which will it be? Will I see Him or won't I see Him? Doesn't
Jesus know?

Or is He too clear? I mean, so clear that at first I miss the meaning
of what He says?

He was talking to His followers, those who knew Him best—the
disciples. And He told them: "I'm going to the Father. In a little
while I'm leaving. I'll be gone from this earth.

"But I'm not going to be away forever. It won't be too long. In
fact, just a little while, and I'll be back. You'll see Me again."

The disciples were there with Him when He said it; He hadn't left
them yet. They couldn't possibly have understood what that second
part meant—"again a little while, and you will see me"—because
He hadn't gone yet.

But I know what He meant, being here during the in-between
times, walking with Him by faith, and longing to know Him by
sight.

Those words probably didn't hit the disciples as they hit me:
"You will see me."

Jesus must have been looking down the line at us, the waiting
ones, because after He said that, He added those five additional
words: ". . . And your hearts will rejoice . . ." (John 16:22).

He's right; they will.

Prayer: Lord, I know the day is coming when I will see You.

NOVEMBER 9

ARTIST

So when you give to the needy, do not announce it with trumpets, as the hypocrites do in the synagogues and on the streets, to be honored by men. I tell you the truth, they have received their reward in full.

Matthew 6:2 NIV

I know people who are artists. They can't paint, sketch, work with plaster, wire, or clay. These artists are givers. They are individuals who can give money without drawing attention to themselves or even without getting tax credit.

There is a quality about their giving, a finesse—they have style. They also have biblical precedent.

Jesus said, "So when you give to the needy, do not announce it with trumpets, as the hypocrites do in the synagogues and on the streets, to be honored by men."

We don't sound trumpets; that's crude. But some of us aren't always silent about it either. There are a lot of ways to let people know we are giving money or time or some other part of our lives and means.

Giving can be fun, out and out pure pleasure, when nobody knows. It's even fun not to tell God about it unless we need His guidance about how large the gift should be.

Even when we keep our giving secret, giving cash instead of checks, not asking for a receipt for taxes, we have enough fun doing it that we need nothing more. Still, God finds out. Artists tend to be noticed by the Master who knows great art when He sees it.

Prayer: Lord, may I enjoy giving because a gift is needed and because You want me to give—not for any other reason.

NOVEMBER 10

SYSTEM

For we have not followed cunningly devised fables, when we made known unto you the power and coming of our Lord Jesus Christ, but were eyewitnesses of his majesty.

2 Peter 1:16 KJV

I know that the day after I take the snow tires off the car we will get one of our biggest storms of the year. It doesn't matter what the weatherman says; I know that a snowstorm is going to hit. I don't think it would matter if I waited until June 15. If that's the day I take off my snow tires, we will get a heavy snow on June 16! The opposite is true when I put the snow tires back on the car. If I intend to do that job on Saturday, I can be certain that Friday night I will drive home in a blizzard, fishtailing all the way.

Some people scoff at my conviction that I'm a snowmaker and laugh at my childish beliefs. Then they turn right around and produce rainstorms by washing their cars—and they admit it. A mother knows exactly which of her daughter's fifteen blouses she will want to wear tonight. It's the only one that didn't get washed and ironed.

Since we know how life works, we adjust pretty well. I get out my umbrella when I see my neighbor washing his car. He gets out his snow shovel when he sees me taking off my snow tires.

It's nice to have life figured out, a system that works. It's nice, but it's wrong. And we are just as wrong when we try to apply God's Word to our system.

God won't be put into our system. His truth comes from outside our system. God isn't "believable because He works." Believing in God isn't the same as believing that it is going to snow tomorrow because of what I do today.

Our nice little systems are comfortable; they work well until we read more Scripture. Then we discover that God won't be limited by systems that we cling to. He is beyond our systems. Jesus knew it and said so over and over again—especially to religious people who had a system. Peter knew it, too, and pointed to Jesus.

Prayer: Lord, help me to see that my system is only that—my system. Help me to let go of my little ideas so that I can be open to You.

🥀 NOVEMBER 11 🥀
UNSOPHISTICATED WEAPONRY

And he divided the three hundred men into three companies, and he put a trumpet in every man's hand, with empty pitchers, and lamps within the pitchers.
Judges 7:16 KJV

Talk about sophisticated weaponry! Gideon didn't have a huge defense budget. He didn't even have a big army. He had 300 faithful men who were willing to look to him for direction. He also had 300 trumpets, 300 empty pitchers, and 300 torches. But in the middle of the night, in the Midianite camp, it was enough.

God's people have never had great armaments or weapons of any kind, except the light of the truth of the Gospel inside earthen vessels. But God's people have always had what Gideon's army had—a commitment to look to Him for direction and to do as they were told.

Prayer: Lord, I'm an earthen vessel, but I have the light You gave me. Show me how I can use it best.

🥀 NOVEMBER 12 🥀
IT FEELS LIKE JET LAG

I have been young, and now am old; yet have I not seen the righteous forsaken, nor his seed begging bread.
Psalm 37:25 KJV

How can I have jet lag? I never left the ground. But I'm tired, just as tired as I am after a trip across the Pacific. All we did was drive from Toledo to Minneapolis, a sixteen-hour trip.

Someone suggested, "Maybe you're just getting old; you can't handle those long trips anymore." Maybe so, but there's a promise in Scripture for me. "I have been young, and now am old; yet have I not seen the righteous forsaken, nor his seed begging bread."

God took care of me when I was young. I wondered some days where the next meal was coming from. He took care of me in supporting a young family. Though we didn't have plenty, we weren't in want. And He's taking care of me now.

One of the pleasures of getting older is the perspective it gives on the goodness of God. Some people look at me and think I don't have much. By their standards I don't. But by the standard that I have, that is, being taken care of day by day, I have everything I want. I have the goodness of God.

But I'm still tired. And even though it's early, I'm going to bed. I don't care what anyone says; it feels like jet lag.

Prayer: Dear Father, Your care was there when I was young; it still is. Thank You.

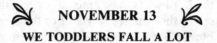 **NOVEMBER 13**

WE TODDLERS FALL A LOT

The Lord upholds all who are falling, and raises up all who are bowed down.

Psalm 145:14

"I'm not a child, you know. I'm a mature, capable, intelligent adult, quite able to stand on my own two feet!"

I usually feel the need to argue that and make it plain to God, because if I read the Bible correctly, He isn't just talking about weak old men with lots of wisdom; He's talking about childlike people with not much experience and the need to be helped, and I resent that!

Still, the word is there: "The Lord upholds all who are falling, and raises up all who are bowed down."

Of course, when I'm honest, I have to admit that I do trip sometimes—well, quite a few times. And I don't always know where I'm going. (But I don't admit it publicly; what would people think?)

If I knew that I could put my hand in the hand of the heavenly Father and always be caught when I tripped (providing nobody knew I was holding His hand), it surely would help a lot.

And if He could pick me up quickly when I'm down and set me on my feet, my friends would marvel at my resiliency. "Nothing gets him down," they'd say. I'd go for that.

In fact, if I did have God with me all the time like that, then I guess I wouldn't care if everybody knew it. I'd go smoothly through life, not being afraid to take some chances, skipping a little, maybe, because God would have hold of my hand.

I guess I have to admit that I'm not so capable. Here I am with scraped knees and a bump on my head, because I wanted to go along all by myself, even when I knew my Father had His hand outstretched.

I'm not very good at walking all by myself. We toddlers fall a lot.

Prayer: Help me to be adult enough to be like a little child.

 NOVEMBER 14

HE'S WAITING

> Therefore the Lord waits to be gracious to you; therefore he exalts himself to show mercy to you. For the Lord is a God of justice; blessed are all those who wait for him.
>
> Isaiah 30:18

That's not a promise!

It's just a plain statement.

Oh? Read it again. In fact, read it five or six times—out loud.

See? It is a promise!

In fact, a lot of God's Word comes like that, taking on a deeper meaning as we read it over and over, and we begin to see or sense or feel that what God is doing is reaching out, trying to communicate not just words about Himself but His own love.

The point is, the Lord has been waiting, and He is waiting now.

And all this time most of us have thought of ourselves as the ones who have done the waiting. Our favorite words are, "Isn't God ever going to be gracious to me?"

Grace, mercy, justice—all ours—and He's waiting. When it comes, at the right moment, it will bless us and exalt Him.

And that's a promise!

Prayer: Thank You for waiting for me to be ready.

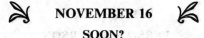

NOVEMBER 15
WEAK AND OVERWEIGHT

When he mentioned the ark of God, Eli fell over backward from his seat by the side of the gate; and his neck was broken and he died, for he was an old man, and heavy. He had judged Israel forty years.

1 Samuel 4:18

There must not have been a YMCA in downtown Shiloh, or a health spa, or even a weight-reducing clinic, because when Eli died, though very little else is said about him, it's clear that he was overweight. But obesity wasn't his only weakness. During his time as a priest and a judge, the ark of God was taken. He didn't have much spiritual discernment, because when Hannah was praying for a son, he thought she was drunk. And he couldn't control his children. His two sons were called ruthless men. They didn't know the Lord (1 Samuel 2:12). Their actions proved it.

Yet Eli wasn't a complete failure, because he was the tutor to young Samuel, who grew in the Lord under Eli's teaching. Eli didn't have much of a life or a ministry, but God entrusted young Samuel to him. Eli may not have been exemplary in human terms, but God saw value in him as a teacher for Samuel, and in the long run, that's what counted.

Eli wasn't the first or the last less-than-admirable clergyman, but who can judge? God used him.

Prayer: Father, when You anoint someone, he's your choice for a particular task, whether or not we admire his life-style. Help us always to look beyond the person, to You.

NOVEMBER 16
SOON?

He who testifies to these things says, "Surely I am coming soon." Amen. Come, Lord Jesus!

Revelation 22:20

Go ahead; try it.
Close the Bible; what's the last promise you remember?

Right—and that's why Jesus said it last, so you would remember. "Surely I am coming soon."

Five words, but they say a whole lot more than a casual "see ya." It's a parting promise, and every believer has been clinging to that promise since the ascension of Jesus.

"I'm coming."

It will be soon!

As secular man sees things, it has been a long time.

As eager children see things, He'll never come.

As mature Christians see things, He has only stepped behind a curtain for a few minutes.

Will Jesus really come back?

He said He would.

Soon?

He said so.

But can I depend on it, build my faith on it?

That's why He added the "surely."

An angel told the followers of Jesus: " . . . Men of Galilee, why do you stand looking into heaven? This Jesus, who was taken up from you into heaven, will come in the same way as you saw him go into heaven" (Acts 1:11).

So there's no point spending your time getting a cramped neck.

But as you watch the days slip by, there will come a quickening of your pulse, a growing excitement as you sense the time getting shorter.

And you'll find yourself smiling (others won't know why), but you'll know—it's that promise.

"I'm coming—soon!"

Prayer: Soon—You are coming soon. I'm ready, Lord, and I'm grateful.

৯১ NOVEMBER 17 ৶
PERSON TO PERSON

And the Word was made flesh, and dwelt among us. . . .
                                              John 1:14 KJV

Really?

I was just told that one of my books has been translated into Korean. Translations surprise me, particularly when the language is something other than European. Why would readers in another culture, using another language, be interested in my writings? But they are, and the reason is that people relate to people, and more especially, all people need God. My books center on God and people.

Jesus Christ is truly transcultural. "The Word was made flesh and dwelt among us." God came, person to person. He relates to us where we are. That has nothing to do with culture or language. He entered our time, space, circumstances. People who think that Christ is strictly Western have forgotten where the Gospel started, where the Church was born, and where it's growing fastest today.

The more I think about it, when I write about Jesus and write about people and put the two together in my books, that can communicate anywhere, in any language. So why am I so surprised? That only proves how small and limited I am. A better grasp of God and what He did in Christ Jesus can take care of that.

Prayer: Lord, my surprise at how You meet people everywhere only shows my own limitations, not Yours.

⤳ NOVEMBER 18 ⤶
SECONDS

The Son of man is come eating and drinking; and ye say, Behold a gluttonous man, and a winebibber, a friend of publicans and sinners.

Luke 7:34 KJV

Tonight we're having chili for supper. I'll probably eat too much; I always do. Then in my repentant moments afterwards, I'll find myself wondering, *Would Jesus have done that?*—and I don't know whether or not He would have. He went to dinners; certainly He was probably served a good meal. Did He go back for seconds? Is that why people called Him a glutton and a winebibber? Or did they do it because they were just trying to find something negative to say about Him?

Obviously Jesus was not in bad physical shape. One who walked the miles He walked and who lived outdoors couldn't have been. And He was doing the Father's will, which means He wouldn't have been anything less than committed to God in His life-style.

But Jesus was totally human. He had to be to be tempted in all

points like me, yet without sin. He had to be to know pain, to identify with me. The love of God called for that. It's a marvelous
thought, God giving His Son for my sake, to redeem me on my
terms where I am. Jesus was totally God but also totally man. I do
wonder sometimes, when I think about the humanity side of His
nature, if He ever went back for a second bowl of chili.

*Prayer: Lord, I thank You that Jésus, though totally God and totally
pure, came to be like me in order to redeem me.*

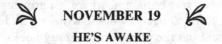

NOVEMBER 19

HE'S AWAKE

> How precious it is, Lord, to realize that you are thinking
> about me constantly! I can't even count how many times a
> day your thoughts turn towards me. And when I waken in
> the morning, you are still thinking of me!
>
> Psalm 139:17, 18 TLB

The day before Thanksgiving, our daughter called at 6:30 in the
morning to tell us, "I'll be picked up for my ride home after 4:00
P.M., so I probably won't be there until after midnight. Don't wait
up." But I told her we probably would wait up, and we did. Who
can sleep with a homebound college-age daughter on the road?
Mentally we traveled with her almost every mile. We wanted her
safely home. We wanted to see her. We couldn't sleep.

Scripture says God cares about each one of us far more than that,
and I am told clearly that God was up all last night, thinking about
me. He never slumbers or sleeps, because He is God and He doesn't
need to, and because He loves us and doesn't want to.

*Prayer: Thank You, Lord, that even when I sleep You're awake,
thinking about me.*

≈ NOVEMBER 20 ≈

SOMETIMES HE SEEMS TO BE SO SLOW

For still the vision awaits its time; it hastens to the end—it will not lie. If it seem slow, wait for it; it will surely come, it will not delay.

Habakkuk 2:3

Run that past me again, a little more slowly, please!

"For still the vision awaits its time. . . . If it seem slow, wait for it; it will surely come, it will not delay" (Habakkuk 2:3).

If all that is true, then what God tells me will definitely be, no matter what seems to be happening or how long He seems to be taking to act.

If I ever get hold of that, I mean really internalize it, maybe I'll no longer push the clock, rush the gates, pace the floor, chew my lip, wear out the armrests of my chair, and crack my knuckles—because all of that is wearing me out.

"Slow," He says, and it surely seems that way most of the time.

"It will not delay," He says; that's the part that I was misunderstanding. It seems that speed (at least my concept of speed) has nothing to do with results.

God has a different measure—His own faithfulness and a total awareness of circumstances that surround the answers that are coming. So regardless of the time that elapses, there will be no delay.

Yet in all honesty, His visions of what will be and His actions do seem slow to me sometimes. It will be difficult to trust the "wait-for-it" part, especially when I think I need an answer or His help right now.

He must know me pretty well, though. Just for me, I think, He added that simple additional note—"It will surely come."

I like that.

Prayer: I get so frazzled with my worries. You, Lord, are so steady. And when You act, Your timing is perfect.

❧ NOVEMBER 21 ❦

POOR RISK?

. . . For Jesus knew from the beginning who they were that
believed not, and who should betray him.

John 6:64 KJV

How do they know?

Yesterday in the mail I received a letter telling me that as a recent
college graduate I am eligible for credit with that company's particular credit-card offer. They told me my credit is good. How do they
know that? Since I graduated from college more than twenty-five
years ago, it is obvious to me that the company hasn't done much
research. And if they are so wrong about when I graduated from
college, how can they know I am such a good credit risk?

I could be a big spender! I could have no self-control when it
comes to credit cards. They don't know. So I threw the letter away.

God knows me. I know that, because out of curiosity I got out my
concordance to see how many times He reminds me that He knows
me. There are a lot of references. He knows me very well, and unlike credit-card companies, He doesn't make any mistakes.

I could be a poor risk for credit, but God knew I wasn't a poor
risk for Him. Even knowing me and what I'm like, He made the
greatest investment in me—Himself.

*Prayer: Thank You, Lord, for redeeming me and trusting me. It's nice
to know I'm not a poor risk.*

❧ NOVEMBER 22 ❦

GOD WILL JUDGE

He shall judge between the nations, and shall decide for
many peoples; and they shall beat their swords into plowshares, and their spears into pruning hooks; nation shall
not lift up sword against nation, neither shall they learn
war any more.

Isaiah 2:4

Sometimes, when political leaders reject God and a government
oppresses the people and introduces "institutional violence," God
will step in.

He may wait for what humanly seems to be a long time. But He will judge.

Isaiah knew it and said, "He shall judge between the nations, and shall decide for many peoples."

There are oppressed peoples in the world (they rarely make the headlines), seeking the face of God in prayer.

They could rebel, take up the sword, and be just like the enemy—no higher, no better. But they rely on God, who has judged and will judge. They wait, and sometimes die, believing.

A day is coming when the prophecy of Isaiah will be fulfilled permanently: "They shall beat their swords into plowshares, and their spears into pruning hooks; nation shall not lift up sword against nation, neither shall they learn war any more." It may not be so very far away now.

There will come a Kingdom where these words will be true. It will be a Kingdom with Christ as head, and there will be peace.

Until then, depending on where a person lives, there are decisions to be made about resistance, becoming a refugee, martyrdom.

Some won't see the day when God judges the oppressors. And someone may wonder why God doesn't act now, thinking that action in time depends on the immediacy of our own torture or death.

But none of us has to live to see God bring His justice.

He will act; that's enough.

Prayer: O God, I know You will keep Your Word. At the right time You will act.

❧ NOVEMBER 23 ❧

TEARS

> And David was greatly distressed; for the people spake of stoning him, because the soul of all the people was grieved, every man for his sons and for his daughters: but David encouraged himself in the Lord his God.
>
> 1 Samuel 30:6 KJV

Some of us have been there once, perhaps twice, and some of us will be there again. It is that point in life when everything has crumbled and there's nothing left. That's when we weep as David wept. David and the people with him had lost their sons, their wives; all were taken captive. "Then David and the people that were with him lifted up their voice and wept, until they had no more power to weep" (v. 4). They cried themselves into exhaustion. There is a sadness that is deeper than any distress ever felt before, and that's where David was. Some of us have been there. We understand.

David had to face something more. People turned on him. They blamed him. They wanted to stone him. Their grief was such that they had to blame somebody, so in the midst of his grief over his own extreme loss, David also had to face the wrath of his people. Then he did what honesty must bring us all to do. He didn't try to "pull himself up by his own bootstraps" or tough it out or "stonewall" it; "David encouraged himself in the Lord his God." He had no resources of his own. He turned to the One who never fails. He was down, but he wasn't out. He knew where to go for help.

Prayer: Lord, let me learn as David learned that You are my encouragement. I need to turn to You.

◈ NOVEMBER 24 ◈
TOO LATE

> . . . Your name shall be Abraham; for I have made you the
> father of a multitude of nations.
>
> Genesis 17:5

Someone said, "God is never late, but He's not especially early either." Abraham must have been thinking that way. If God were going to do what He said, make a great nation from Him, He might have started a little sooner. Abraham had his youth once; it was gone. His was a withered old body, and his wife was in no better shape. *Too late, God,* he must have thought. *Too late; it isn't possible. You had Your chance, but now it's too late.*

I've said that. I have said it about an event that I knew had to take place at a certain time. It didn't. Then in God's timing it did happen, and it happened correctly. I've said it about people I was praying for. *The chance is gone now, God. They're outside of hearing the Gospel.* But it wasn't too late. God knew exactly what He was doing.

Too late? Impossible? Abraham learned that with God neither of those terms fit. Some of us are still trying to learn that.

Prayer: O Lord, why do I keep trying to measure Your ability by my poor strength and Your timetable by my calendar. Abraham was an early Bible lesson, but I'm still learning the lesson.

NOVEMBER 25

ONLY ONE!

And he who sat upon the throne said, "Behold, I make all things new."

Revelation 21:5

No one else could say that!
Only One.
Because only One has the credentials.
"And he who sat upon the throne said, 'Behold, I make all things new.' Also he said, 'Write this, for these words are trustworthy and true.' And he said to me, 'It is done! I am the Alpha and the Omega, the beginning and the end. To the thirsty I will give from the fountain of the water of life without payment' " (Revelation 21:5, 6).
Only One sits on the throne.
Only His words are trustworthy and true.
Only He is the Alpha and Omega.
Only He is the Fountain of the water of life.
And from all that He is comes the promise: "He who conquers shall have this heritage, and I will be his God and he shall be my son" (Revelation 21:7).
No whim or fancy to it. He *will* be my God. I *shall* be His son.
But how do I conquer? In fact, what do I conquer?
Ah, there it is, explained the other way around in verse 8.
Takes a little reading of the Word, doesn't it?
The more we read, the more we know what to conquer, who makes conquering possible, and more of the credentials of the Conqueror.
He doesn't just give a snap formula for "Godship" and "sonship"; He gives the whole Scripture with the whole promise.
No one else could be all that and give all that.
Only One!

Prayer: Father, the more I read Your Word, the more I appreciate You and Your promises.

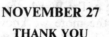

NOVEMBER 26

SOMEONE WAS COMING

... But when he was yet a great way off, his father saw him,
and had compassion, and ran. ...

Luke 15:20 KJV

What would the servants think? All day they labored in the fields,
their loins girded, their legs free for bending and lifting and walking. No long robes for these farm laborers. That was for the landowner, the man with the money, the one who kept the books and
paid them on Friday. If he came out in the sun at all, it was at a gentleman's pace, robe trailing in the dust.

But now the farmhands looked, put down their tools, and looked
again. There was the owner, the boss, the old man, not walking se-
dately but running. He had done what the workers did—reached
down between his legs, pulled the back of his robe up between his
legs, and tucked it into his waistband so that, bare legs exposed, he
could run. What was making that dignified gentleman landowner
run as fast as his pounding heart could make his legs go?

Someone was coming up the road. They could see that. But who
could be so important?

Prayer: O Lord, I know why Jesus told that story. He told it for me.

NOVEMBER 27

THANK YOU

I know that thou canst do every thing, and that no thought
can be withholden from thee.

Job 42:2 KJV

Thankful?

Oh, I say I am. I talk about giving thanks, say table grace, thank
God for my wife and children, appreciate my liberty. ...

But I also plan my own day, expect to eat regularly, forget to rejoice that over my head is a roof that doesn't leak, assume that the
furnace will work (and become irritated when it doesn't), and sel-
dom bother to realize that I have more than most when I stand in
the yard and breathe fresh air. Some people can't stand, some fight
for every breath, some have no yard, some don't have fresh air.

Thankful?

If I were, would I put so much stress on my rights, my needs, my problems, my future, my situation, my feelings? That syndrome captures many of us, even in the church. And it can rob us of genuine thanksgiving.

There's obviously a lot more to being thankful than just using words that have the right sound in church or at the dinner table. Thankfulness comes from an acknowledgment of who God is.

That's why, on a somewhat regular basis, I have to go back to a visit with Job. He learned through his brokenness that God is greater than any human acknowledgment or questioning of Him. God is also greater than what He gives. God is God, alone and apart from everything else.

Job is good for me. He comes to know, as each person must, that God is in Himself our reason for being thankful.

As I reflect on what that means, not as a child looking for a handout, or as an immature adult looking for a "special blessing," but as a created being who needs the Creator and draws life from Him, I have to thank Him that He is God.

So, I do say it. "Thank You." And I mean it.

Prayer: Father, as I think about You and me, I have so many reasons to be thankful.

❧ NOVEMBER 28 ❧
A COMPUTER WON'T LOVE YOU

For I am the Lord, I change not. ...

Malachi 3:6 KJV

Shopping for a computer is awful. I look at all the models, listen to the salesmen, hear about everything that these machines will do—and just about the time I have decided on a particular model, a company comes out with something newer, faster, better, simpler, that does more, and I start all over again. Every week there is something new or improved in the computer world.

How refreshing, then, to listen to God, who tells me that He's the Lord and He never changes. God isn't like a computer or any other gadget. We can't choose the style, size, color, or even function of our God. God is perfection; nobody is going to come out next week with an improved model.

God is all-knowing. I can't add to Him or subtract from Him. His capabilities are complete. He knows more than I do; He always has, He always will, for I can only know what He reveals to me.

God is present everywhere. He doesn't have to be carried with me on a trip or checked through with my luggage to be picked up when I arrive at my destination.

And I cannot assemble God from a selection of types and models, to do what I want Him to do, the way I want Him to do it. He is God. There is no other to choose from. I've listened to the sales pitches of those who have a computer to sell me. Every one is the best. But even when I make my choice, a computer is only something I own.

When God gets hold of my life, He owns me. I'm loved. Try saying that about a computer.

Prayer: Father, we're so impressed with our high-tech world. Then we get a glimpse of Your wonder and realize how silly we are.

NOVEMBER 29

THUMBS UP

That if thou shalt confess with thy mouth the Lord Jesus, and shalt believe in thine heart that God hath raised him from the dead, thou shalt be saved.

Romans 10:9 KJV

He didn't have very long to live. He was seventeen years old, his body full of cancer—no longer able to speak, his hearing almost gone, his face horribly swollen—and his mother asked me to visit him in the hospital. She asked me for her own peace of mind to learn if her son had ever placed his trust in Christ. When I entered his room, I didn't know that he could hear only if I shouted at him, and I didn't know that he couldn't answer back, but I found out.

Later I thought how simple it is for those of us who can confess Christ with our mouths to do so; yet many won't. This young man couldn't.

I asked him if he had ever accepted Jesus Christ as his personal Savior, then tried to read his eyes. I thought I saw an indication of assent, but I couldn't be sure. I asked the question another way, but still wasn't sure of his response. Then, first pointing up and then pointing to my own heart and finally pointing to him, I asked, "Is Jesus living in your heart?" As I asked I gave him a thumbs up sign. Very slowly, with what must have taken a lot of effort, he raised his thumb.

I prayed for him before I left. He didn't hear, of course, but I knew God did. Later, without adding to it or subtracting from it, I told his mother what he did. It was enough.

Prayer: Lord Jesus, while we still have our voices, give us courage to receive You and confess You.

⅏ NOVEMBER 30 ⅏
STILL TIME

> And the angel dictated this sentence to me: "Blessed are those who are invited to the wedding feast of the Lamb." And he added, "God himself has stated this."
> Revelation 19:9 TLB

A party is coming soon, and the invitations are going out.

It's a marriage supper, actually, a party for those united with the Lamb of God, the Lord Jesus Christ.

When God gives an invitation, it's personally dictated, and those who receive one are blessed; He said so.

Don't be jealous if His special-delivery message passes you by and goes next door. If you don't get an invitation to the party, don't blame Him. After all, the Bridegroom knows who His bride is and can't be expected to shun her for someone else.

The question is not, "Will I get an invitation to the marriage supper?" It's "Whose bride am I? To whom am I promised right now?"

But the invitations haven't been sent yet—maybe tomorrow. The Divine Suitor is still calling, "Come unto me."

There is still time for another place to be set at the table.

Prayer: Today, right now, I reaffirm my faith in Your saving work. Lamb of God, thank You for redeeming me.

DECEMBER 1
FIRST MATTERS FIRST

> ... Grace, mercy, and peace, from God the Father and Christ Jesus our Lord.
>
> 2 Timothy 1:2 KJV

If there is any part of Scripture that we usually rush past in order to get what we call the meat of the text, it's usually the opening remarks of an epistle. We think, wrongly, that this is merely a greeting similar to the mail that comes to our house saying, "Dear Friend." But it isn't. Paul, in writing to Timothy, is putting first matters first. No matter what else he speaks about, no matter what else in the epistle is stated, there is first this needed affirmation and proclamation.

He focuses on the basics, the essentials—grace, mercy, and peace. To a people who are waiting eagerly for guidance and spiritual leadership, for a people awaiting answers to how to be a Christian, how to function as a body of believers, this comes first, for this is the Gospel. It's because of God's grace that we have His mercy. It's because of His mercy that we have His peace.

When someone you know is living without peace—emotional peace, spiritual peace—one of the first questions to ask is, has he yet experienced the mercy of God that comes by the grace of God? For grace comes to the hopeless, mercy to the helpless, and peace to the restless.

Prayer: Dear Father, if anyone needs Your grace, your mercy and your peace, I do.

DECEMBER 2
NO NEW HERESY

> And the angel answered and said unto her, The Holy Ghost shall come upon thee, and the power of the Highest shall overshadow thee: therefore also that holy thing which shall be born of thee shall be called the Son of God.
>
> Luke 1:35 KJV

Heresy is a lot like sin; there aren't any new ones, just modern ways to practice old ones. Satan is as clever about heresy as he is about sin: he disguises both in acceptable language.

Lately the old heresy about Jesus not being fully God is rearing its head again, only this time it is couched in Bible terms that nonetheless limit the deity of Jesus to what those who wrote about Him said of Him.

And what of the things He said of Himself? That's limiting, too, these teachers say, since we can only measure what He said about being the Son of God by what He did by the power of God. That He was "a" son of God, they have no doubt.

Sooner or later, these teachers would like us to look only at the function of Jesus, not His essence. They would call Him "Son of God" but only because of what He does for us. That quickly makes us the measurers of His divinity and limits His deity to what we think it is, not what Scripture teaches about His oneness with the Father.

The angel announced to Mary the deity of the child she would bear: "That holy thing which shall be born of thee shall be called the Son of God." We can choose to accept that or argue that Jesus was a man who had the power of God only to the point that it was proven by His involvement with us. Acceptance of His deity leads to a high view of the Trinity; acceptance of the other leads to heresy—the same one the Church has battled for centuries.

Satan hopes we don't know that or won't remember.

Prayer: Lord Jesus, You come to us as very God, very man, one with the Father, yet living among us. I accept that.

❧ DECEMBER 3 ❧
DON'T WAIT

The barrel of meal shall not waste, neither shall the cruse of oil fail. . . .

1 Kings 17:14 KJV

The widow didn't get more meal or a larger jar of oil. What she had she gave, and as a result what she had never ran out.

When we see needy people around us we think, *Lord, if You would only give me more, I could give more.* So we ask for a larger paycheck, more profit, less expenses, and put the responsibility on God: "You give me more, and I'll give more."

Why should He? Maybe what He wants is what He expected of the widow—to give and keep giving so that He can keep supplying what we give away. The widow didn't end up rich, nor were her troubles over. Her son got deathly ill. There was no great reward for her in giving, just faithfulness.

God doesn't promise a reward to us, either. We are to be faithful, to give, because He tells us to. Don't wait until you get a bigger jar of oil. It will never be big enough in your opinion. Start giving now, and then watch and see if that jar of oil ever runs out.

Prayer: Father, I know I'm not trusting You as I would like to and as I know You would like me to. I'd like to change that, starting now.

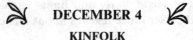

DECEMBER 4

KINFOLK

> I will establish your descendants for ever, and build your
> throne for all generations.
>
> Psalm 89:4

We're related.

Not directly, of course. Some of us are Jewish, and some are not.

But we're related, and that adds quite a dimension to what God told David.

"I have made a covenant with my chosen one, I have sworn to David my servant: 'I will establish your descendants for ever, and build your throne for all generations' " (Psalm 89:3, 4).

That's me. A child of the covenant, one of the "descendants for ever," a part of the "all-generations" group.

He promised it: "I have made a covenant with my chosen one."

He told how: "I will write it upon their hearts" (*see* Jeremiah 31:31–34).

And He did it: ". . . You, a wild olive shoot, were grafted in their place to share the richness of the olive tree" (*see* Romans 11:17).

One thing is certain about all of this—no believer is a drifting loner. None of us in the family is isolated. In God's whole historical plan, we're a continuous line, a family with no orphans—a part of the whole.

Established—that's what God said: His line is established. And any believer in Him is part of that line.

The covenant is a lot older than any of us, and it won't be changed by our doubts about belonging.

It was there long before any of us were ready to be a part of it.

And long before any of us, feeling lonely and sorry for himself, started saying, "I don't belong."

You can't judge an eternal promise by a lonely Saturday night.

Prayer: Thank You for Your eternal promise that far outweighs my lowly feelings.

DECEMBER 5

DIRTY DISHES

Therefore shall a man leave his father and his mother, and shall cleave unto his wife: and they shall be one flesh.

Genesis 2:24 KJV

We have two automatic dishwashers at our house. After supper my wife and I automatically start in on the dishes. (We used to have four dishwashers, but two of them grew up and moved away.) But it isn't so bad, the two of us doing dishes together; there is variety and excitement to it, deciding who will wash and who will dry and then alternating. We help each other.

The Bible talks of a man and a woman leaving their parents and becoming one flesh. Doing dishes together is part of the one-fleshness. There can be a lot of togetherness at the kitchen sink. It might be that more marriages would be healthier if people turned off the dishwasher and stood together at the sink. Dirty dishes can be part of the tie that binds.

Prayer: Lord, may it be in our marriage that we always have time to be together.

DECEMBER 6

BODY LIFE

Not forsaking the assembling of ourselves together, as the manner of some is; but exhorting one another: and so much the more, as ye see the day approaching.

Hebrews 10:25 KJV

We see it all the time; slowly, subtly, Satan pulls people away from the gathering of believers—at worship, Bible study, praise meetings. There are other things to do, perhaps an interesting television program. Pretty soon the interest isn't there anymore. And invariably, those who begin to drift become more and more convinced: "I don't need it. I can serve the Lord other ways. Church doesn't do anything for me." And instead of guilt, they develop more and more pride.

It has always been that way, and it's sad, because there is a whole lot more to the assembly of believers than "going to church." There is life in the Body. Cut off a finger or a hand or a foot and see how long it can live on its own.

Satan is clever, though. He can convince people that they're alive long after he has performed an amputation.

Prayer: Lord, if it breaks my heart to see people becoming weaker and weaker, how much more it must break Your heart when You want people to have life abundantly.

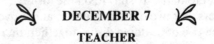

DECEMBER 7
TEACHER

For Ezra had prepared his heart to seek the law of the Lord, and to do it, and to teach in Israel statutes and judgments.

Ezra 7:10 KJV

Recently I read a book by a professor at a theological seminary. He has a brilliant mind. But he wasn't teaching in favor of God and the Scriptures. He was teaching a philosophy that was against the Scriptures. What was in his head gave him the academic qualifications to teach. What was in his heart didn't.

Ezra had a good mind, too. But it is clear in Scripture that Ezra also prepared his heart to seek the law of the Lord, to do it, and to teach it. No one can adequately teach God's Word if he isn't first obeying God's Word, and no one will obey God's Word unless his heart is prepared to seek it. Fortunately, not all teachers are like that seminary professor. There are still a lot of Ezras around—preaching, teaching, and writing God's truth. It's easy to tell the difference.

Prayer: Thank You, Father, for those prepared both in mind and heart to seek Your law, obey it, and teach it. I know that I can learn from them.

DECEMBER 8

IT CAN'T BE WALLED IN

For he looked for a city which hath foundations, whose builder and maker is God.

Hebrews 11:10 KJV

When Nehemiah rebuilt the walls of Jerusalem, it was to keep the enemies out. But also, because that was the city of God, he probably never thought there would be a need to expand it. He didn't have what we call a world vision. God's city is bigger than what Nehemiah built; it can't be walled in.

In the book of Acts, the Scripture says, ". . . And the Lord added to the church daily such as should be saved" (2:47 KJV). The Church, the family of God, has swept around the world, still growing at tremendous rates in some parts of the world. The city of God is expanding, and someday the eternal city of God will be established forever; no walls there, either, no need to keep enemies out. God Himself will be in the city, and He will be the wall around the city. Every believer in Christ who ever lived will be a citizen of that city.

Until then the Church grows, breaking down all the walls that people build to try to contain it.

Prayer: Lord, neither You nor Your people can be contained within walls. Give me opportunity to find others to be added to the number of Your holy city.

DECEMBER 9

STILL GROWING

But we have this treasure in earthen vessels, that the excellency of the power may be of God, and not of us.

2 Corinthians 4:7 KJV

I hear older people saying, "I'm not strong; I can't do what I used to do." I smile at them, because the Bible never told us that we were strong or that we could do anything in ourselves, even in our youth, when we thought we could. Some have more strength than others, but all can have a ministry.

Dr. Herbert Lockyer had a Bible conference ministry until he was in his mid-fifties. Then he started writing. Over the years he wrote more than fifty books. One of his last books was translated into Chinese. When he was ninety-three years old, I asked him for an article for our magazine. He replied excitedly, "Certainly. I just have to do seven radio messages, a few columns for a newspaper, and finish up a book. Then your article will be the very next thing I do."

But not all are as Dr. Lockyer was, right up to his death at age ninety-eight. Some are crippled or bedridden. They spend their time praying for those who still have strength to move about for God.

Whatever we do today or tomorrow, we can still be growing. And we need to be growing in our praying, in our loving, in our serving. The power to do that belongs not to ourselves, but to God. So don't say, "But Lord, I have this treasure in a weak earthen vessel." Because He can rightly reply, "I know that. I made the vessel."

Prayer: Father, I know this earthen vessel that is me. Every day I want to prove the transcendent power that belongs to You, not to me.

ঌ DECEMBER 10 ঌ
IT'S DIFFERENT ON THE MOUNTAIN

"For behold, I create new heavens and a new earth; and the former things shall not be remembered or come into mind."

Isaiah 65:17

That will be something to see!

"The wolf and the lamb shall feed together, the lion shall eat straw like the ox; and dust shall be the serpent's food. They shall not hurt or destroy in all my holy mountain, says the Lord"(Isaiah 65:25).

When God chooses an illustration, He sometimes goes to extremes, but He does make His point. What will come someday is a whole new order.

"For behold, I create new heavens and a new earth."

When this old order of things gets me down with its corruption, hurt, and weariness brought on by the interference of Satan, God's promise becomes all the more beautiful to read.

For those who do not know His holy mountain, who have chosen only what is painfully now, life must be oppressive.

It's not an escape to read Isaiah; it is a refreshing glimpse at what will be. Reading God's promise is like a walk in the mountains before having to return to the smog in the valley. The change isn't permanent, but we know from sampling it what is coming.

Those who have never been to the mountain don't know. They have no concept of what Isaiah means. They've never had the taste of what will someday be forever.

All they've had is the burning and the choking, the corruption and the hurt.

They call us dreamers, because they've never taken the climb.

And so we keep telling them what it will be like, based on what God has promised and what we've already experienced.

And we choke with them for a while—all the time wishing that they would want to breathe freely too, someday.

Prayer: Thank You, Father, for the contrast between mountain air and smog. I know the difference and wait with expectancy.

⅏ DECEMBER 11 ⅏
INSOMNIA

On that night could not the king sleep, and he commanded to bring the book of records of the chronicles; and they were read before the king.

Esther 6:1 KJV

Insomnia is not such a bad thing. Though God may not cause insomnia, more than one believer has found himself praying in the middle of the night and sensing some new direction from God that has altered the course of his life. Ahasuerus may not have known what was happening, but one night he couldn't sleep. Then things began to happen that set in motion the deliverance of God's people.

When you can't sleep some night, get up and pray. God may be about to do something dramatic.

Prayer: Lord, in the middle of the night, when I can't sleep, speak to me. That can be one of my best times for hearing You.

❧ DECEMBER 12 ❦

IMPOSSIBLE!

> The Lord says, "This seems unbelievable to you—a rem-
> nant, small, discouraged as you are—but it is no great thing
> for me."
>
> Zechariah 8:6 TLB

They were dragging their feet.

No wonder! We all do when we are discouraged like that.

God knew how those Jewish people felt and what they were
thinking after their anything-but-triumphant return from Babylon.

So, God did what He usually does. He told them a little of what
He would do for them. Then He paused and waited while they
muttered to themselves and told each other how impossible it was
and how it would never happen and trotted out all of their human
excuses about being too few and having so little to work with and so
on.

God didn't argue with them or beg to be believed. He just told
them, "This seems unbelievable to you . . . but it is no great thing
for me."

He's right!

To my way of thinking, what He promises does seem unbelievable—in fact, impossible. And usually I respond to Him by measuring His promises against my weaknesses, my inability to deliver,
and my concept of the possible.

God must smile a lot as He waits for me to list all of my negatives
and then with flare and finality crown my argument with a very sa-
gacious "Impossible!" When I am finished, He quietly repeats: "But
it is no great thing for Me."

How can you argue with that?

But just watch me. The next time around, I probably will.

Prayer: Nothing is too great for You—and I'm glad.

DECEMBER 13
HAMSTER

If I take the wings of the morning, and dwell in the utter-
most parts of the sea; Even there shall thy hand lead me,
and thy right hand shall hold me.

Psalm 139:9, 10 KJV

Watch a hamster in his cage. He thinks he can push up his chips
and hide from you. But you know where he is. God knows where
you are, too.

We can't hide from God. That saddens those who want to try.
But it gladdens those who don't want to. No person is hidden from
God. When we want to be safe and ask to be, we know that we are
safe in His holy and loving care. We are safe in His powerful right
hand; He holds us.

Yet there are still people who try to hide from God. If you want
to know how silly that is, go watch a hamster.

*Prayer: Thank You, Father, for Your strong right hand and Your de-
sire to lead me. I know I can't hide from You, and I don't want to.*

DECEMBER 14
WE'RE ALL HERE!

And hath raised us up together, and made us sit together in
heavenly places in Christ Jesus.

Ephesians 2:6 KJV

Every Sunday we have a different crowd. I teach a college-and-
career Sunday-school class, and though each Sunday there are
about twenty-five to thirty in attendance, they are not the same ones
two Sundays in a row! Some are home, visiting from out-of-town
colleges, and then they go back. Others leave to take jobs in other
cities but come back at holiday times. Some come and go depending
on whether they're going off that weekend to another church with a
boyfriend or girl friend. So it's always a different crowd. And each
Sunday as we gather it's fun to see who's going to be there. Invariably there's the comment, "If we were ever all here at the same

time, there wouldn't be room for us." That's true, but it would be a nice problem to have!

God isn't going to have that problem. Someday we'll all be together, sitting with Him in heavenly places, because of our oneness in redemption through the Lord Jesus Christ. It will probably be like our Sunday morning. First we'll marvel, "Look who's here!" Then we'll realize we're all here together, and then we'll notice what God had arranged long before—there is plenty of room for us all!

Prayer: Lord, I look forward to that final gathering when forever we will sit together with Christ Jesus in heavenly places.

   DECEMBER 15
HOMECOMING

> I tell you, many will come from east and west and sit at table with Abraham, Isaac, and Jacob in the kingdom of heaven.
>
> Matthew 8:11

Now, there's a reunion for you!

Take every family get-together, homecoming, and welcome-home party that has ever been held, and all together they won't compare to this one.

He's bringing together His own people, the redeemed ones from east and west throughout all the centuries, to sit at table with the patriarchs.

Ministers and missionaries, poets, songwriters, artists, and Bible teachers, the famous and the unknown, will all be present. Anybody and everybody who is committed through obedient faith to the One who is from everlasting to everlasting will be there.

Think of the conversation!

Think of the excitement!

But the highlight will be when those millions of believers stop talking to one another and the voices drop to silence as we all turn to greet the Host when He comes in.

Then we will know what He had in mind when He called us His own—His special guests.

Prayer: What a reunion You have planned for us, Father! Knowing it is coming keeps me going now.

DECEMBER 16
PRAYER LIST

I urge, then, first of all, that requests, prayers, intercession
and thanksgiving be made for everyone.

1 Timothy 2:1 NIV

How are we going to do all that? The people around me are facing surgery, divorce, problems with teenagers, financial setbacks,
job layoffs. To do what Paul told Timothy, I need a carefully noted
prayer list to check off answers as they come, add names to the list,
and subtract others as the need is met.

I was in a group one time when the leader asked, "How many of
you have a prayer list?" One young man raised his hand and asked,
"What's a prayer list?" The leader replied, "Never mind; you've already answered my question."

I have the urging of Paul in 1 Timothy 2:1. Now what I need is a
notebook and a ballpoint pen.

*Prayer: Father, I know that whatever other ministry I have, the great-
est is the ministry of prayer. Keep me faithful to my ministry.*

DECEMBER 17
A LITTLE MORE ROPE

The Lord is slow to anger, and great in power, and will not
at all acquit the wicked: the Lord hath his way in the
whirlwind and in the storm, and the clouds are the dust of
his feet.

Nahum 1:3 KJV

The wicked aren't getting away with anything. They just think
they are. "Nothing has happened so far," they say. "Why should we
be afraid?" Nahum tells us that the Lord is slow to anger. Then he
emphasizes the great power of God and says in a definitive statement that God "will not at all acquit the wicked."

No one takes God's power from Him. He hasn't surrendered it to
anyone. No one outsmarts God or outruns God. Some people think
God is slow to anger because He doesn't know what's going on. He
knows. He's just giving a little more time, playing out a little more

rope. A few will come to their senses and follow that rope back to its source. Others will go a little bit farther, until they've played it out. It will happen; it's only a matter of time. No one gets away with anything. God is on the throne.

Prayer: There are times, Lord, when I need Nahum's statement because I wonder why some people seem to be getting away with so much. I realize that they aren't getting away with anything.

❧ DECEMBER 18 ❧
WHAT WOULD HAPPEN?

O Lord, I have heard thy speech, and was afraid: O Lord, revive thy work in the midst of the years, in the midst of the years make known; in wrath remember mercy.
Habakkuk 3:2 KJV

What would happen if every Christian in every church throughout the world prayed, "O Lord, revive thy work in the midst of the years"?

What would happen if just your church members prayed that way?

What would happen if just you, by yourself, prayed that way?

What might happen? What revival is God waiting to bring? How much does He want to answer the prayers of believers? And when He answers, what impact is that going to make on the world? Think about where you live, where you work, the government. Are society and the world too far gone?

Not for God.

Prayer: O Lord, teach me to pray as Habakkuk prayed, and as I pray teach me to believe that You will act.

﹌ DECEMBER 19 ﹌
WORKING TOGETHER

And they went forth, and preached every where, the Lord working with them. . . .

Mark 16:20 KJV

Look at any church bulletin where there is a line-up of the pastoral staff. As you go down the list, think for a minute: where would you put Jesus? Would He be first, ahead of the senior or executive minister? Somewhere between the Christian education director and the church secretary? After the janitor? Ahead of the church organist? You say, "That's ridiculous. This is the paid ministerial staff. Jesus doesn't work here."

Or go out some evening with the church evangelistic callers. Everybody teams up. Two women might go together, or two men, or an older man and a younger man; sometimes they go by threes. Who gets Jesus? But that's just as silly, we say; Jesus isn't part of the church calling committee. Nobody gave Him any names of visitors. Nobody even asked Him to drive.

After the resurrection there was a reverse of what happened before the crucifixion. Prior to the crucifixion the disciples followed Jesus, working along with Him. After the resurrection wherever they went preaching the Gospel, the Lord worked with them. It's still that way when believers seek His help. His name may not be on a church bulletin or a calling-committee workers' list, but to any who will pray and seek His counsel and His guidance, He's there working with them. And when He is, people see the difference.

Prayer: Thank You, Lord, for working with us in ministry. We see the results of trusting You.

﹌ DECEMBER 20 ﹌
NEW WAY OF THINKING

I will also leave in the midst of thee an afflicted and poor people, and they shall trust in the name of the Lord.

Zephaniah 3:12 KJV

Reading the Bible demands a whole new way of thinking. It isn't always the comfortable who are an example of faith to us. It isn't always the rich. It isn't always those who experience the good things of life or the many gifts of God. But in any circle of acquaintances, some are afflicted, some are poor, and we see them trusting in the name of the Lord. We look at all that they endure and the faith they have, and then we look at ourselves, and we're ashamed.

God can satisfy a heart in ways that many of us have yet to discover.

Prayer: O Lord, we think good gifts and happy times multiply faith and trust. Yet often we see the opposite, both in Your Word and in life around us.

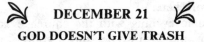

DECEMBER 21

GOD DOESN'T GIVE TRASH

> But my God shall supply all your need according to his riches in glory by Christ Jesus.
>
> Philippians 4:19 KJV

I don't ask, but I receive. And when all that I receive hits my trash basket, it's pressed down and running over. I'm talking about unsolicited mail. I don't want it, but it comes to me anyway. It fills the counter where we put mail before we go through it; then it fills the wastebasket in the study after we go through it; then from there it goes to the trash can out back; and soon the trash cans are pressed down and running over, too. Legally I suppose our mail carrier can't drop all of it into the trash can directly and cut out the middle-man—me—but I wish he could.

What a difference when God opens Himself to me. Not only does His bounty come, but it is more than I hope for. He does do exceedingly abundantly above all that I ask or think. And what God gives isn't trash. God knows my longings, and He fills them. He knows where I hurt; He gives healing and peace. He fills my soul's emptiness; He satisfies.

God doesn't have to ask me to explain where I am or what I need; He knows. And when I pray for His guidance, His wisdom, His strength, His healing, His peace, and His love, too, it all comes. God doesn't have to mail a flyer asking, "Wouldn't you like. . . ?" He knows. When He gives His good gifts, He doesn't have to ask our mail carrier to deliver them for Him. And I never have to ask our trash collector to carry any of it away.

Prayer: Thank You for all that You pour into my life every day.

⅔ DECEMBER 22 ⅄
GOD MUST BE LAUGHING

Great peace have those who love thy law; nothing can make them stumble.

Psalm 119:165

Did you ever notice how God does it? When He gives a gift, it's better than what we would have thought to ask for and it even comes wrapped in pretty circumstances.

Or when He makes a statement about Himself or a promise, it's never plain. God has a lot of color; He enjoys adjectives. "Great peace have those who love thy law; nothing can make them stumble."

Peace is what people pray for. He gives "great" peace.

Just a reasonably smooth path is good enough for most of us, but He promises: "Nothing can make them stumble."

God is more than generous; He's extravagant.

He doesn't just give; He lavishes.

In this case, it's peace. In other promises, it's gifts such as joy or love or comfort—never in small amounts, always more than our outstretched child-sized hands can hold.

God must be laughing as He gives His peace, pouring it out, letting it spill all over you.

Gift getting is fun when you have a happy Father!

Prayer: You keep giving and giving, and You allow me to keep taking and taking. Thank You.

❧ DECEMBER 23 ❧
TELL IT

And immediately his fame spread abroad throughout all
the region round about Galilee.

Mark 1:28 KJV

Word of mouth is always the best promotion of anything. Witness the incarnation. Except for the public announcement by the
angels to the shepherds, the birth of Jesus in Bethlehem was spread
by talk—plain old gossip. Later, during His ministry, the crowds
following Jesus grew because something was happening, and the
news of it was carried by the people.

That still happens, even though this is the twentieth century.
With high-priced hype and media hoopla, the best communication
is still the quiet, personal expression: "Let me tell you what Jesus
means to me." "Let me tell you about my Christ." What one person
tells another person about the Savior, saying, "This is what the Savior did in my life," does more than all the high-priced advertising
we can ever buy. Good news is always good news. No one can improve on it. What we can do is tell it.

*Prayer: Lord Jesus, You are my Savior and my Lord. Help me today
to tell at least one other person what You mean to me.*

❧ DECEMBER 24 ❧
SORRY, NO ROOM HERE

. . . Jesus Christ, the son of David, the son of Abraham.

Matthew 1:1 KJV

No one was there to meet me. I came off a long flight and looked
around for the person who should have met me, but he wasn't there.
So I made my way to the baggage-claim area, got my bags, found
public transportation, and went to the hotel. What an inconvenience.

At the front desk I gave my name. The reply: "Sorry, we don't
have a reservation for you." Now I was really miffed. Then the clerk
smiled and said, "But we can get you a room." That helped—a little.

Joseph and Mary made a longer trip than mine—not by jet, but by donkey. Tired, they approached the innkeeper. Mary's baby is about to be. . . . "Sorry, no room. Push some of the cows aside in the stable and bed down there."

The son of King David is about to be. . . . "Sorry, no room. Try the stable."

The son of Father Abraham is about to be. . . . "Sorry, no room here."

The Son of God, the Savior of the world is about to be. . . . "Sorry."

I opened the door to my room, stepped from the carpeted entryway past the dresser, the chairs, the king-sized bed, the color televison set, the desk, and the telephone. I glanced into the bathroom; a wrapper around the toilet seat said it was sanitized. Then I adjusted the temperature control and noticed a little card on the dresser. It said, "Welcome."

Prayer: Lord Jesus, I can't even begin to fathom the dimensions of Your incarnation, but thank You for leaving heaven for me.

❧ DECEMBER 25 ❦
TRADITIONAL

And she brought forth her firstborn son, and wrapped him
in swaddling clothes, and laid him in a manger; because
there was no room for them in the inn.

Luke 2:7 KJV

They must have been lonely, Mary and Joseph, that night as they were shown into the stable near the inn.

That's the way Christmas began, so many years ago in Bethlehem. It was God's choosing to have it that way. He could have arranged something much different. There could have been the security of home, family, friends, and even a party—there wasn't.

That first Christmas wasn't very "traditional." None of the elements that make a nice Christmas were there—except one. Jesus was born that night.

There was neither party nor laughter, neither warm hearth nor family and friends—it was a lonely night. It is for many people now, too.

These are the ones whose jobs take them away from their relatives. There are the missionaries, too, and the service personnel. Then there are the prisoners and the aged who have no one to care. There are the left-behind ones, who find that there is no one around "who really knows me."

Oh, it's true that acquaintances say, "You can spend Christmas with us." But it isn't the same. They have their own families, their own traditions. So Christmas comes back to the original. A lonely place to celebrate the birth of Jesus.

I'm glad in a way that God put Mary and Joseph alone in that stable. God might have missed identifying with many lonely people, and they with Him, had He ushered in Messiah's birth any other way—especially had He made Christmas the way we tend to celebrate it.

Jesus Christ Himself is the only reason for Christmas. He is the one coming both to the family gathering and to the person alone. He is the one for the frightened or the rejected—and for those who have no place to go. No matter what else we add to Christmas, Jesus Christ came. That's the whole story. And whether we ponder that story surrounded by family, or alone, He must be both reason and focus for Christmas.

Christmas is celebration.

Christmas is worship.

Christmas is Christ—in a crowd, or all alone.

Prayer: Lord Jesus Christ, I worship You and celebrate Your birth today.

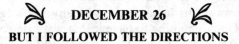

DECEMBER 26
BUT I FOLLOWED THE DIRECTIONS

> Take fast hold of instruction; let her not go: keep her; for she is thy life.
>
> Proverbs 4:13 KJV

Why doesn't it work? It has to be a manufacturer's defect; it can't be me. I followed the instructions.

It's this new ten-speed bicycle. When I bought it I was given a huge cardboard carton and told the bike was inside. It was, but in pieces.

Seat and handlebars I understood; hand brakes I figured out. Gear shifts and derailleur were not designed for a brain past forty years of age.

But carefully I read the instructions and began to work. Finally I got it all together. I called my wife, showed off my mechanical prowess, bragged about how easy it was for me to do, and even used the new ten-speed technical words I'd just learned. The only problem was, I hadn't tested it. What looked right standing still didn't work right in motion.

Some people are like that. They are impressive standing still, but nothing seems to go right when they are moving. Others move fairly well until it's time to shift gears; then they seem to go off their sprocket.

But what a beautiful smooth machine a bicycle is when it operates the way it was designed to operate, put together according to the instructions, by the person who knows what he is doing.

And what a beautiful, smooth instrument we are, too—under the same circumstances.

Prayer: Lord, You designed me; You can make everything in my life fit together and work.

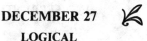

DECEMBER 27
LOGICAL

And Simon Peter answered and said, Thou art the Christ, the Son of the living God. And Jesus answered and said unto him, Blessed art thou, Simon Bar-jona: for flesh and blood hath not revealed it unto thee, but my Father which is in heaven.

Matthew 16:16, 17 KJV

What is logical after we believe sometimes seems illogical before we believe. Even people who want to believe have said, "I want to, but I can't"—meaning logically it doesn't fit together for them. Paul said, "But the natural man receiveth not the things of the Spirit of God: for they are foolishness unto him: neither can he know them, because they are spiritually discerned [understood]" (1 Corinthians 2:14 KJV).

Though we hate to admit it, there is a point of commitment, a leap of faith. It isn't that we accept something that we "know to be untrue." It is that we are willing to take God at His Word and act on it. It is that point of acting on it that is like throwing on a light switch. Once the light comes on, everything becomes so clear that it is logical even though at that point logic is no longer required.

Jesus told Peter that his confession came because it was shown to him by the Father in heaven. The Holy Spirit of God still does the showing. We need to spend more time praying that the Holy Spirit will convict and convince unbelievers and a lot less time trying to be logical.

Save the logic for later. Once the veil is pulled back, then the logic—who Jesus is and what He does—takes on deeper and deeper dimensions, offering one thrilling discovery after another. It's like pulling back the curtain at a theater. It is the beginning of seeing and understanding.

Prayer: Father, help me to learn from what Jesus told Simon Peter, because I know nothing has changed about logic and the ability to understand who You are.

DECEMBER 28

INDIFFERENT

> Then all the Greeks took Sosthenes, the chief ruler of the synagogue, and beat him before the judgment seat. And Gallio cared for none of those things.
>
> Acts 18:17 KJV

What a bother. Gallio didn't care. Religion—the squabbling of Christians and Jews and all that was going on between Paul and the Greeks and the Jews—was no concern of his. He didn't care. He drove them all out.

We've all met Gallio. Every family has one like him. "Have your religion if you want it, but don't bother me with it." Like Gallio, he wouldn't go to a church meeting even if Paul was preaching. He can't be bothered. It's all a bore. "You religious people do whatever it is that you do, but don't try to involve me in it."

Gallio was indifferent, and so far as we know, remained so until the end of his days. I wonder what he's thinking now. He had his opportunity to hear the Gospel. He didn't care.

Prayer: Father, I'm not going to give up on the indifferent ones I know. I'm going to keep praying for the convicting work of the Holy Spirit. They shrug and walk away; they have no idea what the word lost means.

❧ DECEMBER 29 ❦
FUZZY PRAYERS

> The end of all things is at hand; therefore keep sane and sober for your prayers.
>
> 1 Peter 4:7

You what?

You don't drink because of prayer?

Not drinking because you have to drive; that makes sense. Not drinking because it's costly or not drinking because you don't want to become an alcoholic or even not drinking because it makes you dull and a party boor is understandable—but prayer?

Peter knew something many of us have forgotten. He knew it because God made it clear to him. If you are a little fuzzy headed, you can't pray. Oh, you can phrase words, even be aware of God, but your praying won't be adoration, and it won't be based on clear thought. It will probably be selfish, too.

Sound minds produce sound praying; cloudy minds produce cloudy praying. God wants His people to have clear heads, not only for their own sake or for the sake of others, but for conversation with Him.

So the next time someone says, "Have a drink," you can say, "No, thank you. I want to be sane and sober for prayer." Chances are he won't understand.

Prayer: Help me to keep my mind clear for You. Our relationship is important to me.

❧ DECEMBER 30 ❧
HE HAD THE AUTHORITY

. . . When Jesus had ended these sayings, the people were astonished at his doctrine: For he taught them as one having authority, and not as the scribes.

Matthew 7:28, 29 KJV

Being what is called a visiting professor at both a college and a seminary in our community, I can decide which term I want to teach, which evening of the week—or not to teach at all, if I don't care to. Best of all, I don't have to do any of the faculty committee work or attend meetings. And because I teach in my own area of expertise, I find myself stretching and growing by the pushing and pulling of the students even as I teach them from my own experience in the marketplace. That's a pretty good deal.

Jesus wasn't a visiting professor, but He was a visiting rabbi. He was an itinerant. He could teach wherever He felt like teaching, and He didn't have to sit in on rabbinic committee meetings. So I think Jesus must have enjoyed teaching.

As I read through the Gospels, I see that He had compassion for people. I know He loved them. But though no one asked Him, "Master, are you having a good time?" I think He was having a good time. Here were people eager to learn, people with needs. Here were eternally significant concepts to impart and results that could be measured in lives that were changed.

Jesus had authority; He didn't teach as the scribes. Obviously He had that authority because He had the credentials. Look where He came from; look who He was. The visiting rabbi was "God with us."

Prayer: Thank You, Lord, for sending the Lord Jesus to this world and especially to me.

⚡ DECEMBER 31 ⚡

DOWNWIND OF THE KITCHEN

But Daniel purposed in his heart that he would not defile himself with the portion of the king's meat, nor with the wine which he drank: therefore he requested of the prince of the eunuchs that he might not defile himself.

Daniel 1:8 KJV

It wasn't a once-for-all decision. Daniel had to face the consequences of his choice three times a day. There was the table, laden with the king's rich food, but Daniel took none of it. How did he resist? How can anyone resist? New Year's resolutions rarely last into the first week of the year; good intentions are mostly that—good intentions. But Daniel did it, and he wasn't even on a weight-loss plan or a physical-fitness program.

He made a decision in his heart that he wasn't going to defile himself. He would not indulge himself or pander to his appetites. He must have reiterated that vow to God every day, three times a day, especially when he stood downwind of the kitchen window. When Daniel kept his vow, God knew He had a man He could trust.

God knows whom He can trust today, too.

Prayer: Lord, when I make a promise to You and purpose in my heart to keep it, help me to stay with that promise no matter what happens.

TITLE INDEX

∂🙰 **Scripture Index** 🙰∂